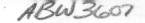

Multithreading Applications in Win32®

The Complete Guide to Threads

Jim Beveridge
Robert Wiener

ADDISON-WESLEY DEVELOPERS PRESS

An imprint of Addison Wesley Longman, Inc.

Reading, Massachusetts • Harlow, England • Menlo Park, California
Berkeley, California • Don Mills, Ontario • Sydney
Bonn • Amsterdam • Tokyo • Mexico City

Many of the designations used by manufacturers and sellers to distinguish their products are, claimed as trademarks. Where those designations appear in this book, and Addison Wesley Longman, Inc. was aware of a trademark claim, the designations have been printed in initial capital letters or all capital letters.

The author and publisher have taken care in preparation of this book, but make no expressed or implied warranty of any kind and assume no responsibility for errors or omissions. No liability is assumed for incidental or consequential damages in connection with or arising out of the use of the information or programs contained herein.

Library of Congress Cataloging-in-Publication Data

Beveridge, Jim
   Multithreading applications in Win32 : the complete guide to threads / Jim Beveridge, Robert Wiener.
      p.   cm.
   Includes index.
   ISBN 0-201-44234-5 (pb)
   1. Operating systems (Computers)   2. Microsoft Win32.   3. Microsoft Windows (Computer file) 4. Microsoft Windows NT.
   I. Wiener, Robert, 1966-   . II. Title.
   QA76.76.063B478   1997
   005.26'8--dc21

96-48106
CIP

Sponsoring Editors: Claire Horne and Ben Ryan
Project Manager: Sarah Weaver
Production Coordinator: Erin Sweeney
Cover Design: Ann Gallager
Set in 11-point Times Roman by Octal Publishing, Inc.

1 2 3 4 5 6 7 8 9 -MA- 0099989796
First printing, December 1996

Addison Wesley Longman, Inc. books are available for bulk purchases by corporations, institutions, and other organizations. For more information please contact the Corporate, Government, and Special Sales Department at (800) 238-9682.

Find A-W Developers Press on the World Wide Web at:
http://www.aw.com/devpress/

For my wife, Anne-Marie, who gave me her love and support all the time I was sitting in front of the computer instead of being with her, and for my parents, who never used the word "impossible."—J.B.

For my parents, who fostered and encouraged my love for computers.—R.W.

Contents

Frequently Asked Questions

Acknowledgments

Putting together a book is always the work of many people and I would be remiss if I did not mention at least a few of them.

Everyone in Developers Press at Addison Wesley Longman has been very helpful. They deserve my thanks for taking on a new author and for guiding me through the process.

Mike Lippert spent many late nights poring over the details in the book and the code and correcting my errors. I take full responsibility for any remaining mistakes. Thank you very much, Mike.

My employer, Turning Point Software, supported me by giving me the time I needed to get this book finished. From TPS, Brian Bodmer took many hours out of his personal schedule to read and mark up these chapters. The book is better for his constructive suggestions.

I'd also like to thank my dad, Dave Beveridge, who read chapters, helped with sample programs, and generally helped me get this manuscript out the door.

Microsoft support deserves mention for spending days and days hunting down answers to the obscure questions I posed to them. To those who helped me, thank you. Microsoft also deserves mention for Word 7.0, whose automatic cross-referencing and on-the-fly spell checking saved me countless hours of drudgery.

Finally, I want to thank IBM, who designed and created the marvelous ThinkPad 701 "Butterfly" that I wrote this book on. After six months, I still love it. How *did* they make the keyboard do that, anyway?

James E. Beveridge
October 1996

Preface

In 1992, I was at the second Microsoft Professional Developers Conference where Win32 was first displayed to a large audience. It was a momentous event, with many fascinating new technologies being rolled out. Time after time the audience applauded at what we were being shown. As I watched, my Unix background said, "About time." My Windows 3.1 background said "Hallelujah!"

Here we are, five years and several versions of Windows NT later. The further I got in this book, the more I realized how little I had originally understood what I saw in 1992. Most of the conventional wisdom I heard, such as using multiple threads for each window in an MDI application, is just plain wrong. Techniques I thought were obvious, such as overlapped I/O, had bizarre twists to them that I never expected.

While researching this book, I discovered many other books and articles that thoroughly described individual Win32 functions, but I discovered very little information on how to use them in an application or how to use related functions. Some functions, such as `MsgWaitForMultipleObjects()`, are central to the workings of Win32 applications, but there are almost no sample programs that correctly use this call. Having been frustrated by the focus of most of the documentation I found, I wrote this book to be as task-oriented as possible so that you can see how various functions in Win32 fit together.

This book is designed for a wide audience, from Win16 and Unix developers transitioning to Win32, to the experienced Win32 developer. You'll find answers to questions not otherwise documented, such as why `_begin-threadex()` really matters. The code samples range from basic examples of synchronization mechanisms to demonstrations of multithreaded COM and ISAPI applications.

This book is about hands-on, get-it-done development using threads in Win32. I will describe the basics of the theory, but you will have to look elsewhere if you want a highly theoretical work. Most problems in the world of threads were solved by people like Dijkstra and Courtois over twenty-five years ago. Their papers are still as applicable today as they were then.

If you have ever despaired of books that seemed to tell the obvious parts and ignore the hard parts, I hope you will find this one an exception. Some of the chapters in this book are the result of many hours of empirical testing, correlating obscure magazine articles and Microsoft Knowledge Base articles, and reading source code. On subjects such as threads in the C run-time library and MFC, I think you will find many gems of information.

Many developers are very ambivalent about threads. The Unix people scoff at them because processes seem just as good. Win16 people scoff at them because `PeekMessage()` loops have always worked for them. One of the key questions that I tried to understand while I wrote this book was, "Why should anyone care about threads?"

If you are doing server development, you should care deeply about threads because I/O completion ports use them. I/O completion ports are the only way to do high-performance I/O with sockets or named pipes in Win32. Run, don't walk, to Chapter 6 to find out more.

If you are doing Web development, extensions for the Internet Information Server are created with multithreaded DLLs. The background for this development is presented throughout the book, and Chapter 16 shows how to apply those concepts.

Part I of this book is written in C. C++ would have added very little to the introductory topics and might have obscured matters by trying to make everything into objects. Starting in Part II we move into C++ and stay there for Part III. As I describe in Chapter 9, C++ development is the way to go, regardless of whether you use MFC or not. If your C++ is shaky I hope you will give Chapter 9 a particular look to see what you are missing.

Who Should Read This Book

This book is aimed at C and C++ developers who have Windows experience in either Win16 or Win32 and are trying to gain a solid understanding of using multiple threads, kernel objects, and overlapped I/O in Win32. This book talks about how the calls are used, what problems you may run into, and how the architecture of Windows affects their usage.

After reading this book you will be equipped to analyze where threads can effectively be applied and where you should stay away from them. Almost the entire emphasis of this book is on creating applications that work. Esoteric and unsafe practices have been pointedly left out.

Unix programmers will find discussions of concepts that are fundamentally different between Win32 and Unix.

How This Book Is Organized

Part I of this book, **Threads in Action,** establishes basic concepts that you will need to know including thread startup and shutdown, kernel objects, the meaning of signaled and nonsignaled, and synchronization mechanisms and their uses. Experienced Win32 developers can probably skip this part, although Chapter 6 discusses concepts such as I/O completion ports that are very important but poorly documented in the world at large.

Part II of this book, **Multithreading Tools and Tricks,** talks about the threading support in the C run-time library and MFC, how to apply multiple threads within the limitations of USER and GDI, how to create a DLL, and how to debug a multithreaded application. Much of the information in these chapters comes from research and experience.

Part III of this book, **Multithreading in Real-World Applications,** talks about how to structure an application to effectively support multiple threads and presents two applications that might be found in the "real world." The first is a freethreaded OLE automation server and the second is a ISAPI extension for the Internet Information Server that shows how to talk to a JET database.

About the Examples

Throughout much of this book I have used command-line based programs to demonstrate concepts. Some people will dislike this choice, but I believe that a 50- or 100-line example that is tightly focused on showing a concept is much better than a 750-line example with a message loop, resource file, window procedure, and other assorted Windows paraphernalia that are irrelevant to the problem at hand. Many of the people who read this book will be looking at servers that have very little user interface. I believe that the examples in this book will be more useful to you in their current state.

I have worked to use extensive error checking throughout the examples. Although this checking tends to clutter the listings, error checking is truly important for creating any real-world application, and creating applications is what this book is about.

Related Reading

There are two things you should have next to you at all times when trying to write anything in Win32. The first is the *Microsoft Developer Network*. This pair of CD-ROMs contains an unbelievable amount of material, including the Microsoft Knowledge Base, the complete set of manuals for the compiler and for Win32, and back issues of the *Microsoft Systems Journal*.

The second is a copy of Jeffrey Richter's excellent book, *Advanced Windows NT: The Developer's Guide to the Win32 API for Windows NT 3.5 and Windows NT* (Redmond: Microsoft Press, 1995). Although it is missing some topics that are new with Windows NT 3.51, it is an otherwise invaluable reference.

Part I

Threads in Action

Chapter 1

Why You Need Multithreading

This chapter explains why multithreading is an important asset for both the developer and the end user. It describes the meaning of terms like thread and context switch and discusses race conditions, the root of problems in multithreading.

Each time a new technology is unleashed in the computer industry, it seems like everyone races around worrying whether it is important. Companies keep an eye on their competitors, delaying using the new technology until the competition starts advertising how important it is. Regardless of whether the technology really is important, everyone makes it sound *terribly* important to the end user. Now the end user demands it, even if he has no idea what it is.

Developing with threads is at the beginning of this cycle. Although threads have been around for decades on various operating systems, it is only with the widespread release of Windows 95 and Windows NT that the technology has become widely available for home and business applications.

In the near future, multithreaded applications will be pervasive. Threads will become a standard tool that every developer uses. Not every application will need to use them. Multithreading, like multimedia or Internet support, will be put into those applications that need it. Threads may improve the "user experience," simplify development, or provide support for hundreds of users at the same time in a server. Users will usually only be aware of the results; they may not realize that an application is multithreaded at all.

A single-threaded program is like a single cashier in a supermarket. That cashier can rapidly ring up small purchases. However, if someone has a cart full of groceries, then that purchase will take a long time to ring up and everyone else will have to wait.

A multithreaded program is like a group of cashiers working together. Some of the lines can be designated for large purchases and others can be designated express. If one line becomes tied up, everyone else does not also stop.

Based on this metaphor, here is a simple definition:

Multiple threads allow a program to be divided into tasks that can operate independently from each other.

Threads are not always required to achieve this result, but they can make the job easier. To understand where threads fit into the development picture, it is worth taking a short look at how the needs of developers have changed since MS-DOS was introduced.

A Twisting, Winding Path

Over the past 15 years, developers writing applications for Microsoft operating systems have had to exert less and less effort to get programs to cooperate. As the needs of users and the size of programs have grown, the operating system has taken more and more responsibility for housekeeping and keeping applications coordinated and running smoothly.

MS-DOS

Originally there was MS-DOS. MS-DOS version 1.0 would be almost unrecognizable to today's users. There was no support for subdirectories, no batch language, not even CONFIG.SYS or AUTOEXEC.BAT files. The operating system did not support the idea of a task or a process. A running program got control of the entire machine. If you were running Lotus 1-2-3, you could not run anything else. Without a process model, it was not possible to have even the concept of a multitasking or multithreaded operating system.

MS-DOS version 2.x had minimal support to allow the installation of operating system extensions called TSRs, and there were small applications, such as Sidekick, that were designed as TSRs to run while another application was running. However, MS-DOS considered these TSRs to be a part of the operating system, not applications or processes in their own right. Internally,

TSRs were intrusive on the application and had to work around the operating system. Some of you may remember spending hours or days trying to get all of your TSRs to work together.

Sometimes even TSRs could not run. If DOS tried to format a floppy, *everything* else, including TSRs, stopped running. In summary, MS-DOS, even today, is *not* multitasking and definitely not multithreaded.

Microsoft Windows

FAQ 1

What is the difference between cooperative multitasking and preemptive multitasking?

Microsoft Windows versions 1, 2, and 3 allowed several applications to run at the same time, but it was the responsibility of each application to share the processor. If one application decided to hog the processor, all other applications would come to a halt. For this reason we say that Windows had **cooperative multitasking.** In the early days of Windows 2 and 3, there were many poorly written applications that refused to share. Gradually, developers learned how to create programs that were well behaved, but it took a great deal of programming effort that would have been better spent on tasks such as fixing bugs.

Because Windows relied on DOS underneath, formatting a floppy disk or copying a file to a floppy disk still caused everything else in the system to stop running.

Meanwhile, operating systems such as Unix, VMS, and AmigaDOS already supported a model called **preemptive multitasking.** This meant that the operating system was able to force applications to share the processor without extra effort on the part of the developer.

DID YOU KNOW...

Multitasking in Windows 3.x

Windows 3.x actually did support preemptive multitasking, but it was not easily available to a developer. Because DOS applications had no concept of sharing, preemptive multitasking was the only way to get them to run without devoting control of the entire machine to each DOS application. All of the Windows apps together were counted as a "single" DOS application, so the Windows apps were preemptively multitasked with the DOS apps, but not with each other.

OS/2, originally created by Microsoft and IBM to be the replacement for Windows, was designed to support many of the features of these other operating systems. OS/2 was a 16-bit operating system that supported memory protection and preemptive multitasking. OS/2's API (Application Programming Interface) was substantially different from the Windows API and so presented a challenging migration path to developers. Microsoft turned over ownership of OS/2 to IBM in 1990.

Windows NT to the Rescue

The release of Microsoft Windows NT, with full support for preemptive multitasking for 32-bit applications, brings us to today's state of the art. Windows NT is able to take control away from an application that has taken too much time and give control to another deserving application. Developers writing applications under Windows NT are freed from writing `PeekMessage()` loops to yield the processor. A clean break was made with the past by creating a new set of APIs called Win32 that is a superset of the APIs available on Windows 3.1.

IMPORTANT!

FAQ 2

Can I use multiple threads in Win32s?

The Win32 API was ported to Windows 3.1 and called **Win32s.** Unfortunately, much of the functionality behind these calls was not ported. Win32s supports neither preemptive multitasking nor multithreading. None of the samples in this book will run on Win32s, so it will not be mentioned again.

Although 16-bit programs continued to be cooperatively multitasked with each other for backwards compatibility, they are preemptively multitasked with the 32-bit programs. In Windows NT, a 16-bit Windows program or even a DOS program cannot take control of the processor.

Windows NT provides a remarkable contrast to the early days of MS-DOS. We have gone from an operating system that did not even provide a process model to a multithreaded, multitasking, secure operating system. Amazingly enough, in NT you can do anything you want to with a floppy disk, including copying files to or from the floppy, and there will be absolutely no impact on the rest of the system. If you are running Word at the same time, you cannot even tell that the floppy drive is running. This, more than anything, shows the power of preemptive multitasking. Even operations that the operating system itself is performing do not prevent applications from running.

Preemptive multitasking, multithreading, and the Win32 API were important enough that they would later become an important addition to Windows 4.0, otherwise known as Windows 95.

When Microsoft Sold Unix
In the mid-80s Microsoft sold a version of Unix called Xenix. Xenix was capable of preemptive multitasking years before either OS/2 or Windows NT was introduced. It was also incompatible with DOS and difficult to learn or maintain. Xenix has long since faded into obscurity.

Cooperative Threads

The evolution from DOS to Windows NT has a close parallel to how today's applications are designed. For example, older versions of Microsoft Word were able to edit and repaginate at the same time. Not very complex. Newer versions were also able to print at the same time. Microsoft Word 95 is usually able to print, spell check, and repaginate, all while the user is working.

Since it does not use threads, Word has to juggle the processor time among all of the tasks for which it is responsible. This is the equivalent of cooperative multitasking, except that everything is happening within the same application. Like applications in Windows 3.x, Word must make sure each operation gets to run. Like applications under DOS, Word must take care of its own task switching. To change from printing to repaginating, Word must save the state of the print operation, then restore the state of repagination. Saving the state of an operation in progress is difficult and requires careful design to support it.

Ideally, we would like the operating system to take care of saving the state of repagination as well as deciding when to switch to background printing. This is the same problem that Windows NT solved with preemptive multitasking. Now we need to solve the same problem *within* an application. That is what threads do.

Why Users Want Threads

Although making an application multithreaded is a cool idea, it takes more than that to convince management that adding multithreading to your application will provide a significant benefit. Here are some examples of threads in action that could not be solved without the use of threads.

If you have ever tried to connect to a busy server using File Manager under Windows NT 3.x, you know that File Manager essentially hangs until the operation is completed. There is nothing that the developer can do to fix this problem because the operation is stopped in the operating system. If it was stopped inside your program you could put in a `PeekMessage()` loop, but you have no such control in the operating system. Therefore it is impossible to return control to the user if a file operation will take a long time.

If File Manager were multithreaded, then one thread would come to a halt while trying to connect to the server, but other threads would keep going and your user interface would remain responsive. A responsive user interface is always important.

This technique was implemented in the Windows 95 desktop. If you copy a file from one folder to another, you can still open and close folders and documents on the desktop. In fact, you can start multiple copies at the same time (see Figure 1-1). You will end up with multiple windows, each of which is animating the copy process. Because most of the work is being done in the operating system, the desktop would not be able to accomplish this feat without multiple threads.

The multithreading in the desktop in Windows 95 is not perfect. Once you start copying a file to a folder, you cannot do anything more with that folder until the copy is finished. This illustrates that multithreading is not an instant cure-all. An application must still be designed to properly use threads, and only those things that the developer chooses will be able to run in parallel.

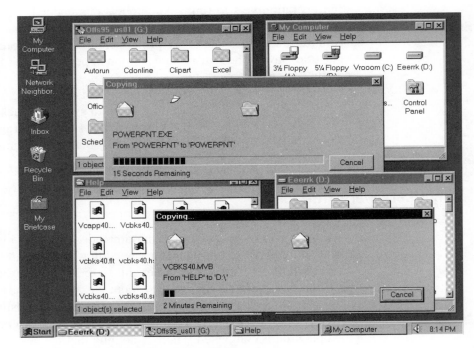

Figure 1-1. Explorer performing multiple copies.

Any application that uses a CD-ROM can also benefit from multithreading. The seek times on CD-ROM drives are on the order of 200 ms. On a processor, such as a Pentium, that runs at tens of millions of instructions per second, waiting around for 200 ms means that a lot of potential processing time goes to waste. This processor time could have been used for updating the display, mixing wave files, preparing buffers, or any number of other activities. Using multiple threads can remove many bottlenecks that have historically existed with CD-ROM drives and network files. We will look at how to do this in Chapter 6.

Win32 Basics

FAQ 3

What is the difference between a thread and a process?

Before looking at how threads work, let's first examine what words like *process* and *thread* mean in the context of Win32. I'll give a very high-level overview of what the low levels are really doing. These explanations are very generalized and the actual implementation, not surprisingly, is much more complex.

Processes

From the perspective of Win32, processes consist of memory and resources. The memory owned by a process can theoretically be up to 2GB. The resources include kernel objects such as file handles and threads, USER resources like dialogs and strings, and GDI resources such as device contexts and brushes.

A process is like a notebook. You can write things in a notebook, you can erase things or rip pages out, but the notebook itself just holds these things. Similarly, a process by itself cannot run. It provides a place for memory and threads to live.

UNIX

This definition is a little bit different than that used by other operating systems such as Unix. In Unix, a process and its main thread of execution are one and the same, no distinction is made. In many versions of Unix that support threads, or lightweight processes as they are sometimes called, the illusion of threads is produced by the runtime library and the operating system itself has no knowledge of them.

Memory

Every process has memory associated with it. Memory is like the writing in a notebook. What it means at any moment is completely dependent on what is written down. This memory can be broken down into three basic types:

- Code
- Data
- Stack

The **code** is the executable part of the program. The memory for code in a process is read only. This is the only kind of memory that the processor is allowed to execute. These restrictions are enforced by the hardware on the Intel architecture as well as the RISC chips that run Windows NT.

The **data** is where all of the variables in your program that are not local to a function are placed. The memory for data is broken down into memory for global and static variables, and memory that is allocated dynamically by a thread with `malloc()` or `new`.

The **stack** is your call stack and local variables. A new stack is allocated for each thread created. The operating system will allocate memory to grow the stack automatically as needed.

All of this memory is available to all threads running in that process. This single fact is the greatest convenience and greatest curse of multithreaded programming.

Threads

By themselves, a process and its memory do nothing. When the processor starts running the code, you have a **thread** of execution. Like rats in a maze, you can have a whole bunch of threads running the same code in the same process at the same time.

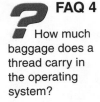

FAQ 4

How much baggage does a thread carry in the operating system?

Very little information is needed to define a thread. The state of a thread at any instant is defined by the memory in the process and a scratch pad in the processor. Other important things, such as the variables and the call stack of the application, are stored in the memory that is common to all threads in the process.

The processor's scratch pad is its internal registers. The registers on most CPUs are not part of memory and cannot be addressed with a pointer. On an Intel Pentium, these registers include the general-purpose registers EAX, EBX, ECX, and EDX; the stack pointer; and the instruction pointer. By examining these registers, the operating system can determine what a thread is working on at any given instant.

The Win32 Operating System
There is no such thing as a "pure" Win32 operating system. In Windows NT, the Win32 API is one of several personalities that can run simultaneously on the Windows NT kernel. Windows 95 is substantially based on 16-bit technology internally, and its Win32 API is layered on top of the 16-bit technology.

Why Not Use Multiple Processes?

The most common question people ask when they are introduced to threads is, "What do threads give me that multiple processes do not?" This can be loosely translated as, "So what?" The most important answer is that threads are cheap. Threads are fast to start up, fast to shut down, and have a minimal impact on system resources. Threads also share ownership of most kernel objects such as file handles.

One of the more difficult problems to solve if you are using multiple processes is that it is difficult to pass window handles between processes. In Win32, a handle is meaningful only within the process that created it. This behavior is a safety precaution to prevent one process from being able to damage the resources in another process. In order to share a window handle, you must explicitly create a copy of a handle that can be used by the other process. In a multithreaded program, all threads can share window handles because both the handles and the threads live in the same process.

A completely different kind of problem occurs in nonwindowed applications. For example, server software would seem to be a prime candidate for multiple processes. After all, with a server each user is doing something different, right? Consider the case of an Internet server for the World Wide Web. A Web server may have to service several million requests per day, and possibly hundreds at the same time. However, Web servers are "stateless." A user does not need to log into a Web server, the user just makes ad-hoc requests. With a few exceptions, each request that comes in is completely unrelated to any other request. Also, each request is typically for a relatively small amount of data.

Although it would be easy to start a new process to service each request, the overhead to do so is tremendous. A new copy of the server software would have to be loaded, requiring large amounts of memory to be allocated and initialized. The state of the new copy would have to be initialized to the state of the first copy. By now several seconds may have passed on a busy server. The new process is now ready to service the request for 8K of data, after which everything must then be torn down again. That's a lot of work to move 8K of data. Internally, the operating system may have had to move several megabytes to service this one request.

In contrast, if you have a single thread servicing all of the requests in turn, then you do not get optimal use out of the hardware. With multiple threads, you always have threads waiting for system resources such as the network and the hard drive. The operating system can process these requests very efficiently because it can look to see who is waiting for what at any moment and decide how best to make that happen. With only a single thread, it becomes much more difficult to keep the hardware fully utilized. If the thread had to do any extensive calculations, then all other requests would have to wait.

The other extreme in client/server computing is a workgroup database server, where a few users create connections that often last several hours. In this case, the overhead of creating a process to support each user is negligible. Unfortunately, everyone still needs to use the same database, so the processes would have to negotiate who can read a record, write a record, or change an index. This is the same problem we would have faced with threads, only now there is the added complexity of trying to share data structures across processes, which the operating system tries very hard to prevent. All of the memory in an application is always shared among all threads.

UNIX   Process creation has much lower overhead under Unix than it does under Win32. However, thread creation in Win32 is much cheaper than either. It is not unreasonable for a single-processor Windows NT machine to have 500 threads. Most Unix machines would have serious performance problems with 500 processes, even if most of them were not active.

Context Switching

FAQ 5

How does a "context switch" work?

In a preemptively multitasked system, the operating system takes care of ensuring that every thread gets to run. It does this with assistance from the hardware and lots of bookkeeping. When a hardware timer decides that a thread has run long enough, an interrupt occurs. The processor takes a snapshot of the thread by copying all registers onto the stack. Then the operating system saves the current state of the thread by copying the thread's registers from the stack into a CONTEXT structure and saving the structure for later use.

To switch to a different thread, the operating system points the processor at the memory of the thread's process, then restores the registers that were saved in the CONTEXT structure of a new thread. This entire procedure is called a **context switch.**

If the second thread is in a different process than the first thread, then the two processes will not share any of their memory. This separation protects the processes from accidentally hurting each other. The really sneaky part is that both processes may think that they are running at the same address. A pointer to location 0x1f000 in one process actually points to a different place than a pointer with value 0x1f000 in another process. Therefore, the only way that threads in the two processes can communicate is if they have been specifically designed to share memory. In contrast, remember that two threads in the same process share all of their memory.

The operating system may make a context switch several hundred times per second. This rapid context switching provides the illusion that your computer is actually doing many things at the same time. Figure 1-2 shows the context switches per second in an idle Windows NT system. The chart shows that between 296 and 1126 context switches are being made per second.

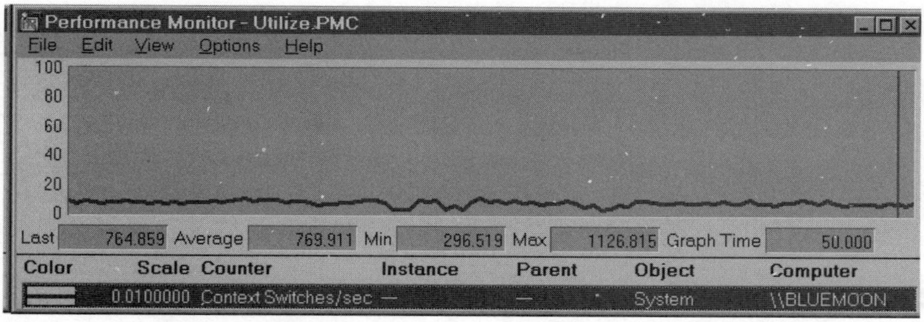

Figure 1-2. Context switches on Windows NT Workstation 4.0.

Context Switch Performance

There is a small performance penalty paid for each context switch. If your application is broken down into 500 threads, then you are potentially paying a big performance penalty.

If two threads were running and both were trying to calculate pi to a million digits, then they would both run slightly less than half as fast than if one of the threads were running by itself. This is because it takes a finite amount of time for the processor to perform the context switch from one thread to another. Therefore it takes longer for two threads to calculate pi at the same time than if one thread were to do it twice in a row.

From the user's perspective, preemptive multitasking makes it look like the computer is doing many things at the same. In reality, the processor is working on only one thing at a time. However, it is also possible to buy machines with multiple processors. The more processors, the more threads that can run at the same time without context switching.

Multiple processors are supported under Windows NT with **Symmetric Multi-Processing** (**SMP**). Each processor executes a different thread, although any particular thread could be running on any processor at any time. A process is not bound to any particular processor. In a two-processor system, each processor could be running threads that both belong to the same process, or to different processes. In an SMP system, it is possible for multiple threads to be executing at exactly the same time. Figure 1-3 shows an SMP system about to schedule Thread 3 to run on Processor 1.

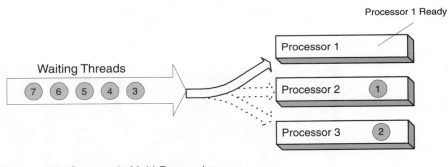

Figure 1-3. Symmetric Multi-Processing.

Race Conditions

Context switching is the heart of a preemptively multitasked system. In a cooperatively multitasked system, the operating system changes threads whenever the program allows it to. But in a preemptive system, control is forcibly taken away from the current thread and the order of execution between multiple threads becomes unpredictable. This unpredictability is the heart of what is called a **race condition.**

The easiest way to define a race condition is to show an example. Say you are editing a list of phone numbers on the file server. When you open the file, the list looks like this:

```
Joe       555-3765
Elaine    555-9300
Tom       555-2040
```

You add a new entry for Karl. While you are typing in Karl's phone number, someone else opens the same file and adds Ted. Each of you saves your changes.

The question is, whose changes will be left? The answer, of course, is the changes made by the last person to save the file will be kept, and the other person's changes will have been overwritten. The two people in this example have encountered a race condition.

The Linked List Example

The same problem happens in code. For example, suppose you had a routine that adds a new entry to a linked list:

```
struct Node
{
    struct Node *next;
    int data;
};

struct List
{
    struct Node *head;
};

void AddHead(struct List *list, struct Node *node)
{
    node->next = list->head;
    list->head = node;
}
```

Simple, straightforward, just like it's been written for years. So let's assume we start with a list with one node, as shown in Figure 1-4 below.

But look what happens if Thread 1 calls this routine to add Node B, and then a context switch occurs between the two lines of code in `AddHead()`. The linked list is left in the state shown in Figure 1-5.

Figure 1-4. Linked list with one node.

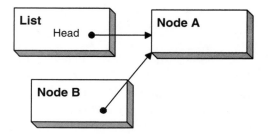

Figure 1-5. Linked list after context switch.

Now Thread 2 tries to add Node C to the same list. It successfully completes (Figure 1-6).

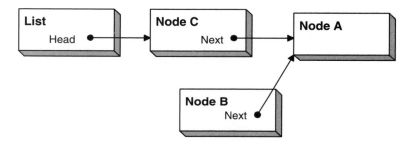

Figure 1-6. Linked list after Thread 2 completes.

Finally, Thread 1 is allowed to finish. It continues from where it left off, so it sets *head* to Node B. Node C is cut out of the list and probably becomes a memory leak. Because of the preemptive multitasking, there is no way for Thread 1 to realize that something changed behind its back. Finally you are left with the mess shown in Figure 1-7.

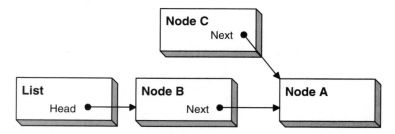

Figure 1-7. Damaged linked list after Thread 1 completes.

It would seem that a problem like this has only a one-in-a-million chance of happening. The odds seem to be so small that the problem is not worth worrying about. However, your processor is executing 20 to 50 million instructions per second. For a linked list that is used often throughout a program, the odds are very good that the race condition will cause problems several times a day.

Atomic Operations

It is necessary to plan for and prevent race conditions while you are writing code. The hard part is identifying where race conditions can happen. After working in C or C++ for any length of time, it is often hard to remember that you are working in a high-level language and that the processor is operating at a much lower level. When you are concerned about race conditions, forgetting about the "low levels" just *once* can lead to a bug that is extremely difficult to find and fix.

It would seem that the simplest solution for fixing the linked list example above is to put a flag around the code to see if it is safe to go on.

```
int flag;

AddHead(struct List *list, struct Node *node)
{
    while (flag != 0)
        ;
    flag = 1;
    node->next = list->head;
    list->head = node;
    flag = 0;
}
```

Now let's look at the assembly language that is generated for this code.

Listing 1-1. Assembly language generated for AddHead()

```
1    ;        : {
2
3                    xor    eax, eax
4    $L86:
```

Listing 1-1 (continued)

```
5
6       ;       :       while (flag != 0)
7
8               cmp     DWORD PTR _flag, eax
9               jne     SHORT $L86
10
11      ;       :               ;
12      ;       :       flag = 1;
13
14              mov     eax, DWORD PTR _list$[esp-4]
15              mov     ecx, DWORD PTR _node$[esp-4]
16              mov     DWORD PTR _flag, 1
17
18      ;       :       node->next = list->head;
19
20              mov     edx, DWORD PTR [eax]
21              mov     DWORD PTR [ecx], edx
22
23      ;       :       list->head = node;
24
25              mov     DWORD PTR [eax], ecx
26
27      ;       :       flag = 0;
28
29              mov     DWORD PTR _flag, 0
30
31      ;       : }
32
33              ret     0
```

IMPORTANT!

> It is very important to see how simple C statements expand out to many machine instructions. It is *never* safe to assume that a statement in C will completely finish without a context switch happening somewhere in the middle.

There are several ways that the routine as written could fail. It is possible that a context switch could happen between the comparison on line 8 and the jump on line 9. Another thread could enter this routine even though this thread was about to set the flag. The routine could then fail if a context switch happened after lines 20 or 21.

An operation that will complete without ever being interrupted is called an **atomic** operation. Checking and setting the flag in the example above must be an atomic operation. If it ever got interrupted, then it would create a race condition when it was trying to solve one.

Checking and setting a flag is such a common operation that it is implemented in hardware on many processors. It is called the **Test and Set** instruction. In practice, only the operating system will use the Test and Set instruction. The operating system provides high-level mechanisms that your program may use instead of Test and Set.

The first part of this book goes over techniques that manage situations in which race conditions could happen. In Parts II and III we will put some of those techniques to work.

How Threads Communicate

A problem closely related to race conditions is making threads communicate. In order for a thread to be useful, you have to tell it what to do. Win32 provides a simple way to give a thread start-up information, as we'll see in Chapter 2, but striking up a conversation between two threads can be quite tricky. How do the threads know where the data will be put?

An obvious solution is to use global data since all threads can read and write it. But if Thread A writes to a global variable, how would Thread B know that the data was there? When Thread B does read the data, how does Thread A know that Thread B has gotten the information? What if Thread A needs to write more information before Thread B has read anything?

The problem gets more complex because threads can be continually created and destroyed. What if Thread B exits while Thread A waits for Thread B to read something?

In short, communicating between threads can be quite tricky. In Part II of this book we will look at how to solve these problems by using various facilities in the operating system.

Good News/Bad News

Using threads is not without a price. You did not think this was going to be free, did you? There are several potentially significant problems with using threads. Unless very carefully designed, multithreaded programs tend to be unpredictable, hard to test, and hard to get right.

If you have ever tried working in the kitchen with someone else, you know that the extra help can sometimes hurt more than it helps. If both of you are working on the same thing, then you must constantly talk to the other person, find out what's been done, whether the sauce needs stirring or if the rolls need to go in the oven. Eventually it becomes easier for the two of you to work on completely separate tasks—for example, one of you prepares the vegetables while the other makes the salad. Even then there are problems because there are only a finite number of knives and bowls and a limited amount of space in the refrigerator. You have to plan ahead, figure out who gets which utensils and which bowls, and sometimes you have to wait because what you need is in use.

Writing multithreaded applications is just like that. If you have multiple threads working on exactly the same thing, then there is a high probability that something will go wrong unless the tasks are very carefully coordinated. If you have multiple threads that are working on separate tasks, they will still need to share a few data structures, or dialogs, or files, or many other things. The recipe for success is to very carefully plan who does what, when, and how.

Chapter 2

Getting a Feel for Threads

This chapter introduces the Win32 calls for creating, monitoring, and exiting threads, shows you some threads in action, and presents a functioning background printing application. This chapter also introduces MTVERIFY, a macro to help debug the sample programs.

If I were asked to describe my attempts in the past to implement background printing in Win16, I would sum up the process with one word: aggravating. I think you'll find the same problem to be much easier to solve in Win32.

To implement background printing in Win32, you need to learn how to create a thread and how to exit a thread. I'll also show you how a multithreaded program behaves, because multithreaded programs tend to exhibit some surprising behavior.

> **Console Applications**
> In this chapter and throughout the book, I will use **console applications** to introduce the use of SDK functions, then put everything together in a Windows application. Console applications are text-based applications that look like a DOS window. Unlike Windows 3.x and 16-bit Windows applications, calls such as `printf()` are fully supported in console applications. It is a little-known fact that 32-bit Windows applications also can have a text window associated with them. We will use this feature to help illustrate what

an application is doing. Console applications can be started using File Manager, Explorer, or the command prompt. A text window will automatically be created if needed.

Creating a Thread

Creating a thread, and therefore a multithreaded application, starts with the CreateThread() call, which looks like this:

HANDLE CreateThread(
LPSECURITY_ATTRIBUTES lpThreadAttributes,
DWORD dwStackSize,
LPTHREAD_START_ROUTINE lpStartAddress,
LPVOID lpParameter,
DWORD dwCreationFlags,
LPDWORD lpThreadId
);

Parameters

lpThreadAttributes   Describes the security attributes that should be applied to the new thread. Use NULL to get the default security attributes. This parameter is ignored under Windows 95. This book will not discuss security attributes.

dwStackSize   The new thread has its own stack that is different from the current thread's stack. The default size of one megabyte can be used by passing zero.

lpStartAddress   The start address is the address of the function where the new thread will start.

lpParameter   The parameter provides a way for the current thread to give arguments to the new thread.

dwCreationFlags   The creation flags allow you to create a suspended thread. The default is for the thread to start immediately.

lpThreadId   The thread ID of the new thread will be returned here.

Return Value

`CreateThread()` returns a handle to a thread if it succeeds, otherwise it returns FALSE. On failure, call `GetLastError()` to find out why.

IMPORTANT!

> If the thread ID is not needed, the parameter *lpThreadId* may be NULL on Windows 95, but not on Windows NT. If you are writing a program that must run on Windows NT, do not pass NULL for *lpThreadId*.

The way this function works can be tricky to grasp at first because it is unlike anything else in conventional programming. To provide a starting point I'll contrast the use of `CreateThread()` with how a function call works. Listing 2-1 shows a function call side by side with a thread startup. The numbers in parentheses indicate the order of execution of the code.

Listing 2-1. Function call vs. thread startup

Standard Function Call	*Thread Startup*
`#include <stdio.h>`	`#include <windows.h>`
`int square(int n);`	`DWORD WINAPI ThreadFunc(LPVOID);`
`void main()`	`void main()`
`{`	`{`
`    int result;                (1)`	`    HANDLE hThread;            (1)`
	`    DWORD threadId;`
`    result = square(5);    (2)`	`    hThread = CreateThread(NULL,`
	`                   0,`
	`                   ThreadFunc,`
	`                   0,`
	`                   0,`
	`                   &threadId ); (2)`
`    printf("%d\n",result);(5)`	`    printf("Thread running") (4)`
`}`	`}`
`int square(int n)`	`DWORD WINAPI ThreadFunc(LPVOID p)`
`{`	`{`
`    int product = n*n;     (3)`	`    // ...                     (4)`
`    return product;        (4)`	`}`
`}`	

In a function call, control is transferred to the function, which executes and then returns control to the caller. In order to print the squared value, the function `square()` must return to `main()`.

What happens when a thread is created is very similar, but there is a twist. In the example in the left column we call `square()` directly. In the multi-thread version in the right column, instead of calling `ThreadFunc()` directly, we call `CreateThread()` and pass the address of `Thread-Func()`. `CreateThread()` starts the new thread of execution, which then calls `ThreadFunc()`. The original thread continues executing. In other words, `ThreadFunc()` gets called **asynchronously.** This means that `ThreadFunc()` does not necessarily complete before `main()` continues on, so the return value cannot be passed back in the conventional way.

There is no magic to the name `ThreadFunc()`. You can call your startup function anything you want, even `Fred()`. The connection is established by what you pass to `CreateThread()`.

Notice in Listing 2-1 that there are *two* statements numbered (4). They will both be executed at approximately the same time. The ordering is not predictable. Once `ThreadFunc()` starts up, it is completely separated from the caller.

To try to get a feel for what is going on under the hood, let's look at a program that does something. Listing 2-2 starts five threads and passes each thread a number from 0 to 4. Each new thread will print out a row of its number ten times, then exit.

Listing 2-2. NUMBERS.C—Multiple threads in action

```
/*
 * Numbers.c
 *
 * Starts five threads and gives visible feedback
 * of these threads running by printing a number
 * passed in from the primary thread.
 * Build with the command line: cl Numbers.c
 * Note: This program was purposely built
 *       without the multithread run-time library
 *       for demonstration purposes.
 */

#include <stdio.h>
#include <stdlib.h>
#include <windows.h>
```

Listing 2-2 (continued)

```
DWORD WINAPI ThreadFunc(LPVOID);

int main()
{
    HANDLE hThrd;
    DWORD threadId;
    int i;

    for (i=0; i<5; i++)
    {
        hThrd = CreateThread(NULL, 0,
            ThreadFunc,
            (LPVOID)i,
            0,
            &threadId );
        if (hThrd) {
            printf("Thread launched\n");
        }
    }
    // Wait for the threads to complete.
    // We'll see a better way of doing this in Chapter 3.
    Sleep(2000);
}

DWORD WINAPI ThreadFunc(LPVOID n)
{
    int i;
    for (i=0;i<10;i++)
        printf("%d%d%d%d%d%d%d%d\n",
                n,n,n,n,n,n,n,n);
}
```

Especially notice the function definition for `ThreadFunc()`:

```
DWORD WINAPI ThreadFunc(LPVOID n)
```

The function prototype for `CreateThread()` expects a pointer to a specific kind of function; the function returns a DWORD, is of calling convention WINAPI, and takes an LPVOID as an argument. In other words, if you do not declare your thread startup function in exactly this manner, you will get an error when you compile the program. It is much better to get the declaration exactly right than to try to cast the function when you pass it to

CreateThread(). By not using a cast, you let the compiler perform the appropriate type checking and you know that your function declaration is correct. If, for example, you forget to put WINAPI on the function declaration, but force the program to compile with a cast, then the thread will crash when it starts up because the calling convention will be wrong.

You will also notice that there is a prototype for ThreadFunc() at the beginning of the listing so that you can use the identifier in the call to CreateThread().

Consequences of Using Multiple Threads

Figure 2-1 shows the results from running this program a couple of times. The column on the left, "Normal Function Calls," shows what we might expect if we called ThreadFunc() five times in a row with a normal function call instead of using threads (the equivalent C code is not shown).

The other two columns show what happened when I ran the sample program. For the first run, the results were shown on the screen. For the second run, the results were redirected to a file. The results in Figure 2-1 demonstrate some of the most important aspects of multithreading.

Normal Function Calls	Run #1 (to screen)	Run #2 (to file)
Calling Function	Thread launched	Thread launched
00000000	00000000	00000000
00000000	00000000	00000000
00000000	00000000	00000000
00000000	00000000	00000000
00000000	00000000	00000000
00000000	Thread launched	00000000
00000000	11111111	00000000
00000000	11111111	00000000
00000000	11111111	00000000
00000000	11111111	00000000
Calling Function	11111111	Thread launched
11111111	22222222	11111111
11111111	22222222	11111111
11111111	22222222	11111111
11111111	22222222	11111111
11111111	Thread launched	11111111
11111111	Thread launched	11111111
11111111	00000000	11111111
11111111	00000000	11111111

```
11111111         00000000         11111111
11111111         00000000         11111111
Calling Function 11111111         Thread launched
22222222         11111111         Thread launched
22222222         11111111         Thread launched
22222222         11111111         22222222
22222222         11111111         22222222
22222222         22222222         22222222
22222222         22222222         22222222
22222222         22222222         22222222
22222222         22222222         22222222
22222222         33333333         22222222
22222222         33333333         22222222
Calling Function 33333333         22222222
33333333         33333333         22222222
33333333         33333333         44444444
33333333         Thread launched  44444444
33333333         44444444         44444444
33333333         44444444         44444444
33333333         00000000         44444444
33333333         22222222         44444444
33333333         22222222         44444444
33333333         33333333         44444444
33333333         333344444444     44444444
Calling Function 44444444         44444444
44444444         44444444         33333333
44444444         44444444         33333333
44444444         3333             33333333
44444444         33333333         33333333
44444444         33333333         33333333
44444444         33333333         33333333
44444444         44444444         33333333
44444444         44444444         33333333
44444444         44444444         33333333
44444444         44444444         33333333
```

Figure 2-1. Results of running NUMBERS.

Multithreaded Programs Are Unpredictable

First, the results from a program running multiple threads can be very unpredictable. You can see that column 2 shows different results than column 3. Every time NUMBERS is run, you get different output.

Many developers have spent their careers expecting results from computers to be exactly reproducible. In a multithreaded program, the results are dependent on the speed of the processor, what the threads are doing, how busy the processor is, and numerous other factors.

This unpredictability means that a particular result, such as a crash, can be very hard to reproduce. One of the key goals of this book is to teach you how to get predictable results from a multithreaded program.

Order of Execution Is Not Guaranteed

The second important point is that the order of execution of multiple threads is not guaranteed. In column 3, you can see that Thread 4 finished before Thread 3 started, even though Thread 3 was created first. The order of execution of multiple threads in relation to each other should be considered random.

Task Switches Can Happen Anywhere, Anytime

If you look carefully near the end of column 2, you will see that there is one row that looks like this:

```
333344444444
```

The numbers are mixed up because a context switch happened while the thread was in the middle of displaying its results. This behavior is a type of race condition. A race condition occurs any time a result depends on which thread finishes an operation first.

Further down the listing in column 2, you can see that Thread 3 was allowed to continue and it finished displaying the line that it started:

```
3333
```

This problem can be solved by compiling the program with /MT or /MD to use the multithreaded version of the C run-time library (discussed in Chapter 8). The multithreaded version of the library takes steps internally to make sure that your output is not intermingled as shown above. However, the example serves to illustrate one of the many potential problems of multithreading.

UNIX

Unix Line Mode

This problem would never happen to a Unix program that was running in line mode (cbreak). Because Windows is not designed to run on terminals, the Windows program's output is not internally buffered on a line-by-line basis before being output. If you have ever tried a command like this under Unix:

```
ls & ; ls &
```

the output from the two commands will be intermingled on a line-by-line basis, but a single line will never contain the results of both programs.

Threads Are Sensitive to Small Changes

You will notice that the output of the various threads is better grouped together in column 3 than in column 2. This happened because column 3 was redirected to a file and column 2 was shown on the screen. Output redirected to a file could be sent to the disk much faster than it could be displayed on the screen.

The differences in grouping show how much the program was affected by changing just one thing that wasn't even part of the program. In preemptive scheduling, a thread is allowed to run for a fixed amount of time before control is taken away and given to another thread. Because displaying on the screen is a relatively slow process, each thread processes fewer lines during each **timeslice**, which is a single interval that a thread is allowed to run before being preempted. Even though the order in which the program runs changes, everything still runs to completion.

Because multithreaded programs are so sensitive, small changes in code can cause dramatic changes in results. For example, if you put the following line after the `printf()` in `ThreadFunc()`, you will cause the output to be substantially more random than either column 2 or column 3:

```
int j;
for (j=0; j<100000; j++)
    ;
```

Although you are not likely to put a delay loop like this in one of your programs, the effect is the same as inserting any lengthy calculation or expensive function call. This sensitivity can cause another problem you may not expect. The time-honored tradition of putting in calls to `printf()` to help debug can completely change the behavior of the program.

Threads Do Not Always Start Immediately

In both column 2 and column 3, threads 0 and 1 started printing their results as soon as they were created by the primary thread in `main()`. This behavior is not guaranteed. In column 3, threads 2, 3, and 4 were created all at once before any of them were allowed to start running. We'll go over this point in more detail later in this chapter.

Kernel Objects

`CreateThread()` returns two values to refer to each new thread created. The first value is a HANDLE that is the return value of `CreateThread()`. This HANDLE is local to your process and cannot be used by anyone else. Most API functions that work with threads take a handle. The second value is the thread ID returned with *lpThreadId*. The thread ID is a global value that uniquely refers to the thread from any process in the system. The thread ID is used by Win32 API functions such as `AttachThreadInput()` and `PostThreadMessage()`. These functions allow threads to affect each other's message queues. The thread ID is also used by debuggers and process viewers. To enforce security, it is not possible to obtain a thread handle from a thread ID.

The handle returned by `CreateThread()` refers to a kernel object. A kernel object is like a GDI object such as a brush or a DC, except that the object is managed by KERNEL32.DLL instead of GDI32.DLL. There are many similarities between the two kinds of objects.

GDI objects are a fundamental part of Windows. In both Win16 and Win32, they are managed by the operating system. You usually do not know the format of the data. For example, you manipulate a device context with calls such as `SelectObject()` and `ReleaseObject()`. Windows hides the implementation details from you by giving you an HDC or an HBRUSH that is a handle to the object.

Kernel objects are referred to with a HANDLE. Unlike GDI, with HBRUSH, HPEN, HPALETTE, and other kinds of handles, there is only one kind of handle that refers to kernel objects. A handle is a pointer to something in the operating system's memory space that your program is not allowed to use directly. Your program is prevented from accessing it to maintain system integrity and security.

The following is a partial list of the various kinds of kernel objects in Win32. This book will cover everything on this list except pipes.

- Processes
- Threads
- Files
- Events
- Semaphores
- Mutexes
- Pipes (named and anonymous)

We will talk about events, semaphores, and mutexes in Chapter 4. These kernel objects are used for coordinating the actions of multiple threads or processes so they can safely work in concert.

There is one major difference between kernel objects and GDI objects. GDI objects have a single owner, either a process or a thread. Kernel objects can have multiple owners, even across processes. To keep track of the owners, kernel objects use a reference count to count how many handles refer to the object. The object also keeps track of which thread or process owns each handle. The reference count is incremented by `CreateThread()` and other functions that return a handle, and the count is decremented when you call `CloseHandle()`. (You'll see more about `CloseHandle()` in a moment.) When the reference count drops to zero, the kernel object is automatically destroyed.

The distinction between whether the thread or the process owns the handle to the open object is important because it determines when the system cleans up. Cleanup consists of decrementing the reference counts on all objects owned by that process or thread. The objects are destroyed as necessary. The developer does not get to choose whether the thread or process owns an object; it depends on the kind of object.

Because of the reference count, it is possible for an object to outlive the process that created it. There are a variety of mechanisms in Win32 by which other processes can get a handle to a kernel object. If another process has a handle to the object when the original process terminates, the kernel object will not be destroyed.

The Importance of CloseHandle()

The `CloseHandle()` API is shown here. You need to use it to release kernel objects when you are finished using them.

BOOL CloseHandle(

HANDLE hObject
);

Parameters

hObject   Identifies the handle to an open object.

Return Value

CloseHandle() returns TRUE if it succeeds, otherwise it returns FALSE. On failure, call GetLastError() to find out why.

FAQ 6

Why should I call Close-Handle()?

If a process exits without calling CloseHandle() on all the kernel objects it has open, then the operating system will automatically drop the reference counts of those objects. Although you can rely on the kernel to handle the physical cleanup properly, the logical cleanup is an entirely different matter, especially if you are using multiple processes. The kernel doesn't know what the object means, so it also cannot know such things as whether the order of destruction is important.

If a process frequently creates worker threads without closing the thread handles, the process could end up with hundreds or thousands of thread kernel objects still open, leaving the operating system to manage all of these objects that are not needed. Such **resource leaks** can have a significant negative impact on system performance.

It is also important to realize that you cannot rely on thread termination to clean up all the kernel objects created by that thread. Many objects, such as files, are owned by the process and will not be cleaned up until the process exits.

To be correct, the NUMBERS program in Listing 2-2 needs to be updated a little. Here is the revised version of main() that calls CloseHandle().

```
int main()
{
    HANDLE hThrd;
    DWORD threadId;
    int i;

    for (i=0; i<10; i++)
    {
        hThrd = CreateThread(NULL, 0,
            ThreadFunc,
            (LPVOID)i,
            0,
            &threadId );
```

```
        if (hThrd)
        {
            printf("Thread launched\n");
            CloseHandle(hThrd);              // ***
        }
    }
    // Wait for the threads to complete.
    // We'll see a better way of doing this in Chapter 3.
    Sleep(2000);
    return 0;
}
```

The Difference Between a Thread Object and a Thread

FAQ 7

Why can you close a handle to a thread without terminating the thread?

An important distinction for thread objects is that the HANDLE is to a thread kernel object, not to the thread itself. For most API functions, the distinction does not matter. However, when you call `CloseHandle()` with a handle to a thread, you are merely indicating that you wish to disassociate yourself from the kernel object. All `CloseHandle()` does is decrement the reference count of the object. If the count drops to zero, the object itself is destroyed.

The thread that the kernel object refers to also has the kernel object open. Therefore the default reference count on a thread object is two. When you call `CloseHandle()` the count drops and when the thread terminates the count drops. Only when both of these things happen, regardless of the order, will the object actually be destroyed.

The reference-counting mechanism guarantees that the new thread will have a place to write its return value. The mechanism also guarantees that the old thread will be able to read that return value as long as it does not call `CloseHandle()`.

Because the handle returned by `CreateThread()` is owned by the process and not the thread, it is possible for the newly created thread to call `CloseHandle()` instead of the original thread. The function `_beginthread()` in the Microsoft Visual C++ C run-time library does this, as discussed in Chapter 8.

The Thread Exit Code

I cheated in the NUMBERS sample program in Listing 2-2 by putting a `Sleep()` in `main()` to give the threads time to exit. Ideally we would like to make sure that the threads have finished and examine their exit values before exiting the program. If the processor was extremely busy, it is possible that the `Sleep()` call could return before the threads have completed.

The installation program for Windows NT is a case in point. While the primary thread copies from the CD to the hard drive, a second thread creates the boot disks simultaneously by copying files to the floppy. Either of these operations could finish first, so the primary thread must make sure that the second thread has finished before continuing. Otherwise either the floppy or the hard drive would not have a complete copy of its data.

This information can be obtained using the thread handle returned by `CreateThread()` and calling the function `GetExitCodeThread()`:

BOOL GetExitCodeThread(

HANDLE hThread,
LPDWORD lpExitCode
);

Parameters

hThread   The handle to the thread, returned by
                           `CreateThread()`.

lpExitCode   Pointer to DWORD to receive the exit status.

Return Value

`CloseHandle()` returns TRUE if it succeeds, otherwise it returns FALSE. On failure, call `GetLastError()` to find out why. If the thread has exited, then the thread's exit value will be written at *lpExitCode*. If the thread is still running, then the value STILL_ACTIVE will be written at *lpExitCode*.

The sample program in Listing 2-3 starts two threads, then asks you to "Press any key to exit." When you press a key, it checks to make sure that the threads have both exited. If both threads have exited, the program displays their exit status and exits the primary thread. Otherwise you are told which threads are still running.

Although the example looks contrived, the background printing sample later in this chapter has exactly the same problem. What if the user selects File / Exit while a background thread is still printing? For the purposes of this chapter, we will just refuse to exit until the threads complete.

Listing 2-3. EXITCODE.C—Demonstration of GetExitCodeThread()

```
/*
 * ExitCode.c
 *
```

Listing 2-3 (continued)

```
 * Start two threads and try to exit
 * when the user presses a key.
 */

#include <stdio.h>
#include <stdlib.h>
#include <windows.h>

DWORD WINAPI ThreadFunc(LPVOID);

int main()
{
    HANDLE hThrd1;
    HANDLE hThrd2;
    DWORD exitCode1 = 0;
    DWORD exitCode2 = 0;
    DWORD threadId;

    hThrd1 = CreateThread(NULL,
        0,
        ThreadFunc,
        (LPVOID)1,
        0,
        &threadId );
    if (hThrd1)
        printf("Thread 1 launched\n");

    hThrd2 = CreateThread(NULL,
        0,
        ThreadFunc,
        (LPVOID)2,
        0,
        &threadId );
    if (hThrd2)
        printf("Thread 2 launched\n");

    // Keep waiting until both calls to
    // GetExitCodeThread succeed AND
    // neither of them returns STILL_ACTIVE.
    // This method is not optimal - we'll
    // see the correct way in Chapter 3.
    for (;;)
    {
        printf("Press any key to exit..\n");
        getch();
```

Listing 2-3 (continued)

```
            GetExitCodeThread(hThrd1, &exitCode1);
            GetExitCodeThread(hThrd2, &exitCode2);
            if ( exitCode1 == STILL_ACTIVE )
                puts("Thread 1 is still running!");
            if ( exitCode2 == STILL_ACTIVE )
                puts("Thread 2 is still running!");
            if ( exitCode1 != STILL_ACTIVE
                && exitCode2 != STILL_ACTIVE )
                break;
        }

    CloseHandle(hThrd1);
    CloseHandle(hThrd2);

    printf("Thread 1 returned %d\n", exitCode1);
    printf("Thread 2 returned %d\n", exitCode2);

    return EXIT_SUCCESS;
}

/*
 * Take the startup value, do some simple math on it,
 * and return the calculated value.
 */
DWORD WINAPI ThreadFunc(LPVOID n)
{
    Sleep((DWORD)n*1000*2);
    return (DWORD)n * 10;
}
```

PROGRAM OUTPUT:

```
Thread 1 launched
Thread 2 launched
Press any key to exit..
Thread 1 is still running!
Thread 2 is still running!
Press any key to exit..
Thread 2 is still running!
Press any key to exit..
Thread 1 returned 10
Thread 2 returned 20
```

`GetExitCodeThread()` will return the return value from the thread function, which is `ThreadFunc()` in this program. However, `GetExitCodeThread()` has the bad behavior of returning TRUE for success even if the thread is still running and no exit code is available yet. When this happens, `GetExitCodeThread()` sets *lpExitCode* to the value STILL_ACTIVE. You have to be very careful of this behavior. It is not possible to tell from the return values whether the thread is still running, or if it terminated but returned the numeric equivalent of STILL_ACTIVE.

IMPORTANT!

> In this chapter, we will use `GetExitCodeThread()` to wait for a thread to exit. However, `GetExitCodeThread()` is *not* the right way to do this. Chapter 3 describes the correct solution in detail.

Exiting a Thread

In the last two sample programs we have exited threads by returning from the thread function. It is sometimes necessary to exit a thread without returning all the way up to the thread function. In this case you can use the API function `ExitThread()`.

VOID ExitThread(
    DWORD dwExitCode
);

Parameters

dwExitCode   Exit code for this thread.

Return Value

None, this function never returns.

This function is similar to the function `exit()` in the C Run-time Library because it can be called at any time and it never returns. Any code that comes after this call will never execute.

Listing 2-4 shows `ExitThread()`. The thread will always have an exit code of 4 because `AnotherFunc()` never returns.

Listing 2-4. EXITTHRD.C—Demonstration of ExitThread()

```c
/*
 * ExitThrd.c
 *
 * Demonstrate ExitThread
 */

#include <stdio.h>
#include <stdlib.h>
#include <windows.h>

DWORD WINAPI ThreadFunc(LPVOID);
void AnotherFunc(void);

int main()
{
    HANDLE hThrd;
    DWORD exitCode = 0;
    DWORD threadId;

    hThrd = CreateThread(NULL,
        0,
        ThreadFunc,
        (LPVOID)1,
        0,
        &threadId );
    if (hThrd)
        printf("Thread launched\n");

    for(;;)
    {
        BOOL rc;
        rc = GetExitCodeThread(hThrd, &exitCode)
        if (rc && exitCode != STILL_ACTIVE )
            break;
    }

    CloseHandle(hThrd);

    printf("Thread returned %d\n", exitCode);

    return EXIT_SUCCESS;
}
```

Listing 2-4 (continued)

```
/*
 * Call a function to do something that terminates
 * the thread with ExitThread instead of returning.
 */
DWORD WINAPI ThreadFunc(LPVOID n)
{
    printf("Thread running\n");
    AnotherFunc();
    return 0;
}

void AnotherFunc()
{
    printf("About to exit thread\n");
    ExitThread(4);
    // It is impossible to get here, this line
    // will never be printed
    printf("This will never print\n");
}
```

PROGRAM OUTPUT:

```
Thread launched
Thread running
About to exit thread
Thread returned 4
```

Exiting the Primary Thread

FAQ 8

What happens if there are threads running when my program exits?

The thread that is running when a program starts up is the primary thread. This thread is special in two ways. First, it is responsible for the main message loop in a GUI (Graphical User Interface) application. Second, exiting this thread by returning from `main()` or calling `ExitProcess()` will cause all threads to be forcibly terminated and therefore the application itself will terminate. The other threads are not given a chance to clean up.

If you take out the call to `Sleep()` at the end of NUMBERS in Listing 2-2, then the program will print out a partial list of numbers and then stop. The C run-time library causes this behavior because of what it does when the primary thread returns from `main()`. This behavior is discussed in more detail in Chapter 8, but the point to remember is to always wait for your threads to exit before returning from `main()` or `WinMain()`. In Chapter 3, you'll see how to do this properly.

It is possible to call `ExitThread()` in the primary thread, and thereby exit the primary thread but keep the workers running. However, doing so bypasses the cleanup functions in the run-time library and prevents them from cleaning up open files and calling cleanup functions. I do not recommend doing so.

Error Handling

FAQ 9

? What is MTVERIFY?

Before jumping into background printing, it is worth taking a look at how Win32 handles errors. Especially in Windows NT, virtually anything that goes wrong in an API function can be described by calling `GetLast-Error()`. Experience has shown that it is easy to make a mistake when calling the various thread functions, and proper error handling will prevent frustration and create a more reliable application.

For this book, we will be using a macro called `MTVERIFY()` that works in both GUI applications and in console applications. This macro will be placed around Win32 calls that report errors with `GetLastError()`. If the Win32 function fails, `MTVERIFY()` will print out a short textual description of what `GetLastError()` reported and then exit. You can find the source code for MTVERIFY in Appendix A.

Although these sample programs have been tested, you will find this error checking invaluable if you make modifications to these programs and try things out for yourself.

The sample in Listing 2-5 shows MTVERIFY in action. This sample is similar to the last listing, except that the call to `CloseHandle()` has been switched around with the call to `GetExitCodeThread()` in order to cause `GetExitCodeThread()` to fail.

Listing 2-5. ERROR.C—Demonstration of Error handler

```
/*
 * Error.c
 *
 * Demonstrate the MTVERIFY macro.
 */

#include <stdio.h>
#include <stdlib.h>
#include <windows.h>
#include "MtVerify.h"
```

Listing 2-5 (continued)

```
DWORD WINAPI ThreadFunc(LPVOID);

int main()
{
    HANDLE hThrd;
    DWORD exitCode = 0;
    DWORD threadId;

    MTVERIFY( hThrd = CreateThread(NULL,
        0,
        ThreadFunc,
        (LPVOID)1,
        0,
        &threadId )
    );
    if (hThrd)
        printf("Thread launched\n");

    MTVERIFY( CloseHandle(hThrd) );

    for(;;)
    {
        BOOL rc;
        MTVERIFY( rc = GetExitCodeThread(hThrd, &exitCode) );
        if (!rc && exitCode != STILL_ACTIVE )
            break;
    }

    printf("Thread returned %d\n", exitCode);

    return EXIT_SUCCESS;
}

DWORD WINAPI ThreadFunc(LPVOID n)
{
    printf("Thread running\n");
    return 0;
}
```

PROGRAM OUTPUT:

```
Thread launched
Thread running
```

```
The following call failed at line 38 in Error.c:
    rc = GetExitCodeThread(hThrd, &exitCode)

Reason: The handle is invalid.
```

Background Printing

Of all the devices attached to your computer, the printer is often the slowest. An ink-jet or dot-matrix printer can take several minutes to print a page, and a fast laser printer can print 24 pages per minute. But neither of these comes close to the 300 megabytes per minute that a hard drive is capable of transferring.

Printing in the background is so enticing that it was the impetus for the first multitasking hooks for TSRs in MS-DOS version 2. The Print Manager in Windows now takes care of printing the document once an application finishes spooling the data, but just creating the data for the printer can take several minutes. Using multiple threads, we can let one thread produce the data for the printer while another thread controls the user interface.

With the three calls you have learned, you now have enough functionality to write a small application that does background printing.

The Microsoft Threading Model

The Win32 documentation recommends that multithreaded applications have GUI threads and worker threads. The GUI thread takes care of putting up windows and handling the main message loop. The worker threads take care of performing time-consuming tasks, such as recalculation or repagination, that would cause the primary thread's message queue to become unresponsive. Generally the GUI thread never does anything that cannot be accomplished quickly.

The definition of a GUI thread is a thread that has a message queue. The messages for any particular window on the screen are always handled by the thread that created that window. All changes to that window should be handled by that thread.

If a worker thread creates a window, a message queue is created and attached to that thread and the thread becomes a GUI thread. This means that worker threads should not put up main windows, dialogs, or message boxes, among other things.

If a worker thread needs input or must display an error, the task should be delegated to the UI thread and the results reported back to the worker thread. We will look at these problems in detail in Chapter 11.

Description of the Printing Example

On the samples CD-ROM you will find an application called BACKPRNT. When the application starts up, you see an edit control and a menu. Enter some text in the edit control, and then press either "Display" or "Print." The text is rendered into a bitmap, italicized, and then redisplayed in either the window or onto the printer, depending on which button you pressed. If you selected "Print," you are also presented with the Print common dialog box.

As soon as a worker thread is launched, the application will be ready for you to enter a new message. The application will create as many worker threads as you have the patience to type in.

Architecture of the Printing Example

Although you have seen in this chapter how potentially difficult it is to make multithreaded applications work properly, this example shares a common design goal with most of the big examples in this book:

Prefer simplicity and safety over complexity and speed.

Throughout this book, I will try to show you how to design applications with low **surface area** between threads. By surface area, I mean the number of data structures that threads must share. As a rule, the more closely related the threads are in an application, the greater the chances for errors and race conditions.

To meet these goals, the primary thread for BACKPRNT is responsible for bundling together all the information that the worker thread will need, then creating the worker thread and handing it the new thread. The thread startup code is in the routine `PrintText()`, shown here:

Listing 2-6. Excerpt from BACKPRNT, PrintText() routine

```
//
// Asks user which Printer to use, then creates
// background printing thread.
//
HANDLE PrintText(HWND hwndParent, char *pszText)
{
    ThreadPrintInfo *pInfo;
    HANDLE hThread;
    DWORD dwThreadId;
    int result;
    DOCINFO docInfo;
```

Listing 2-6 (continued)

```
PRINTDLG dlgPrint;

// Put up Common Dialog for Printing and get hDC.
memset(&dlgPrint, 0, sizeof(PRINTDLG));
dlgPrint.lStructSize = sizeof(PRINTDLG);
dlgPrint.hwndOwner = hwndParent;
dlgPrint.Flags = PD_ALLPAGES | PD_USEDEVMODECOPIES
        | PD_NOPAGENUMS | PD_NOSELECTION | PD_RETURNDC;
dlgPrint.hInstance = hInst;
if (!PrintDlg(&dlgPrint))
    return NULL;

// Initialize Printer device
docInfo.cbSize = sizeof(DOCINFO);
docInfo.lpszDocName = "Background Printing Example";
docInfo.lpszOutput = NULL;
docInfo.lpszDatatype = NULL;
docInfo.fwType = 0;
result = StartDoc(dlgPrint.hDC, &docInfo);
result = StartPage(dlgPrint.hDC);

pInfo = HeapAlloc(GetProcessHeap(),
                  HEAP_ZERO_MEMORY,
                  sizeof(ThreadPrintInfo));
pInfo->hDlg = hwndParent;
pInfo->hWndParent = hwndParent;
pInfo->hDc = dlgPrint.hDC;
pInfo->bPrint = TRUE;
strcpy(pInfo->szText, pszText);

MTVERIFY( hThread = CreateThread(NULL, 0,
    BackgroundPrintThread, (LPVOID)pInfo,
    0, &dwThreadId ));

// keep track of all background printing threads
gPrintJobs[gNumPrinting++] = hThread;

return hThread;
}
```

The flow of control in this function goes like this:

1. **Present the Print common dialog.** It is important to do this in the primary thread. Otherwise, if the user clicked "Print" several times

rapidly, each worker thread would display its own Print common dialog at the same time. Showing the user multiple copies of the common dialog is not very useful.

2. **Create a data block of information on the heap.** A global variable could be overwritten and a stack variable might go out of scope. The only safe place to pass data to the new thread is on the heap.

3. **Initialize the data block, including making a copy of the string to print.** If we let the worker thread read the data from the edit control directly, it might be possible for the user to change the edit box before the worker thread finished starting up. This would be a race condition.

4. **Start the thread.**

5. **Save the thread handle.** We will need the thread handle to make sure that the user does not exit the application while threads are still running.

By making the primary thread get all the data ready for the worker thread, we guarantee that everything will happen in the right order and that the worker thread will receive data that is not out-of-date or corrupt. Once the worker thread has started, it does not need any information from the dialog, the program's global data, or the primary thread to finish its work.

BACKPRNT keeps track of all threads that have been created. If the user tries to exit, the GUI thread waits for the worker threads to exit before leaving the program. The following code does the waiting:

```
for (index = 0; index < gNumPrinting; index++)
    {
        DWORD status;
        do
        {   // Wait for thread to terminate
            MTVERIFY(
                GetExitCodeThread(gPrintJobs[index], &status));
            Sleep(10);
        } while (status == STILL_ACTIVE);
    } // end for
```

This is *not* a very good way to wait. You will see a much better solution in the next chapter. However, it does demonstrate that you need to take responsibility for running threads. If you exit without waiting, the threads will be terminated and your printed results will be less than desirable.

The Background Thread

The background thread is completely separate from the main thread. It uses separate data structures, separate device contexts, and is noninteractive. Anything that must be drawn to the screen is rendered by sending a message to the primary GUI thread to tell it to do the work. The printer DC can be written to directly because it was created especially for this thread. The code for the background thread is shown in Listing 2-7.

Listing 2-7. Excerpt from BACKPRNT, BackgroundPrintThread() routine

```
DWORD WINAPI BackgroundPrintThread(LPVOID pVoid)
{
    ThreadPrintInfo *pInfo = (ThreadPrintInfo*) pVoid;
    RECT rect;
    RECT rectMem;
    int iHeight;
    HDC hDcMem;
    HBITMAP bmpMem;
    HBITMAP bmpOld;
    int x, y;
    int counter = 0;
    HFONT hFont;
    HFONT hFontOld;

    // Get dimensions of paper into rect
    rect.left = 0;
    rect.top = 0;
    rect.right =  GetDeviceCaps(pInfo->hDc, HORZRES);
    rect.bottom = GetDeviceCaps(pInfo->hDc, VERTRES);

    // Create Font
    hFont = CreateFont(-64, 0,
        0, 0, FW_DONTCARE,
        FALSE, FALSE, FALSE,
        ANSI_CHARSET,
        OUT_TT_PRECIS,
        CLIP_DEFAULT_PRECIS,
        PROOF_QUALITY,
        VARIABLE_PITCH,
        "Arial");
    MTASSERT( hFont != 0);

    // Draw into memory device context
    hDcMem = CreateCompatibleDC(pInfo->hDc);
    hFontOld = SelectObject(hDcMem, hFont);
```

Listing 2-7 (continued)

```
iHeight = DrawText(hDcMem, pInfo->szText, -1,   &rect,
        DT_LEFT | DT_NOPREFIX | DT_WORDBREAK | DT_CALCRECT);
rectMem = rect;
rectMem.left = rect.left + iHeight;

rectMem.right = rect.right + (iHeight*2);
bmpMem = CreateCompatibleBitmap(hDcMem,
                        rectMem.right, rect.bottom);
bmpOld = SelectObject(hDcMem, bmpMem);
OffsetRect(&rect, iHeight, 0);
DrawText(hDcMem, pInfo->szText, -1,   &rect,
        DT_LEFT | DT_NOPREFIX | DT_WORDBREAK);

// Italicize bitmap. We use GetPixel and
// SetPixel because they are horribly inefficient,
// thereby causing the thread to run for awhile.
for (y = 0; y < iHeight; y++)
{   // Italicize line y
    for (x = rectMem.right; x > iHeight; x--)
    {   // Move specified pixel to the right.
        COLORREF color;
        int offset;
        offset = y - iHeight;
        color = GetPixel(hDcMem, x + offset, y);
        if (color != 0)
            counter++;
        SetPixel(hDcMem, x, y, color);
    } // end for x
} // end for y
MTASSERT( counter > 0);

// Copy bitmap of italicized text from memory to device
if (pInfo->bPrint)
    BitBlt(pInfo->hDc, 50, 50, 50+rect.right, 50+rect.bottom,
        hDcMem, iHeight, 0, SRCCOPY);
else
    SendMessage(pInfo->hDlg, WM_SHOWBITMAP, 0, (LPARAM) bmpMem);

SelectObject(hDcMem, hFontOld);
SelectObject(hDcMem, bmpOld);
DeleteDC(hDcMem);

if (pInfo->bPrint)
{   // Finish printing
    int result;
```

Listing 2-7 (continued)

```
            result = EndPage(pInfo->hDc);
            MTASSERT (result != SP_ERROR);
            result = EndDoc(pInfo->hDc);
            MTASSERT (result != SP_ERROR);
            DeleteDC(pInfo->hDc);
    }
    else
        ReleaseDC(pInfo->hWndParent, pInfo->hDc);
     // free data structure passed in.
    HeapFree(GetProcessHeap(), 0, pInfo);
    return 0;
}
```

Tips for Success

Even this relatively simple example illustrates the key concepts behind successfully writing a multithreaded program:

1. Separate the data between threads. Avoid global variables.
2. Do not share GDI objects between threads
3. Make sure you know the state of your threads. Do not exit without waiting for them to shut down.
4. Let the primary thread handle the user interface.

You can find more information on sharing GDI objects between threads in Chapter 11. You will find more information on waiting for threads to exit in Chapter 3.

Chapter 3

Hurry Up and Wait

This chapter shows how the processor gets shared and how programs can reduce their impact on system resources. The performance monitoring tools are introduced. This chapter introduces signaled objects and the various Wait...() *functions.*

In Chapter 2 you saw that you could use GetExitCodeThread() to determine whether a thread was still running. By continually checking the return from GetExitCodeThread() you could wait for a thread to exit. Failing to wait for a thread to exit caused the thread to be forcibly terminated before it was done.

   With one or two threads waiting like this, there does not seem to be much of a problem, but what happens if you have *two hundred* threads that are waiting by continually calling GetExitCodeThread()? Suddenly, a minimal amount of CPU usage by each thread adds up to a *lot* of CPU usage overall. Making this waiting efficient becomes a critical task. This chapter talks about how to keep your threads from being processor hogs and shows you tools to help find problems when they occur.

   Waiting for something to happen is something that threads need to do frequently. Whenever you read user input or access a disk, your thread must wait. Because the disk drive and the user are each thousands to millions of times slower than the processor, waiting is something that applications need to be very good at.

Busy Waiting

I used two techniques to wait in Chapter 2. The first technique was the Win32 `Sleep()` function. This function causes the operating system to "pause" the thread and not restart it again until the requested amount of time has elapsed. Although `Sleep()` worked for the simple example, in practice it is impossible to predict how long something will take. Even a "quick" task could take several minutes if there is a high priority process running somewhere else in the system.

The next technique I used was to create a **busy loop** that continually called `GetExitCodeThread()` and kept retrying until the result was no longer STILL_ACTIVE. Busy loops are also sometimes called **busy waits.** A busy loop is usually reliable, but it has the significant drawback that it wastes a *lot* of CPU time. This point is so important that I'll say it again:

Do not ever use a busy loop in Win32.

Let's look at the impact on the system of using a busy loop. The sample in Listing 3-1 calculates pi twice and displays the amount of time it takes to make each of the two calculations. The first run uses a normal function call, so it works in the way you are used to. The second run has a worker thread do the calculation while the primary thread sits in a busy loop waiting for the worker thread to finish.

Listing 3-1. BUSYWAIT.C—Effect of busy loop on performance

```
/*
 * BusyWait.c
 *
 * Sample code for "Multitasking in Win32"
 * This is from Chapter 3, Listing 3-1
 *
 * Demonstrate the effect on performance
 * of using a busy loop. First call the
 * worker routine with just a function call
 * to get a baseline performance reading,
 * then create a second thread and a
 * busy loop.
 *
 * Build command: cl /MD busywait.c
 */
```

Listing 3-1 (continued)

```c
#include <stdio.h>
#include <stdlib.h>
#include <windows.h>
#include <time.h>
#include "MtVerify.h"

DWORD WINAPI ThreadFunc(LPVOID);

int main()
{
    HANDLE hThrd;
    DWORD exitCode = 0;
    DWORD threadId;
    DWORD begin;
    DWORD elapsed;

    puts("Timing normal function call...");
    begin = GetTickCount();
    ThreadFunc(0);
    elapsed = GetTickCount()-begin;
    printf("Function call took: %d.%.03d seconds\n\n",
                elapsed/1000, elapsed%1000);

    puts("Timing thread + busy loop...");
    begin = GetTickCount();

    MTVERIFY( hThrd = CreateThread(NULL,
        0,
        ThreadFunc,
        (LPVOID)1,
        0,
        &threadId )
    );
    /* This busy loop chews up lots of CPU time */
    for (;;)
    {
        GetExitCodeThread(hThrd, &exitCode);
        if ( exitCode != STILL_ACTIVE )
            break;
    }

    elapsed = GetTickCount()-begin;
    printf("Thread + busy loop took: %d.%.03d seconds\n",
                elapsed/1000, elapsed%1000);
```

Listing 3-1 (continued)

```
MTVERIFY( CloseHandle(hThrd) );

    return EXIT_SUCCESS;
}


/*
 * Cute little busy work routine that computes the value
 * of PI using probability.  Highly dependent on having
 * a good random number generator (rand is iffy)
 */
DWORD WINAPI ThreadFunc(LPVOID n)
{
    int i;
    int inside = 0;
    double val;

    UNREFERENCED_PARAMETER(n);

    /* Seed the random-number generator */
    srand( (unsigned)time( NULL ) );

    for (i=0; i<1000000; i++)
    {
        double x = (double)(rand())/RAND_MAX;
        double y = (double)(rand())/RAND_MAX;
        if ( (x*x + y*y) <= 1.0 )
            inside++;
    }
    val = (double)inside / i;
    printf("PI = %.4g\n", val*4);
    return 0;
}
```

PROGRAM OUTPUT:

```
Timing normal function call...
PI = 3.146
Function call took: 7.993 seconds

Timing thread + busy loop...
PI = 3.14
Thread + busy loop took: 15.946 seconds
```

Surprised? The second run with the busy loop took almost twice as long to run as the normal function call. This effect is caused by preemptive multi-tasking. The operating system cannot tell that one thread is doing something useful and the other is doing something not-so-useful, so each thread is given equal amounts of processor time. The primary thread uses its processor time to frantically check the return value over and over again, potentially doing so several million times per second. Not very productive.

The problem is even worse if the worker thread is doing something that does not use much CPU time. On the samples CD-ROM, there is a program called BUSY3 that does just this. The busy loop will spend all available processor cycles checking to see if the thread is done. If that program was the only application running, using all the processor cycles would not be a big deal. However, the user could be running other programs or using Explorer, and your busy loop would be taking valuable CPU time away from other programs that really need it. The impact of a busy loop on a server that is trying to handle dozens or hundreds of users would be disastrous.

Although the busy loop in Listing 3-1 is obvious, it is easy to unintentionally use familiar algorithms from Win16 that were implemented with busy loops. Win16 had no facilities in the operating system for helping you wait, so it encouraged poor solutions such as writing busy loops. For example, the following code fragment shows a common technique in Win16 programs for waiting around for a short amount of time.

```
void Wait(DWORD ms)
{
    DWORD begin = GetTickCount();
    while (GetTickCount()-begin < ms)
        ;    /* Do Nothing */
}
```

This code will use all available CPU time to do nothing but wait for something to happen. Although Win16 does provide timers, it is necessary to return to the main message loop to use them. Sometimes this technique was a lot simpler. In summary, keep in mind that busy loops can creep into your code even if you are not using threads.

Performance Monitors

Fortunately, both Windows NT and Windows 95 provide tools that can warn you when your application is using excessive CPU time. I used these tools at one point when I was trying to program an animated selection bounding rectangle.

Programmed properly, a small animated rectangle should take almost no CPU time. When I used the performance monitoring tools, I discovered that the animation was using up all available CPU time, even when the application was minimized. Clearly there was a problem in the code.

My first fix brought the CPU usage down to acceptable levels. Then I clicked on another application and ZOOM! The CPU usage of the animated rectangle shot back up, even though the application was not supposed to be doing anything. It took a substantial amount of tweaking and adjusting, but I finally was able to fix the idle time handling to use a minimal amount of CPU time regardless of whether the application had the focus.

Let's take a look at these tools, because they are important for verifying performance in any Win32 application, and they are invaluable for developing multithreaded applications.

Windows NT Performance Monitor

In Windows NT you can use the Performance Monitor to provide a real-time graph of most of the things happening inside the operating system. You can find the Performance Monitor by opening Administrative Tools in either the Program Manager or the Start menu, depending on whether you are running Windows NT 3.x or 4.x, respectively. The icon looks like this:

Perfmon.exe

Once Performance Monitor is running, click on the "+" sign on the toolbar. You will see the criteria "Processor" and "Processor Utilization" in the combo boxes on the left. If you just click OK, Performance Monitor will start creating a graph of how busy the processor is. Normally the chart looks something like Figure 3-1. The ups and downs in this example reflect the processor responding to what the user is doing.

As long as the line is not at 100 percent, there is spare computing power "left over." When the line hits 100 percent, then the operating system starts dividing the available CPU cycles among all the processes, and the net result is that everything slows down. This is exactly the behavior we saw in BUSYWAIT.

Because the Performance Monitor can tell us how busy the processor is, it is an important tool in making sure that a program you have written is

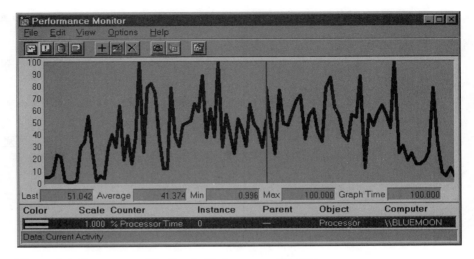

Figure 3-1. Processor utilization in Performance Monitor.

behaving as expected. If the CPU utilization goes to 100 percent and stays there when you start a program, it is a clear warning that you may have a busy loop.

You can use Performance Monitor to see how processor time is being divided between threads by watching what happens inside BUSYWAIT. The first problem is to keep BUSYWAIT running long enough to watch its behavior. In the sample program BUSY2, I modified the loop at the end to run to 100 million instead of 1 million and took out the function call example. These changes keep the program running long enough to watch what it is doing. (Note: You can abort BUSY2 while it is running by typing Ctrl-C.)

First run BUSY2, then change to Performance Monitor. Click the "+" again to add more entries to the chart. If you select "Thread" from the "Object" list, then a list of all threads running in the system will be shown in the "Instance" list box on the right (Figure 3-2).

Both of the threads in BUSY2 are shown in the list. Click on the first and click "Add." Then select the second thread and click "Add" again. Finally, click "Done." The chart should show something like Figure 3-3.

You can see from this chart that each thread is getting a little bit less than half of the available CPU time. The other 10 percent of the system time is being lost to overhead and to other processes. The two threads appear to start at different times in this example because it took me some time to add the second thread to the chart.

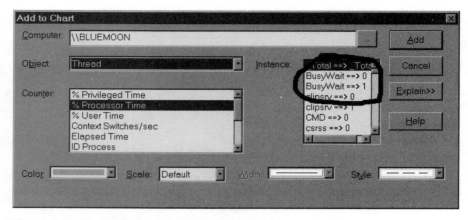

Figure 3-2. Monitor threads in Performance Monitor.

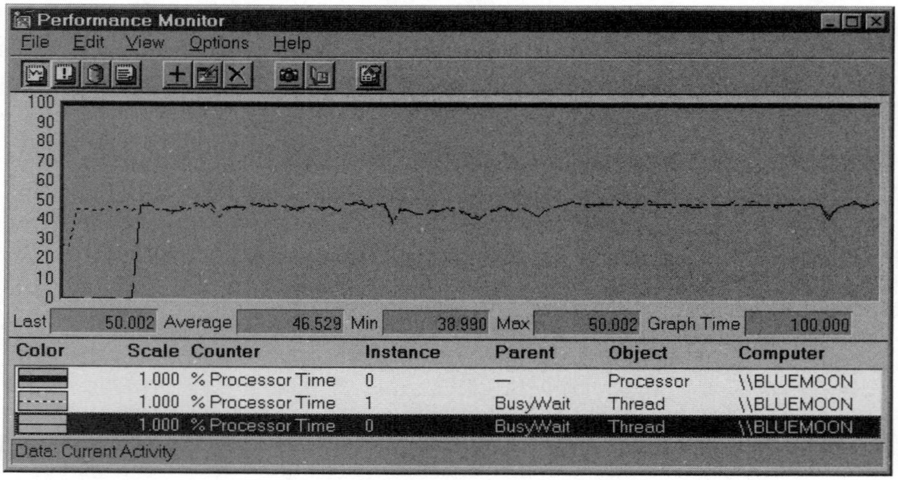

Figure 3-3. BUSY2 threads in Performance Monitor.

Windows 95 System Monitor

In Windows 95, there is a program called the System Monitor that allows you to do a few of the things that Performance Monitor does in NT. To start it, open the Start menu and choose:

Programs / Accessories / System Tools / System Monitor

Sysmon.exe

If the program is not installed, start the Control Panel, choose Add/ Remove Programs, click Accessories, then press the Details button. Near the end of the list, make sure that "System Monitor" is checked, and click OK.

Once you have the System Monitor running, choose "Add Item" from the Edit menu. In the Add Item dialog, choose "Kernel" on the left and "Processor Usage (%)" on the right. Click OK. You should now see a chart as shown in Figure 3-4.

The System Monitor in Windows 95 is much more limited than the Performance Monitor in Windows NT. You can only display the overall CPU usage, you cannot display the CPU usage for each thread as you can in Performance Monitor. However, the tool is still useful to warn you when your program is hogging the CPU when it should not.

If the chart is staying steady at 100 percent as soon as you start System Monitor, then you are probably running a 16-bit Windows application or a

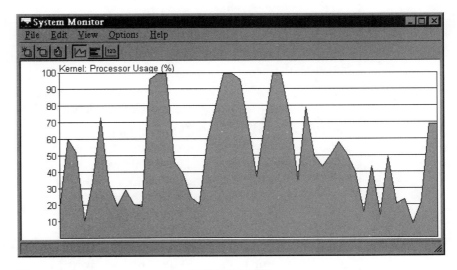

Figure 3-4. Processor usage in SYSMON.EXE.

DOS application that is using up processor cycles. The next sample program will make more sense if you can find the offending program(s) and shut them down.

Waiting for a Thread to Exit

Now that you have seen why using busy loops is a bad idea, let's look at the approved Win32 way of doing things. What we really need is a version of the `Sleep()` call that wakes up when a certain thread exits instead of after a certain amount of time has elapsed. Since the operating system is responsible for thread shutdown, it seems reasonable that the operating system would be able to tell other threads when a given thread shuts down.

Win32 provides a function called `WaitForSingleObject()` that does exactly that. The first argument to `WaitForSingleObject()` is a handle to a kernel object such as a thread. For the purposes of this discussion, let's call the waiting thread Thread 1 and the running thread Thread 2. The thread kernel object is for Thread 2.

Calling `WaitForSingleObject()` with the handle to the thread kernel object will put Thread 1 to sleep until Thread 2 exits. Like the `Sleep()` call, `WaitForSingleObject()` also takes a timeout for the maximum length of time to wait.

DWORD WaitForSingleObject(

    HANDLE hHandle,
    DWORD dwMilliseconds
);

Parameters

hHandle
    Handle to the kernel object to wait for. In this case, the handle to the thread.

dwMilliseconds
    If this amount of time elapses, the function will return even if the handle did not become signaled. This value may be zero to perform a test-and-return, or INFINITE if no time-out is desired.

Return Value

If this function fails it returns WAIT_FAILED. Use `GetLastError()` to get more information. `WaitForSingleObject()` can succeed for any one of three reasons:

1. If the object becomes signaled, WAIT_OBJECT_0 is returned.
2. If the time-out elapses before the object becomes signaled, WAIT_TIMEOUT is returned.
3. Finally, if a thread that owns a mutex exits without releasing the mutex, then WAIT_ABANDONED is returned. Mutexes will be discussed in more detail in Chapter 4.

When given a handle to a thread object, `WaitForSingleObject()` asks the operating system to put Thread 1 to sleep until either:

• Thread 2 exits.

OR

• The amount of time given by *dwMilliseconds* goes by. The count starts from the moment the call is made.

Because the operating system is keeping track of Thread 2, `WaitForSingleObject()` will work correctly even if Thread 2 crashes or is forcibly terminated.

In Listing 2-3 in Chapter 2, we used the following code to wait for a worker thread to exit:

```
for(;;)
{
    int rc;
    rc = GetExitCodeThread(hThrd,&exitCode)
    if (!rc && exitCode != STILL_ACTIVE )
        break;
}
```

This busy loop can now be replaced with this single line of code:

```
WaitForSingleObject( hThrd, INFINITE );
```

? FAQ 10

How do I test if a kernel object is signaled?

There is one particularly important use for the time-out that may not be obvious. Setting the time-out to zero allows you to check the state of a handle and immediately return without waiting. If the handle is "ready," then the function succeeds and returns WAIT_OBJECT_0. Otherwise the function immediately returns with the return value WAIT_TIMEOUT.

There are other reasons why you might want to specify a time-out parameter. The simplest one is that you do not want to become "stuck," especially during the course of debugging. If the thread you are waiting for gets in an endless loop, you can provide a warning by checking the return value and seeing if the time-out expired.

In the example above, you could use the time-out to provide an animation that you are waiting for threads to exit. You would time out every 500 milliseconds, update the icon, and start waiting again.

`WaitForSingleObject()` works on many kinds of handles other than thread handles. In fact, most things in Win32 that are represented by a HANDLE can be used with `WaitForSingleObject()`. Depending on what kind of object you have, the system waits for different things to happen. Formally stated, the system waits for the object to become signaled.

Ding-Dong: Signaled Objects

In Chapter 2 I mentioned the various kinds of kernel objects in Win32, such as files, threads, and mutexes. Each of these objects has state information that may be of interest to running threads. Semaphores and mutexes can report a "green light" to the next waiting thread. Files can tell when an I/O operation is complete, and threads, as we have seen, can tell when they have exited.

Threads can use calls like `WaitForSingleObject()` to efficiently wait for any of these things to happen. The question is, what exactly would we be waiting *for*?

FAQ 11

What is a signaled object?

Kernel objects that can be used with `WaitForSingleObject()` have two states: **signaled** and **nonsignaled.** `WaitForSingleObject()` wakes up when an object becomes signaled. In fact, we will use that as the definition for signaled.

> *When a kernel object is signaled it causes* `WaitForSingleObject()` *to wake up. (As well as other* `Wait()` *functions you will see shortly.)*

In the case of threads, the thread object is nonsignaled while the thread is running, and signaled when the thread terminates. Therefore, any thread waiting on the thread object will wake up when the thread exits because the thread object automatically becomes signaled.

UNIX

Signals in Unix and signaled objects in Win32 are completely different concepts. A signal in Unix is an asynchronous event that usually has an immediate impact on your application. In Win32, when an object becomes signaled it means that its internal state changes. There will be no impact on the application unless a thread is waiting on the object.

Several threads can wait on the same thread handle, and all of the threads will be woken up when that thread handle becomes signaled. However, with other kinds of kernel objects you may only want to wake up one of the waiting threads. Which behavior you get depends on what kind of object you are waiting on. Some objects will only stay signaled long enough to wake a single thread. Other objects stay signaled until explicitly reset. In the next chapter you'll see the sample program EVENTTST that will let you play with how threads respond to signaled objects.

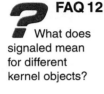

FAQ 12

What does signaled mean for different kernel objects?

Table 3-1 shows what signaled and nonsignaled mean for the various kinds of kernel objects in Win32.

Table 3-1.   Meaning of signaled for kernel objects

Object	Description
Thread*	Signaled when the thread terminates; nonsignaled while the thread is running. Thread objects are created with `CreateThread()` or `CreateRemoteThread()`.
Process*	Signaled when the process terminates; nonsignaled while the process is running. A handle to a process object is returned by `CreateProcess()` or `OpenProcess()`.
Change Notification	Signaled when a particular kind of change occurs in a particular directory. Change notification objects are created with `FindFirstChangeNotification()`.
Console Input*	Signaled when there is input available in the console's input buffer. Handles to the console are returned by `CreateFile()` and `GetStdHandle()`. See Chapter 8.
Event*	The state of an event object is directly controlled by the application using `SetEvent()`, `PulseEvent()`, and `ResetEvent()`. Handles to event objects are returned by `CreateEvent()` and `OpenEvent()`. Event objects can also be set by the system when used in overlapped operations. See Chapter 4.
Mutex*	A mutex is signaled when it is not owned by any thread. When a wait on a mutex returns, the mutex automatically becomes nonsignaled. Handles to mutexes are returned by `CreateMutex()` and `OpenMutex()`. See Chapter 4.
Semaphore*	A semaphore is like a mutex that contains a count of how many threads are allowed to own it. A semaphore is signaled when the count is greater than zero and nonsignaled when the count is zero. Handles to semaphores are returned by `CreateSemaphore()` and `OpenSemaphore()`. See Chapter 4.

*Objects followed by a star are covered in this book.

Waiting for Multiple Objects

Now let's write a program that uses at most three threads to do six tasks. In Listing 3-2, which shows the sample program TaskQueS, there is a function called `ThreadFunc()` that performs some task and returns. The task doing work is simulated by calling `Sleep()` to wait around for a few seconds. Whenever a thread exits, a new thread will be created to do the next task.

Listing 3-2. TASKQUES.C—Dispatch tasks and wait with WaitForSingleObject()

```c
/*
 * TaskQueS.c
 *
 * Call ThreadFunc NUM_TASKS times, using
 * no more than THREAD_POOL_SIZE threads.
 * This version uses WaitForSingleObject,
 * which gives a very suboptimal solution.
 *
 * Build command: cl /MD TaskQueS.c
 */

#include <stdio.h>
#include <stdlib.h>
#include <windows.h>
#include "MtVerify.h"

DWORD WINAPI ThreadFunc(LPVOID);

#define THREAD_POOL_SIZE 3
#define MAX_THREAD_INDEX THREAD_POOL_SIZE-1
#define NUM_TASKS 6

int main()
{
    HANDLE  hThrds[THREAD_POOL_SIZE];
    int     slot = 0;
    DWORD   threadId;
    int     i;
    DWORD   exitCode;

    /*              i=   1 2 3 4 5 6 7 8 9
     * Start Thread     X X X X X X
     * Wait on thread         X X X X X X
     */
```

Listing 3-2 (continued)

```
    for (i=1; i<=NUM_TASKS+THREAD_POOL_SIZE; i++)
    {
        if (i > THREAD_POOL_SIZE)
        {
            WaitForSingleObject(hThrds[slot], INFINITE);
            MTVERIFY( GetExitCodeThread(hThrds[slot], &exitCode) );
            printf("Slot %d terminated\n", exitCode );
            MTVERIFY( CloseHandle(hThrds[slot]) );
        }
        if (i <= NUM_TASKS)
        {
            MTVERIFY( hThrds[slot] = CreateThread(NULL,
                0,
                ThreadFunc,
                (LPVOID)slot,
                0,
                &threadId ) );
            printf("Launched thread #%d (slot %d)\n", i, slot);
        }
        if (++slot > MAX_THREAD_INDEX)
            slot = 0;
    }

    return EXIT_SUCCESS;
}

/*
 * This function just calls Sleep for
 * a random amount of time, thereby
 * simulating some task that takes time.
 *
 * The param "n" is the index into
 * the handle array, kept for informational
 * purposes.
 */
DWORD WINAPI ThreadFunc(LPVOID n)
{
    srand( GetTickCount() );

    Sleep((rand()%10)*800+500);
    printf("Slot %d idle\n", n);
    return ((DWORD)n);
}
```

There is a serious problem with the program as written. It is extremely inefficient, because it assumes that the threads will exit in the order that they were started. Here is the output from a typical run, which immediately shows the assumption to be false.

The primary thread prints "Launched thread" whenever a new thread is started. Each thread prints "Slot x idle" when it exits, and the primary thread prints "Slot x terminated" when it notices that a thread has terminated.

PROGRAM OUTPUT:

```
Launched thread #1 (slot 0)
Launched thread #2 (slot 1)
Launched thread #3 (slot 2)
Slot 1 idle
Slot 2 idle
Slot 0 idle
Slot 0 terminated
Launched thread #4 (slot 0)
Slot 1 terminated
Launched thread #5 (slot 1)
Slot 2 terminated
Launched thread #6 (slot 2)
Slot 2 idle
Slot 0 idle
Slot 1 idle
All slots terminated
```

You can see in the beginning of the output that, by the time the primary thread noticed that the first worker thread (Slot 0) had exited, the second and third worker threads had also exited. Although the goal is to keep three threads running, for a while there were no threads running at all. What we really need is a way to watch for any of the currently running threads to exit.

Introducing WaitForMultipleObjects()

The Win32 call `WaitForMultipleObjects()` allows you to wait for more than one object at the same time. You pass the function an array of handles, the size of the array, and whether to wait on one or all of the handles. Here is what the call looks like:

DWORD WaitForMultipleObjects(

DWORD nCount,
CONST HANDLE *lpHandles,
BOOL bWaitAll,
DWORD dwMilliseconds
);

Parameters

nCount	Number of handles in the array pointed at by *lpHandles*. The maximum allowed count is MAXIMUM_WAIT_OBJECTS.
lpHandles	Pointer to an array of object handles. The handles do not need to all be the same type.
bWaitAll	If this is TRUE, then all of the handles must be signaled before this function returns. Otherwise the function returns when any one of the handles becomes signaled.
dwMilliseconds	If this amount of time elapses, the function will return even if none of the handles became signaled. This value may be zero to perform a test-and-return, or INFINITE if no timeout is desired.

Return Value

The return value from `WaitForMultipleObjects()` is somewhat complicated.

- If the function times out, the return value is WAIT_TIMEOUT, just like `WaitForSingleObject()`.
- If *bWaitAll* is TRUE, then the return value is WAIT_OBJECT_0.
- If *bWaitAll* is FALSE, then the return value minus WAIT_OBJECT_0 tells you which object becomes signaled.
- If you are waiting on any mutexes, then the return value can also be from WAIT_ABANDONED_0 up to WAIT_ABANDONED_0 + *nCount* - 1
- If the function fails, it returns WAIT_FAILED. Use `GetLastError()` to find out why.

It is important to notice that there is a limit to the number of objects you can wait for at one time with `WaitForMultipleObjects()`. The parameter *nCount* can be no larger than MAXIMUM_WAIT_OBJECTS. In Windows NT 3.x and 4.0, this value was 64.

This function can be used to rewrite the TaskQueS example so it operates more efficiently. Instead of `WaitForSingleObject()`, we will call `WaitForMultipleObjects()` with *bWaitAll* equal to FALSE. Now the operating system will watch all of the handles at the same time. The primary thread will be notified immediately when a worker thread exits instead of having to blindly wait for the threads to complete in order.

The next change is to clean up at the end of the program by using `WaitForMultipleObjects()` with *bWaitAll* equal to TRUE (Listing 3-3). We do not want to exit `main()` until all worker threads have completed. This call says to wait for all threads to exit before returning.

Listing 3-3. TASKQUEM.C—Dispatch tasks, wait with WaitForMultipleObjects()

```
/*
 * TaskQueM.c
 *
 * Call ThreadFunc NUM_TASKS times, using
 * no more than THREAD_POOL_SIZE threads.
 * This version uses WaitForMultipleObjects
 * to provide a more optimal solution.
 *
 * Build command: cl /MD TaskQueM.c
 */

#include <stdio.h>
#include <stdlib.h>
#include <windows.h>
#include "MtVerify.h"

DWORD WINAPI ThreadFunc(LPVOID);

#define THREAD_POOL_SIZE 3
#define MAX_THREAD_INDEX THREAD_POOL_SIZE-1
#define NUM_TASKS 6

int main()
{
    HANDLE  hThrds[THREAD_POOL_SIZE];
    int     slot = 0;
    DWORD   threadId;
    int     i;
    DWORD   rc;
```

Listing 3-3 (continued)

```c
for (i=1; i<=NUM_TASKS; i++)
{
    /* Until we've used all threads in *
     * the pool, do not need to wait   *
     * for one to exit                 */
    if (i > THREAD_POOL_SIZE)
    {
        /* Wait for one thread to terminate */
        rc = WaitForMultipleObjects(
            THREAD_POOL_SIZE,
            hThrds,
            FALSE,
            INFINITE );
        slot = rc - WAIT_OBJECT_0;
        MTVERIFY( slot >= 0
            && slot < THREAD_POOL_SIZE );
        printf("Slot %d terminated\n", slot );
        MTVERIFY( CloseHandle(hThrds[slot]) );
    }
    /* Create a new thread in the given
     * available slot */
    MTVERIFY( hThrds[slot++] = CreateThread(NULL,
        0,
        ThreadFunc,
        (LPVOID)slot,
        0,
        &threadId ) );
    printf("Launched thread #%d (slot %d)\n", i, slot);
}

/* Now wait for all threads to terminate */
rc = WaitForMultipleObjects(
    THREAD_POOL_SIZE,
    hThrds,
    TRUE,
    INFINITE );
MTVERIFY( rc >= WAIT_OBJECT_0
        && rc < WAIT_OBJECT_0+THREAD_POOL_SIZE);
for (slot=0; slot<THREAD_POOL_SIZE; slot++)
    MTVERIFY( CloseHandle(hThrds[slot]) );
printf("All slots terminated\n");

return EXIT_SUCCESS;
}
```

Listing 3-3 (continued)

```
/*
 * This function just calls Sleep for
 * a random amount of time, thereby
 * simulating some task that takes time.
 *
 * The param "n" is the index into
 * the handle array, kept for informational
 * purposes.
 */
DWORD WINAPI ThreadFunc(LPVOID n)
{
    srand( GetTickCount() );

    Sleep((rand()%10)*800+500);
    printf("Slot %d idle\n", n);
    return ((DWORD)n);
}
```

PROGRAM OUTPUT:

```
Launched thread #1 (slot 1)
Launched thread #2 (slot 2)
Launched thread #3 (slot 3)
Slot 1 idle
Slot 0 terminated
Launched thread #4 (slot 1)
Slot 2 idle
Slot 3 idle
Slot 1 terminated
Launched thread #5 (slot 2)
Slot 2 terminated
Launched thread #6 (slot 3)
Slot 1 idle
Slot 2 idle
Slot 3 idle
All slots terminated
```

Waiting in a GUI Program

The main message loop is the one place in 16-bit Windows programs that allows a program to wait for something to happen without resorting to busy loops. The standard message loop in a Windows program looks like this:

```
while (GetMessage (&msg, NULL, 0, 0))
{
    TranslateMessage(&msg);
    DispatchMessage(&msg);
}
```

GetMessage() is like a specialized version of WaitForSingleObject() that waits for messages instead of waiting for a kernel object. The call to GetMessage() does not return until a message shows up in your program's queue. Meanwhile, Windows is free to give the processor to another application. GetMessage() is the heart of Win16 cooperative multitasking.

FAQ 13

How do I wait on a handle in the primary thread?

Returning to the main message loop frequently is extremely important. If you do not, your window stops redrawing, your menus stop working, and other things that users do not like start happening. The problem is that if you are waiting in a call to WaitForSingleObject() or WaitForMultipleObjects(), there is no way you can return to your message loop.

Here is how *not* to solve the problem: Do not use a second thread that waits on the handles while the primary thread handles the main message loop. This solution just moves the problem because you still have to figure out when the new thread exits by either polling or using a Win32 Wait…() function.

To solve this problem, the main message loop needs to be modified so that it can wait for a message *or* for a kernel object to be signaled. You need to use a call named MsgWaitForMultipleObjects(). The call is very similar to WaitForMultipleObjects() except that it will wake up if an object is signaled *or* if a message arrives in the queue. MsgWaitForMultipleObjects() also takes a parameter telling what kind of messages to look for.

DWORD MsgWaitForMultipleObjects(
DWORD nCount,
LPHANDLE pHandles,
BOOL fWaitAll,
DWORD dwMilliseconds,
DWORD dwWakeMask
);

Parameters

dwWakeMask   Types of user input to look for. One or more of the following values:

QS_ALLINPUT

QS_HOTKEY

QS_INPUT

QS_KEY

QS_MOUSE

QS_MOUSEBUTTON

QS_MOUSEMOVE

QS_PAINT

QS_POSTMESSAGE

QS_SENDMESSAGE

QS_TIMER

Return Value

`MsgWaitForMultipleObjects()` has one additional return value compared to `WaitForMultipleObjects()`. To indicate that a message has arrived in the queue, the return value is WAIT_OBJECT_0 + *nCount*.

The correct way to use `MsgWaitForMultipleObjects()` is to rewrite the main message loop so that signaled handles are treated like messages. Depending on the return value from `MsgWaitForMultipleObjects()`, the message loop either calls `GetMessage()` and processes the next message, or it acts on one of the signaled handles using code you provide. The outline in Listing 3-4 is a skeleton similar to what would be needed to use `MsgWaitForMultipleObjects()` in your main message loop.

Listing 3-4. Sample main message loop with MsgWaitForMultipleObjects()

```
DWORD  nWaitCount;
HANDLE hWaitArray[4];
BOOL quit;
int exitCode;

while (!quit)
{
    MSG msg;
    int rc;

    rc = MsgWaitForMultipleObjects(
            nWaitCount,
            hWaitArray,
```

Listing 3-4 (continued)

```
                FALSE,
                INFINITE,
                QS_ALLINPUT );

    if (rc == WAIT_OBJECT_0 + nWaitCount)
    {
        while (PeekMessage(&msg, NULL, 0, 0, PM_REMOVE))
        {   // Get Next message in queue
            if (msg.message == WM_QUIT)
            {
                quit = TRUE;
                exitCode = msg.wParam;
                break;
            } // end if
            TranslateMessage(&msg);
            DispatchMessage(&msg);
        } // end while
    }
    else if (rc >= WAIT_OBJECT_0
             && rc < WAIT_OBJECT_0 + nWaitCount)
    {
        int nIndex = rc - WAIT_OBJECT_0;
        /* We now know that the handle at array position */
        /* nIndex was signaled. */
        /* We would have had to keep track of what those */
        /* handles mean to decide what to do next. */
    }
    else if (rc == WAIT_TIMEOUT)
    {
        /* Timeout expired */
    }
    else if (rc >= WAIT_ABANDONED_0
             && rc < WAIT_ABANDONED_0 + nWaitCount)
    {
        int nIndex = rc - WAIT_ABANDONED_0;
        /* A thread died that owned a mutex */
        /* More about this in Chapter 4 */
    }
    else
    {
        /* Something went wrong */
    }
}
```

There is one final problem that is not solved by this sample code. It may be necessary to wait for handles to be signaled even after the application receives WM_QUIT. For example, in the BACKPRNT example from Chapter 2, the user can select "Exit" while there are still threads running. Unless you wait for all the threads to be signaled, all of the background threads would be prematurely terminated when the main loop exited.

Using `MsgWaitForMultipleObjects()`, we can rewrite that main loop in BACKPRNT so that the Exit menu will be disabled if there are worker threads running. Here is the message loop from BACKPRNT in Chapter 2. It is a very typical main message loop.

```
while (GetMessage(&msg, NULL, 0, 0))
    {   // Get next message in queue
        if (hDlgMain == NULL
            || !IsDialogMessage(hDlgMain,&msg))
        {
            TranslateMessage(&msg);
            DispatchMessage(&msg);
        }
    } // end while
```

The PRNTWAIT Sample Program

In the samples on the CD-ROM you will find an example called PRNT-WAIT. This sample is a new version of BACKPRNT that allows the user to choose File/Exit at any time, then automatically waits for all threads to terminate before exiting the application. PRNTWAIT also displays a count of how many threads are currently running.

Listing 3-5 shows the main message loop from PRNTWAIT that uses `MsgWaitForMultipleObjects()`. As you can see, it is significantly more complex. This example only handles a few of the cases shown in the skeleton in Listing 3-4. For example, PRNTWAIT does not use mutexes so the message loop does not need to handle WAIT_ABANDONED.

Listing 3-5. Excerpt from PRNTWAIT, main message loop

```
while (!quit || gNumPrinting > 0)
{   // Wait for next message or object being signaled
    DWORD   dwWake;
    dwWake = MsgWaitForMultipleObjects(
                        gNumPrinting,
                        gPrintJobs,
                        FALSE,
```

Listing 3-5 (continued)

```
                                        INFINITE,
                                        QS_ALLEVENTS);

        if (dwWake >= WAIT_OBJECT_0
                && dwWake < WAIT_OBJECT_0 + gNumPrinting)
        {   // Object has been signaled
            // Reorder the handle array so we do not leave
            // empty slots. Take the handle at the end of
            // the array and move it into the now-empty slot.
            int index = dwWake - WAIT_OBJECT_0;
            gPrintJobs[index] = gPrintJobs[gNumPrinting-1];
            gPrintJobs[gNumPrinting-1] = 0;
            gNumPrinting--;
            SendMessage(hDlgMain, WM_THREADCOUNT, gNumPrinting, 0L);
        } // end if
        else if (dwWake == WAIT_OBJECT_0 + gNumPrinting)
        {
            while (PeekMessage(&msg, NULL, 0, 0, PM_REMOVE))
            {   // Get Next message in queue
                if(hDlgMain == NULL || !IsDialogMessage(hDlgMain,&msg))
                {
                    if (msg.message == WM_QUIT)
                    {
                        quit = TRUE;
                        exitCode = msg.wParam;
                        break;
                    } // end if
                    TranslateMessage(&msg);
                    DispatchMessage(&msg);
                }
            } // end while
        }
    } // end while
```

There are several cases that this loop must handle that were not obvious when it was first written.

1. Windows still sends you messages after WM_QUIT. If you wait for your threads to die after receiving WM_QUIT, you must continue processing messages or the window becomes unresponsive and stops painting.

2. MsgWaitForMultipleObjects() does not allow "gaps" in the array of handles, so you should compact the handle array when a handle is

signaled before calling the wait again. Do not just set the handle to NULL in the handle array. If you look at the code, handles are removed from the array by moving the handle at the end of the array to the empty slot and decreasing the array size.

3. If another thread updates the list of objects that you are waiting on, you need a way to force `MsgWaitForMultipleObjects()` to return and be restarted to include the new handle. The sample in Listing 3-5 solves this problem using the message WM_THREADCOUNT.

The third case requires a little more discussion. Usually, there is only one place in the program that calls `MsgWaitForMultipleObjects()`, and this call is inside the message loop. The array of handles you use to call `MsgWaitForMultipleObjects()` is entirely under your control. If you need to wait on more kernel objects, just add more entries to the array. The third case above discusses the situation where another thread needs to update the handle array. Obviously it cannot just write the array directly because the array has already been passed to `MsgWaitForMultipleObjects()`. Therefore you must force `MsgWaitForMultipleObjects()` to exit so you can update the array and restart the call.

Summary

In this chapter we went over the damaging effects of using busy loops and saw how to use the Performance Monitor in Windows NT to catch such problems. We looked at what a signaled object is and how to wait for one or several in a worker thread or in a GUI thread. Finally, we saw how to rebuild a main message loop to properly use `WaitForMultipleObjects()`.

Chapter 4

Synchronization

This chapter discusses the Win32 synchronization mechanisms with particular emphasis on performance in a multitasking environment.

One of the trickiest problems when writing a multithreaded application is getting the threads to cooperate with each other. Unless you coordinate the threads, you end up with race conditions and data corruption, as seen in Chapter 2.

In the typical office bureaucracy, coordination is performed by a manager. A similar solution, with one thread being the "boss," could be implemented in software, but it has the serious drawback of requiring every thread to get in line whenever it needs guidance. As anyone knows who has waited in such lines, they are usually long and slow, clearly not a useful solution for a high-performance computing system.

The coordination of threads and processes in Win32 is performed by **synchronization mechanisms**. A synchronization mechanism is the equivalent of a traffic light for threads. You design a set of threads to use the same "traffic light," and the traffic light takes care of giving one thread a green light and giving all other threads a red light. The traffic light also makes sure that every thread eventually gets a green light.

There are a wide range of synchronization mechanisms available. Which one you use depends on the kind of problem you are trying to solve. As I discuss each kind of mechanism in this chapter, I will describe when and why it should be used.

These synchronization mechanisms are often combined in various ways to produce more sophisticated mechanisms. If you view these functions as building blocks you will be able to design synchronization mechanisms that are much better suited to your particular problems.

Critical Sections

One of the easiest synchronization mechanisms to use in Win32 is the **critical section.** A critical section is that portion of the code that accesses a shared resource. A resource in this case is *not* a resource from a resource file. The resource could be a single memory location, a data structure, a file, or anything else where **mutual exclusion** must be enforced so that only one thread is allowed to access the resource at a time.

There could be multiple places in your application that access the shared resource. Together, all of these pieces of code make up a single critical section. To prevent problems, only one thread at a time is allowed to be executing any of these pieces of code that reference a particular protected resource. In other words, only one thread at a time is allowed to be "inside" the critical section of code. This restriction is enforced by adding code that requests permission to enter and leave the critical section. A thread will not be given permission to enter a critical section if another thread is currently inside it.

In Win32 you declare a variable of type CRITICAL_SECTION for each resource that needs to be protected. This variable is the traffic light that allows only one thread at a time into the critical section.

A critical section is not a kernel object. Therefore, there is no such thing as a handle to a critical section. Unlike kernel objects, critical sections exist in the process's memory space. You do not use a "Create" API call to get a handle to a critical section. Instead you initialize a local variable of type CRITICAL_SECTION by calling `InitializeCriticalSection()`.

VOID InitializeCriticalSection(
    LPCRITICAL_SECTION lpCriticalSection
);

Parameters

lpCriticalSection   Pointer to variable of type
                                   CRITICAL_SECTION to be initialized. This
                                   variable should be defined in your program.

Return Value

This function returns void.

When you are finished with the critical section, you clean it up by calling
`DeleteCriticalSection()`. `DeleteCriticalSection()` only works on
the contents of the structure; it does not free the object itself. Do not be confused
by the similarity of the name to the C++ *delete* operator.

VOID DeleteCriticalSection(
    LPCRITICAL_SECTION lpCriticalSection
);

Parameters

lpCriticalSection   Pointer to variable of type
                                   CRITICAL_SECTION that is no longer needed.

Return Value

This function returns void.

For example, here is the basic sequence to create and destroy a critical
section. Notice that *gCriticalSection* is declared at the top of the program as
a regular variable that any thread can access.

```
CRITICAL_SECTION gCriticalSection;

void CreateDeleteCriticalSection()
{
    InitializeCriticalSection(&gCriticalSection);
        /* Do something here */
    DeleteCriticalSection(&gCriticalSection);
}
```

Once the critical section has been initialized, each thread that wants to
enter it must ask permission by calling `EnterCriticalSection()`.

VOID EnterCriticalSection(

> **LPCRITICAL_SECTION** lpCriticalSection

);

Parameters

lpCriticalSection   Pointer to variable of type CRITICAL_SECTION that should be locked.

Return Value

This function returns void.

When the thread is ready to leave the critical section of code, it must call `LeaveCriticalSection( )`.

VOID LeaveCriticalSection(

> **LPCRITICAL_SECTION** lpCriticalSection

);

Parameters

lpCriticalSection   Pointer to variable of type CRITICAL_SECTION that should be unlocked.

Return Value

This function returns void.

To continue the example above, here is a routine that uses the critical section we defined:

```
void UpdateData()
{
    EnterCriticalSection(&gCriticalSection);
        /* Update the resource */
    LeaveCriticalSection(&gCriticalSection);
}
```

You will often find several functions are all part of the same critical section, and are all bounded with Enter/Leave calls that use the same argument. In this case, you would put Enter/Leave calls in every function that accesses the global data. Under some circumstances, the Enter/Leave sequence could even appear several times in one function if that function took a long time to run.

If you remember the corrupted linked list example from Chapter 1, the problem was that operations such as *insert* and *add* need to be prevented from updating the linked list at the same time. Let's look at how to use critical sections to prevent this corruption. Each access to the list must be surrounded by a request to enter and leave the critical section. An example is shown in Listing 4-1.

Listing 4-1. Linked list with critical section

```c
typedef struct _Node
{
    struct _Node *next;
    int data;
} Node;

typedef struct _List
{
    Node *head;
    CRITICAL_SECTION critical_sec;
} List;

List *CreateList()
{
    List *pList = malloc(sizeof(pList));
    pList->head = NULL;
    InitializeCriticalSection(&pList->critical_sec);
    return pList;
}

void DeleteList(List *pList)
{
    DeleteCriticalSection(&pList->critical_sec);
    free(pList);
}

void AddHead(List *pList, Node *node)
{
    EnterCriticalSection(&pList->critical_sec);
    node->next = pList->head;
    pList->head = node;
    LeaveCriticalSection(&pList->critical_sec);
}
```

Listing 4-1 (continued)

```
void Insert(List *pList, Node *afterNode, Node *newNode)
{
    EnterCriticalSection(&pList->critical_sec);
    if (afterNode == NULL)
    {
        AddHead(pList, newNode);
    }
    else
    {
        newNode->next = afterNode->next;
        afterNode->next = newNode;
    }
    LeaveCriticalSection(&pList->critical_sec);
}

Node *Next(List *pList, Node *node)
{
    Node* next;
    EnterCriticalSection(&pList->critical_sec);
    next = node->next;
    LeaveCriticalSection(&pList->critical_sec);
    return next;
}
```

With the addition of the critical section, there can be a maximum of one person reading or writing each list at any one time. Notice that I put the CRITICAL_SECTION variable in the List structure. It could have been a global variable instead, but we want each instance of the linked list to be read and written independently. A single global critical section would have meant that only one linked list could be accessed at a time, which could potentially be a serious performance problem.

You might ask why `Next()` needs to be surrounded by a critical section since it is only accessing a single value. Remember from Chapter 1 that the statement `return node->next` could internally be compiled into separate machine instructions that would not be executed as an atomic operation. By putting the code into the critical section, we have forced the operation to be atomic.

A subtle point here is that there is nothing to protect the returned node from being deleted by another thread after `Next()` leaves the critical section but before it returns. This problem can be solved by locking at a higher level using something like a readers/writers lock. We will see how to do this in Chapter 7.

This short example also illustrates the other feature of critical sections in Win32. Once a thread enters a critical section, it is allowed to reenter the critical section over and over again. That is why `Insert()` is able to call `AddHead()` without calling `LeaveCriticalSection()` if the node is at the beginning of the list. The only caveat is that every Enter must be matched by a corresponding Leave. If a thread calls `EnterCriticalSection()` five times, the critical section will not be released until the thread calls `Leave-CriticalSection()` five times.

Minimizing Lock Time

In any discussion of synchronization mechanisms, whether on Win32, Unix, or any other operating system, there is one rule you will hear over and over:

Don't lock a resource for a long time.

If you keep the resource locked, you can prevent other threads from running and bring the application to a complete halt. With critical sections, a resource is locked whenever a thread is inside a critical section.

It is very hard to define the meaning of "a long time." If you are doing operations on a network, especially over a dial-up network connection, a long time could be a couple of minutes. If you are accessing a key resource in an application, then a long time could be defined as a few milliseconds.

The closest to hard and fast advice I can give you is that you should almost never call `Sleep()` or any of the `Wait…()` APIs inside of a critical section.

When you protect a resource with a synchronization mechanism, it is important to keep in mind how often the resource will be used and how quickly a thread must release the resource to keep the application running smoothly.

FAQ 14

What if a thread stays inside a critical section for a long time?

A question that really seems to concern some people is, "What if I never release the resource (or leave the critical section, or release the mutex, and so on)?" The answer is, "Nothing."

The operating system will not crash. The user will not be given any error messages. The worst thing that will happen is that the application will hang if the primary GUI thread needed to use the locked resource. But really, there is nothing magic about the synchronization mechanisms.

Avoid Dangling Critical Sections

FAQ 15

?

⬛ What if a thread terminates inside the critical section?

A disadvantage to critical sections is that there is no way to tell if the thread currently inside a critical section is still alive. In other words, since the critical section is not a kernel object, the kernel does not clean it up if a thread inside the critical section exits or crashes without calling `LeaveCritical-Section()`. If you need this functionality, you should use a mutex, which will be covered later in this chapter.

Jeffrey Richter, in his *Win32 Q&A* column in the July, 1996, *Microsoft Systems Journal,* says that there is a fundamental difference in how Windows NT manages dangling critical sections versus how Windows 95 manages them. In Windows NT, if a thread exits that has a critical section locked, the critical section will still be locked forever. In Windows 95, if the same thing happened, then the threads waiting on that critical section will be allowed to continue. This is potentially a serious problem because you could enter the critical section while your application is in an unstable state.

Deadlock

By choosing to have a single critical section per linked list, I've opened the way to a new type of problem. Take a look at the following function designed to swap the contents of two lists:

```
void SwapLists(List *list, List *list2)
{
    List *tmp_list;
    EnterCriticalSection(list1->critical_sec);
    EnterCriticalSection(list2->critical_sec);
    tmp_list = list1->head;
    list1->head = list2->head;
    list2->head = tmp_list;
    LeaveCriticalSection(list1->critical_sec);
    LeaveCriticalSection(list2->critical_sec);
}
```

Do you see the problem? Suppose the following two calls were made at about the same time by different threads:

Thread A `SwapLists(home_address_list, work_address_list);`

Thread B `SwapLists(work_address_list, home_address_list);`

If a context switch occurs in Thread A after the first `EnterCritical-Section()` in `SwapLists()`, and then Thread B makes its call, the two threads will end up waiting on each other forever. Thread A needs *work_address_list,* Thread B needs *home_address_list,* and each has what the other needs. This situation is called **deadlock**, or "The Deadly Embrace."

FAQ 16

How do I avoid deadlock?

Any time a section of code requires two or more resources, there is a potential for deadlock. It is possible for deadlock situations to be quite complex, wherein many threads make up a complex pattern of interdependencies. Although there are algorithms to detect and arbitrate deadlock situations, they are quite complex. For most applications, the best policy is to find a way to make sure that deadlock will not happen by allocating all the resources you need as a single operation with `WaitForMultipleObjects()`. As you will see in the next section, forcing resource locking to be an all-or-nothing proposition prevents the sequencing problems that lead to deadlock.

The Dining Philosophers

There is a well-known thought problem for demonstrating the problem of deadlock called the "dining philosophers." Although you will find this problem mentioned in every book about operating systems or multithreading, I think you will find this particular discussion one of the best because I can show you the philosophers in action. You can see the philosophers in action by running the sample program DINING on the CD-ROM.

The dining philosophers problem goes like this. Several philosophers are sitting around a table. Each philosopher is either thinking, waiting to eat, or eating. In order to eat, a philosopher must pick up two chopsticks. Unfortunately, there are an equal number of chopsticks and philosophers, so each chopstick is shared by two philosophers. The situation is shown in Figure 4-1.

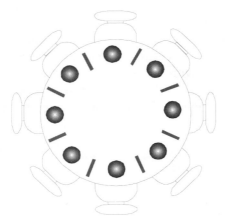

Figure 4-1. The table set for the dining philosophers.

Philosophers being somewhat stubborn people, they do not want to put down a chopstick before they have eaten. Therefore, if every philosopher were to pick up the chopstick to their left, it would be impossible to pick up any right chopsticks because the next person would be using it and would refuse to give it up.

In the DINING sample on the CD-ROM, you decide when you run the program how to approach the dining philosophers problem. If you allow deadlock, then the philosophers will pick up chopsticks one at a time. You can see a philosopher waiting when only one hand is on a chopstick. If you do not allow deadlock, the philosophers will only pick up both chopsticks at a time.

When you run DINING, you will see that usually the philosophers take turns eating. Sometimes there is a problem when everyone picks up one chopstick and the philosophers deadlock.

FAQ 17

? Can I wait for multiple critical sections?

As in the `SwapLists()` routine, the problem occurs because it is necessary to wait for one critical section, then the other. What needs to happen is that the philosophers need some way of picking up both chopsticks at the same time. In terms of the sample application, we need to ask the operating system to give us both critical sections, or neither. Unfortunately, critical sections cannot be used in this fashion.

BY THE WAY

The problem could be solved by using a single critical section and allowing only one philosopher at a time to pick up or put down his or her chopsticks. The solution is not optimal because it restricts the philosophers' free will and makes them wait unnecessarily, a situation the philosophers find unacceptable.

If you remember the call `WaitForMultipleObjects()` from the last chapter, it lets you ask the operating system to wait and not return until all of the objects are signaled. Picking up both chopsticks at the same time instead of one at a time is the key to solving this problem. But `WaitForMultiple-Objects()` only works with kernel objects, and a critical section is not a kernel object (it has no HANDLE). Therefore we need to look at another kind of synchronization mechanism in Win32, called a mutex.

Mutexes

A mutex inWin32 is used to do many of the same things as a critical section, but it sacrifices speed for increased flexibility. As you may have guessed,

mutex stands for MUTual EXclusion. Only one thread at a time is allowed to own a mutex, just as only one thread at a time can enter a critical section.

Although mutexes and critical sections do the same thing, there are some differences in how they operate:

- It takes almost 100 times longer to longer to lock an unowned mutex than it does to lock an unowned critical section because the critical section can be done in user mode without involving the kernel.
- Mutexes can be used between processes. Critical sections can only be used within the same process.
- You can specify a timeout when waiting on a mutex, but not a critical section.

The comparison of the functions used by the two calls is shown here:

CRITICAL_SECTION	*Mutex Kernel Object*
InitializeCriticalSection()	CreateMutex() OpenMutex()
EnterCriticalSection()	WaitForSingleObject() WaitForMultipleObjects() MsgWaitForMultipleObjects()
LeaveCriticalSection()	ReleaseMutex()
DeleteCriticalSection()	CloseHandle()

To allow using a mutex across processes, a mutex has a name you optionally assign when you create it. Given the name, which can be hard coded, any thread anywhere in the system can access the mutex just by knowing the name. You must use the name because you cannot pass a handle to another process that is already running.

Remember that other applications are using this mechanism, too. Names are global across all applications running in the system. Do not name your object with a name like "Object" or "Mutex." Use something more unique like the company name and the application name.

Creating a Mutex

Unlike critical sections, you actually have some options when you create a mutex. A mutex is a kernel object. Therefore it is kept within the kernel and keeps the same kind of reference count as other kernel objects. Although the functionality of a mutex is very similar to a critical section, mutexes can be harder to understand because of the confusing Win32 terminology. First, the easy part. You create a mutex by calling `CreateMutex()`:

HANDLE CreateMutex(
    LPSECURITY_ATTRIBUTES lpMutexAttributes,
    BOOL bInitialOwner,
    LPCTSTR lpName
);

Parameters

lpMutexAttributes	Security attributes. Use NULL to get the default security attributes. Ignored in Windows 95.
bInitialOwner	Set to TRUE if you want the thread that called `CreateMutex()` to own the mutex.
lpName	Text name of the mutex. Any thread or process can refer to this mutex object by this name. The name can be anything you want as long as it does not contain a backslash (\).

Return Value

`CreateMutex()` returns a handle if it succeeds, otherwise it returns NULL. `GetLastError()` returns a valid result in either case. `CreateMutex()` succeeds if a mutex by that name already exists, in which case `GetLastError()` returns ERROR_ALREADY_EXISTS.

When you are finished with a mutex, you should close your handle to it by calling `CloseHandle()`. Like other kernel objects, mutexes have a reference count that is decremented whenever you call `CloseHandle()`. The mutex will be automatically deleted when the reference count reaches zero. This sample function `CreateAndDeleteMutex()` creates a mutex and then deletes it. The mutex has no security attributes, is not owned by the current thread, and is named "Demonstration Mutex."

```
HANDLE hMutex;

void CreateAndDeleteMutex()
{
    hMutex = CreateMutex(NULL, FALSE, "Demonstration Mutex");
        /* Do something here */
    CloseHandle(hMutex);
}
```

Opening a Mutex

If a mutex has already been created with a particular name, then any other thread or process can open it using that name (subject to security restrictions that we will not get into here.)

If you call `CreateMutex()` with the name of an existing mutex, then Win32 will pass back a handle to the existing mutex instead of creating a new mutex. As described above, `GetLastError()` returns ERROR_ ALREADY_EXISTS after calling `CreateMutex()` if this happens.

You can also use an API called `OpenMutex()` if you want to open the mutex if it exists, but not create it. You might do this if you are writing a client process that talks to a server process on the same machine, and only the server should create the mutex because it protects server-defined structures.

See the *Win32 Programmer's Reference* for more information on `Open-Mutex()`. It is available as part of the online help in Visual C++.

Locking a Mutex

To acquire ownership of the mutex, use one of the Win32 `Wait...()` functions. The `Wait...()` does the same thing for mutexes that `EnterCriticalSection()` did with a critical section. This is where the terminology gets confusing.

A mutex is signaled when no thread owns it. Therefore a call to `Wait...()` succeeds if no thread owns the mutex. Conversely, a mutex is nonsignaled when a thread owns it. If a thread waits on a nonsignaled mutex then the thread will **block.** This means that the thread is not allowed to run until the mutex is released and becomes signaled. The `Wait...()` calls will all cause a thread to block if the timeout is greater than zero and the requested handle is not available.

So here is the scenario:

1. We have a mutex, which at the moment is nonsignaled and therefore no one owns it.
2. A thread calls `WaitForSingleObject()` (or any of the other `Wait...()` functions) with a handle to a mutex.
3. Win32 gives the thread ownership of the mutex, then briefly sets the state of the mutex to signaled so that the `Wait...()` will return.
4. The mutex is immediately returned to the nonsignaled state so that anyone else waiting will not be given ownership.
5. The thread releases ownership of the mutex by calling `Release-Mutex()`. The cycle starts all over again.

The `ReleaseMutex()` call looks like this:

BOOL ReleaseMutex(
    HANDLE hMutex
  );

Parameters

hMutex   Handle to mutex object to release.

Return Value

Returns TRUE if it succeeds; otherwise FALSE.

The ownership of a mutex is the second area where the terminology is confusing. The ownership of a mutex is not determined by who created it. Instead, the owner of a mutex refers to whichever thread last did a `Wait...()` on the mutex and has not yet called `ReleaseMutex()`. Saying that a thread owns a mutex means the same thing as a thread having entered a critical section. Only one thread can own a mutex at a time.

Ownership has nothing to do with determining when a mutex will be destroyed. Like most other kernel objects, a mutex is destroyed when its reference count drops to zero. The reference count is decremented whenever a thread calls `CloseHandle()` with the handle to a mutex, or when the thread exits.

If a thread that owns a mutex terminates, the mutex is automatically destroyed *only* if that thread was the last thread with a handle to the mutex. Otherwise the reference count of the object is still greater than zero and other threads (and processes) will still have a valid handle to the mutex. However, there is special handling for the case where a thread exits without releasing a mutex.

Handling Abandoned Mutexes

In a properly written program a thread should never own a mutex when it terminates because that would mean that the thread did not properly clean up its resources. Unfortunately, it is not a perfect world and sometimes, for one reason or another, a thread may not call `ReleaseMutex()` before exiting. To help solve this problem, there is one very important feature of mutexes that is unique among the various synchronization objects. If a thread that owns a mutex exits without calling `ReleaseMutex()`, the mutex is *not* destroyed. Instead, it is marked as unowned and nonsignaled, and the next waiting thread will be notified with the special flag WAIT_ABANDONED_0. This is true regardless of whether the thread terminated either explicitly by calling `ExitThread()` or implicitly by crashing.

If other threads are waiting on the mutex with `WaitForMultipleObjects()`, the function will return a value between WAIT_ABANDONED_0 and (WAIT_ABANDONED_n - 1), where n is the number of handles passed in the array. These threads can use this value to figure out exactly which mutex was abandoned. `WaitForSingleObject()` will return WAIT_ABANDONED_0.

Although it is handy to know that a mutex has been abandoned, figuring out what to do about it can be extremely difficult. After all, the mutex was created in the first place to make sure that a set of operations were done atomically. If a thread dies in the middle of this operation, it is entirely possible that the data structures being protected are irreparably damaged.

Letting the Philosophers Eat

Let's go back and revisit the dining philosophers, still patiently trying to eat and think. The sample code in DINING creates a set of mutexes to represent the chopsticks. The code that creates the mutexes looks like this:

```
for (i = 0; i < PHILOSOPHERS; i++)
    gChopStick[i] = CreateMutex(NULL, FALSE, NULL);
```

The arguments to `CreateMutex()` say that the mutex will have default security attributes, no initial owner, and no name. One mutex is created for each chopstick on the table. We are using unnamed mutexes because the chopstick array is global data that every thread is able to access.

Just like critical sections, mutexes are used to protect a resource. Before accessing a protected resource, your code must receive ownership of the mutex by calling one of the `Wait…()` functions.

The dining philosophers can be set to use `WaitForSingleObject()`, which makes it work just like critical sections (with the same problem of deadlock), or to use `WaitForMultipleObjects()`, which fixes the deadlock problem we saw with `EnterCriticalSection()` and `WaitForSingleObject()`.

In effect, we are using `WaitForMultipleObjects()` to say that we want to pick up both chopsticks at exactly the same time. If only one chopstick is available, then the other should be left alone until the other is available, too. The code looks like this:

```
WaitForMultipleObjects(2, myChopsticks, TRUE, INFINITE);
```

The arguments to `WaitForMultipleObjects()` say that there are two handles in the array *myChopsticks*, the call should only return if all handles are signaled, and there is no timeout.

If you run the DINING sample program using `WaitForMultiple-Objects()`, you will find that the philosophers are able to continue eating and deadlock never occurs.

Fixing SwapLists

The same technique we used for the dining philosophers will also cure the deadlock we encountered in `SwapLists()`. Any time you lock more than one synchronization object in a row you have the potential for deadlock. By always locking all of them at the same time the problem goes away. Listing 4-2 shows the new version of `SwapLists()`:

Listing 4-2. `Swaplists()` using `WaitFor Multiple Objects()`

```
struct Node
{
    struct Node *next;
    int data;
};

struct List
{
    struct Node *head;
    HANDLE hMutex;
};

struct List *CreateList()
{
    List *list = malloc(sizeof(struct List));
    list->head = NULL;
    list->hMutex  = CreateMutex(NULL, FALSE, NULL);
    return list;
}
```

Listing 4-2 (continued)

```
void DeleteList(struct List *list)
{
    CloseHandle(list->hMutex);
    free(list);
}

void SwapLists(struct List *list, struct List *list2)
{
    struct List *tmp_list;
    HANDLE arrhandles[2];

    arrHandles[0] = list1->hMutex;
    arrHandles[1] = list2->hMutex;
    WaitForMultipleObjects(2, arrHandles, TRUE, INFINITE);
    tmp_list = list1->head;
    list1->head = list2->head;
    list2->head = tmp_list;
    ReleaseMutex(arrHandles[0]);
    ReleaseMutex(arrHandles[1]);
}
```

Why Have an Initial Owner?

The second argument to `CreateMutex()` is *bInitialOwner,* which allows you to specify whether the creating thread should immediately acquire ownership of the mutex. At first this flag may seem to be nothing more than a convenience, but in fact it prevents a race condition.

Unlike critical sections, mutexes can be used across processes as well as across threads. The mutex can be opened by its name, so another process can find the mutex without talking to the creating process at all. Without the *bInitialOwner* flag, you would have to write the code like this:

```
HANDLE hMutex = CreateMutex(NULL, FALSE, "Sample Name");
int result = WaitForSingleObject(hMutex, INFINITE);
```

This arrangement creates a race condition. If a context switch occurred to another process after the `CreateMutex()` call, then the other process could lock the object before the creating process could call `WaitForSingleObject()`.

Semaphores

Semaphores get a lot of press because they have the most history in computer science, they are absolutely mired in theory, and professors love asking obscure questions about them. You may be hard pressed to figure out useful examples of where to apply semaphores off the top of your head, so I'll spoil the surprise and tell you that they are the key ingredient in solving various producer/consumer problems where a buffer is being read and written at the same time.

A semaphore in Win32 may be locked at most n times, where n is specified when the semaphore is created. Frequently n will end up being the number of threads that can lock a resource, but there is no reason why a single thread cannot own all of the locks.

Here's an example of why you might need a semaphore. Consider the plight of someone I'll call Steve, who was trying to rent a car in California. There were several car rental agents working behind the counter responsible for renting the cars. Steve told the agent that he wanted a convertible. The helpful agent looked out the window, saw that there were three convertibles available, and wrote up the order for one of them. Unfortunately, at that very moment three other people had also asked for a convertible, and their rental agents had all done the same thing that Steve's agent had done. There were now *four* people for three cars and *someone* there was going to be the loser in the inevitable ugly dispute that followed.

We'll leave this little cliffhanger and hope the best for Steve. The problem at this car rental agency was that it was not possible to instantaneously write up a car rental agreement and give the customer the keys. The entire process took long enough that it was possible for several agents to accidentally rent the same car. This is the same problem we have seen with multiple threads over and over again. If multiple threads are accessing the same resource(s), then some mechanism must be used to prevent the threads from conflicting with each other.

If we were trying to write code that would solve the car rental problem, one solution would be to protect each car with its own mutex. This would work, but you might have to create hundreds or thousands of mutexes for a large rental agency.

Another solution would be a single mutex that applied to all cars, or perhaps just to convertibles, but only one clerk at a time would be able to rent convertibles. This might cut down on the number of employees, but in a busy rental agency, the customers would be making a quick trip to the competition.

The solution is to recognize that all of the convertibles are essentially identical. (Since when did you ever get a choice in colors when renting a car?) Until the keys are finally handed over to a customer, it is only necessary to know how many convertibles are currently available. A semaphore maintains this count, assuring that increments and decrements are handled in an atomic fashion. When a semaphore count gets to zero, whoever was asking for the resource has to wait.

For you theory lovers, it turns out that a mutex is a degenerate form of a semaphore. If you create a semaphore and set the maximum count to one, you get mutual exclusion behavior. Therefore a mutex is often referred to as a **binary semaphore.** If one thread owns a binary semaphore, then no other thread can acquire ownership. In Win32, the ownership semantics of how the two operate are quite different, so they cannot be used interchangeably. With semaphores, unlike mutexes, there is no specific state called "wait abandoned" that can be detected by other threads.

In many systems, semaphores are used quite frequently because mutexes do not exist as a separate primitive. In Win32, semaphores are used more rarely because of the existence of the mutex.

Creating Semaphores

To create a semaphore in Win32, use the `CreateSemaphore()` call:

HANDLE CreateSemaphore(
    LPSECURITY_ATTRIBUTES lpAttributes,
    LONG lInitialCount,
    LONG lMaximumCount,
    LPCTSTR lpName
);

Parameters

lpAttributes	Security attributes. Use NULL to get the default security attributes. Ignored in Windows 95.
lInitialCount	Initial value of the semaphore. Must be greater than or equal to zero and less than *lMaximumCount*.
lMaximumCount	Specifies the maximum value of the semaphore. This is effectively the maximum number of threads that can lock the semaphore at the same time.

| *lpName* | Text name of the semaphore. Any thread or process can refer to this semaphore object by this name. This value may be NULL to create an unnamed semaphore. |

Return Value

`CreateSemaphore()` returns a handle if it succeeds, otherwise it returns NULL. `GetLastError()` returns a valid result in either case. `CreateSemaphore()` succeeds if a semaphore by that name already exists, in which case `GetLastError()` returns ERROR_ALREADY_EXISTS.

Acquiring Locks

The terminology for the semaphore is even more obscure than the terminology for the mutex. First, understand that the current value of the semaphore represents the number of resources currently available. If the semaphore's value is currently one, then only one more lock will be allowed. If the value is five, then five more locks will be allowed.

Every time a lock succeeds, the count decrements. You acquire a lock on a semaphore by using any of the `Wait...()` functions, such as `WaitForSingleObject()`. Therefore, if the current count of a semaphore is non-zero, then the `Wait...()` will return immediately. This is similar to the mutex, where the `Wait...()` returns immediately if no one else owns the mutex.

FAQ 18

Who owns a semaphore?

You do not receive ownership of the semaphore when the lock succeeds. Because several threads can lock a semaphore at the same time, talking about semaphore ownership is not very meaningful. There is no such thing as an exclusive lock on a semaphore. Because there is no concept of ownership, a thread that repeatedly calls one of the `Wait...()` functions will create a new lock for each successive call. This is in contrast to the mutex, where the thread that owns the mutex will not block no matter how many times it calls a `Wait...()` function.

At some point the semaphore's count will reach zero, indicating that the supply of resources has been exhausted. When the count is zero, any thread that tries to call `Wait...()` *will* wait until one of the locks is released.

Releasing Locks

To release a lock, call `ReleaseSemaphore()`. This function increments the semaphore's value by the given amount, usually one, and returns the previous value of the semaphore.

`ReleaseSemaphore()` is the equivalent to `ReleaseMutex()`. You would use it after calling `WaitForSingleObject()` to obtain a lock on a semaphore. Semaphores are often used to protect fixed-size ring buffers. Programs that want to read from the ring buffer would wait on the semaphore. The thread that writes to the ring buffer may write more than one thing to the buffer, in which case the release count would be the number of things written to the buffer.

BOOL ReleaseSemaphore(

    HANDLE hSemaphore,
    LONG lReleaseCount,
    LPLONG lpPreviousCount
);

Parameters

hSemaphore	Handle to the semaphore.
lReleaseCount	Increment the value of the semaphore by this amount. This value may not be negative or zero.
lpPreviousCount	Return the previous value of the semaphore. Note that there is no way to get the current value.

Return Value

`ReleaseSemaphore()` returns TRUE if it succeeds, otherwise it returns FALSE. On failure, call `GetLastError()` to find out why.

`ReleaseSemaphore()` will not increment a semaphore's count past *lMaximumCount* as passed to `CreateSemaphore()`.

Remember that the value returned in *lpPreviousCount* was a snapshot at that moment. You cannot add *lReleaseCount* to **lpPreviousCount* and come up with the current value because other threads could have already changed that value.

Unlike mutexes, the thread that calls `ReleaseSemaphore()` does not have to be the same thread that called `Wait...()`. Any thread can call `ReleaseSemaphore()` at any time to release the locks that were made by other threads.

Why Have an Initial Count?

The second argument to `CreateSemaphore()` is *lInitialCount*. It exists for the same reason that `CreateMutex()` has *bInitialOwner*. By setting the initial count to zero, the thread that creates the semaphore can take care of any necessary initialization. When initialization is complete, a single call to `ReleaseSemaphore()` can increment the count up to its maximum.

With the ring buffer example, the semaphore would usually be created with a release count of zero so that any thread waiting would block. As things are added to the buffer, the semaphore is incremented with `Release-Semaphore()` and threads waiting would be allowed to run.

The very unexpected result here is that the thread writing the ring buffer calls `ReleaseSemaphore()` before it or any other thread calls one of the `Wait...()` functions. In a sense, it is completely backward from the way a mutex works.

Event Objects

The most flexible type of synchronization object in Win32 is the **event object.** The event object is a kernel object whose only purpose is to be either signaled or nonsignaled. This state is under direct program control. It does not change as a side effect of calling a `Wait...()` function.

FAQ 19

What are event objects useful for?

Event objects are useful because their state is under your control. Unlike mutexes and semaphores, whose state changes as a by-product of calls like `WaitForSingleObject()`, you can tell an event object exactly what to do and when to do it.

Event objects are used in many types of advanced I/O operations. You will see this in Chapter 6. Event objects can also be used to design your own synchronization objects.

To create an event object, use `CreateEvent()`.

HANDLE CreateEvent(
LPSECURITY_ATTRIBUTES lpEventAttributes,
BOOL bManualReset,
BOOL bInitialState,
LPCTSTR lpName
);

Parameters

lpEventAttributes	Security attributes. Use NULL to get the default security attributes. Ignored in Windows 95.
bManualReset	Determines whether the event resets itself automatically to nonsignaled after waking up a single thread.

bInitialState	Set TRUE if the initial state of the event should be signaled, FALSE if the initial state is nonsignaled.
lpName	Text name of the event object. Any thread or process can refer to this event object by this name.

Return Value

If the call is successful a handle to an event object will be returned and `GetLastError()` will return zero. If an object of the given *lpName* already exists, `CreateEvent()` will return that object instead of creating a new one. In this case `GetLastError()` returns ERROR_ALREADY_ EXISTS. If `CreateEvent()` fails it returns NULL. Use `GetLastError()` to get more information.

The sample program on the CD-ROM called EVENTTST demonstrates event objects. It creates three threads whose job it is to wait on a single event object and tell us when they wake up. The behavior of the event object is under user control. The overall structure of the program is such that it creates the event object, then creates the threads, then waits for you to push a button.

If you press "SetEvent," "ResetEvent," or "PulseEvent," then EVENTTST calls the equivalent API function. These functions are discussed in more detail below, but the short description is as follows.

Function	Description
`SetEvent()`	Set the event object to the signaled state.
`ResetEvent()`	Set the event object to the nonsignaled state.
`PulseEvent()`	*Manual Reset Event:* Set the event object to the signaled state, wake everything up that is currently waiting, then return to the nonsignaled state.
	Auto Reset Event: Set the event object to the signaled state, wake up a single waiting thread (if any), then return to the nonsignaled state.

If you select a new event type, either "Automatic" or "Manual," then the existing threads and event object are destroyed and new threads and event object are created.

The behavior of the application using the various settings is quite instructive. Try pushing each of the three buttons using both "Automatic" and "Manual."

In "Automatic" the event object is always nonsignaled, and therefore reset, so pushing "ResetEvent" does nothing. Both "SetEvent" and "PulseEvent" wake up a single waiting thread.

In "Manual," the event object stays either set or reset, depending on whether `SetEvent()` or `ResetEvent()` was called. Pressing "SetEvent" causes the waiting threads to wake up as soon as they try to wait, as shown by the rapidly filling list box if you try this. `PulseEvent()`, on the other hand, wakes up everything that is currently waiting.

The other important point you will see from watching this program run is that the operating system forces waiting threads to take turns. This is an important behavior with all the synchronization objects you have seen in this chapter. If the operating system did not enforce some level of fairness, then a single thread might get to run over and over again, thereby preventing the other threads from ever running. This situation is called **starvation.**

FAQ 20

What happens with an event object if I call `PulseEvent()` and nothing is waiting?

The application does not demonstrate what happens if you call `SetEvent()` with auto-reset, or `PulseEvent()`, and there are no threads waiting. In this case, the event will be lost. The event will *not* be saved until a thread waits. This behavior makes it easy to "lose" wakeup requests. For example, Thread A might increment a counter, then call `WaitForSingleObject()` on the event object. If a task switch occurred between these actions, then Thread B could check that counter and call `PulseEvent()` on the event object. The wakeup would be lost because the pulse is not saved.

Another example that would create deadlock is when a receiving thread checks to see if there are characters in the queue (context switch), a sender pulses an event object (context switch), and the receiver calls `WaitForSingleObject()`. Because the receiver called `WaitForSingleObject()` *after* the sender pulsed the event, the event will be lost, the receiver will never wake up, and the app will deadlock. This is what semaphores were invented to solve.

Displaying Output from Worker Threads

I want to take a short detour at this point and look at how EVENTTST allows the worker threads (the three waiting threads) to put information into the list box. The list box message loop is always handled by a single thread, which is the primary thread in this application. Although not strictly necessary in this case, it is a good example of letting the primary thread do all screen updates.

I defined a message in the application called WM_PLEASE_UPDATE that worker threads send to the primary thread when a new entry should be placed in the results list box. The worker thread uses `SendMessage()` to make a sort of "function call" into the primary thread's message loop. `SendMessage()` will not return until the primary thread has processed the message, so we can guarantee that updates will not occur out of order.

Notice that I rely on the fact that all data is accessible to all threads. I use `sprintf()` to create a string on a thread's stack, then I pass this address in `SendMessage()`. The primary thread uses the string at this address when it updates the list box. When the primary thread is finished with that message, `SendMessage()` allows the worker thread to continue.

Now imagine what would happen if I used `PostMessage()` instead of `SendMessage()`. `PostMessage()` returns immediately, so by the time the primary thread got around to processing the message, the string that was originally in the buffer has probably been overwritten. This is a common example of the trade-off between optimal implementation speed and optimal safety when writing a multithreaded application. In this case, I chose the "slower" way because it is much easier to guarantee that it will work properly.

Interlocked Variables

The simplest type of synchronization mechanism is using the interlocked functions that operate on a standard 32-bit long variable. These functions provide no ability to wait; they simply guarantee that access to a particular variable will be sequential. I present these functions last because you can only see how useful they are when you compare them to other synchronization mechanisms.

Consider what you would need to do to maintain mutual exclusion with access to a single 32-bit counter. You would need to create a critical section or a mutex, acquire ownership, do your operation, and release ownership. That is quite a bit of work for a 32-bit variable whose total access time will be two or three machine operations. The overhead is likely to be over two orders of magnitude compared to the work that needs to be done.

A prime example of where a counter like this would need to be used is for reference counting, such as the handles inside the kernel. Typically, when a reference count drops to zero, the object is destroyed. You could either decrement the variable or test for equality with zero with a single operation, but not both. The function `InterlockedDecrement()` does this all at once. It subtracts one from the variable, then compares the result with zero and returns the result of the comparison.

The interlocked functions are:

- `InterlockedIncrement()`
- `InterlockedDecrement()`

These functions only compare against zero. There is no way to compare against any other number.

LONG InterlockedIncrement(
    LPLONG lpTarget,
);

LONG InterlockedDecrement(
    LPLONG lpTarget,
);

Parameters

lpTarget   Address of 32-bit value. Value will be incremented or decremented and the result compared against zero. This address must be long word aligned.

Return Value

Returns zero if *Target* was equal to zero after being incremented, a negative number if *Target* was less than zero, and a positive number if *Target* was greater than zero.

The `Interlocked...()` functions return a comparison against zero. This is very important for implementing the reference counting that we discussed because it is necessary to know when the count reaches zero. Without this comparison, you would have the same problem of having to lock the object to do the decrement and compare as an atomic operation.

FOR THE EXPERTS...

If you are using the newer versions of OLE with the apartment model or the free-threading model, you should use the `Interlocked...()` functions to maintain your object reference count. In `AddRef()` call `Interlocked-Increment()` and in `Release()` call `InterlockedDecrement()`.

The function `InterlockedExchange()` sets a new value and returns the old value. Like Increment/Decrement, it provides a thread-safe way of accomplishing a common fundamental operation.

LONG InterlockedExchange(

LPLONG lpTarget,
LONG lValue
);

Parameters

lpTarget   Address of 32-bit value. This address must be
                            long word aligned.

lValue   New value to place where *lpTarget* is pointing.

Return Value

Returns the value that was formerly pointed at by *lpTarget*.

Summary of Synchronization Mechanisms

Critical Section

A critical section is used to enforce mutual exclusion between threads within a single process. A critical section:

- Is a local object, not a kernel object.
- Is fast and efficient.
- Cannot be waited on more than one at a time.
- Cannot determine if it was abandoned by a thread.

Mutex

A mutex is a kernel object that will enforce mutual exclusion between threads even if they are in different processes. A mutex:

- Is a kernel object.
- Generates an "abandoned" error if the owning thread terminates.
- Can be used in `Wait...()` calls.
- Is named, and can be opened across processes.
- Can only be released by the thread that owns it.

Semaphore

The semaphore is used to keep track of a limited resource. A semaphore:

- Is a kernel object.
- Has no owner.
- Is named, and can be opened across processes.
- Can be released by any thread.

Event Object

Event objects are used for overlapped I/O (see Chapter 6) and for some custom-designed objects. An event object:

- Is a kernel object.
- Is completely under program control.
- Is good for designing new synchronization objects.
- Does not queue up wake-up requests.
- Is named, and can be opened across processes.

Interlocked Variable

The `Interlocked...()` calls are only a synchronization mechanism if they are used for a spin-lock, which is a busy loop that is expected to be running for such a short time that it has minimal overhead. The kernel uses these occasionally. Other than that, interlocked variables are primarily useful for reference counting. They:

- Allow basic operations on 4-byte values without having to use a critical section or mutex.
- Work even in SMP systems.

Chapter 5

Keeping Your Threads on a Leash

This chapter describes how to initialize a new thread, how to stop a running thread, and how to understand and adjust thread priorities.

After reading this chapter, you will be able to answer one of the most basic questions about using threads under Win32. You will see this question over and over on the Win32 newsgroups on Usenet. This simple question drove me nuts when I started using threads in Win32. I searched for the answer for days, even weeks, secure in the knowledge that there must be a good answer.
The question is:

How do I stop a currently running thread from within another thread?

In this chapter we'll look at the answer to this question and similar problems of controlling one thread from within another.

Stopping a Thread Cleanly

In Chapter 2 we created a background thread to print to an off-screen bit-map. One of the more complex problems we needed to solve was what to do if the user tried to exit the application while the background thread was still printing. The solution in that chapter was to prevent the user from exiting the application if any worker threads were still running. This was accomplished by modifying the main message loop so that it would not leave the message loop before all worker threads had terminated. This solution had the advantage of simplicity, but if a lengthy rendering operation was in progress the application would appear to hang for a while before the application actually exited.

Aborting a Thread with TerminateThread()

This situation illustrates a common question in Win32. How do I safely shut down any threads that are currently running? The first and most obvious solution to this problem is to use `TerminateThread()`.

BOOL TerminateThread(
    HANDLE hThread,
    DWORD dwExitCode
);

Parameters

hThread	Handle to the thread to terminate. The "target thread."
dwExitCode	Exit code that should be reported by the thread's handle.

Return Value

If the function succeeds it returns TRUE. If it fails it returns FALSE, in which case `GetLastError()` can be used to find out why the call failed.

`TerminateThread()` seemed like a good solution until I read the documentation, which said, "**TerminateThread** is a dangerous function that should only be used in the most extreme cases." That seemed like a fairly unambiguous directive to stay away from this call.

`TerminateThread()` will forcibly abort a thread without allowing that thread to have any say in the matter. The side effects of this call can be devastating. The target thread is given no chance to clean up after itself. This call does *not* throw an exception in the target thread; the thread is simply erased at the kernel level. There is nothing the target thread can do to "catch" the termination request and clean up.

There are other unpleasant aspects to this call. The target thread's stack is not deallocated, thereby causing a large memory leak. Any DLLs that are attached to the thread will not be notified that the thread is detaching.

About the only thing that you can rely on with this call is that the thread's handle will become signaled and will return the exit code as specified by *dwExitCode*.

There are other more insidious problems that can be caused by using `TerminateThread()`. If that thread was in the middle of a critical section, then the critical section will stay permanently locked. Recall that critical sections, unlike mutexes, do not have an "abandoned" state. Also, if the target thread was in the middle of updating a data structure, then the data structure will be left permanently in an unstable state. There is nothing that can be done to prevent these problems.

The summary of this call is: Stay away from it.

Using Signals

The next idea that seemed possible was to use signals. In Unix, signals are the standard way of sending notifications across processes. In Unix, the signal SIGTERM is a request to "please exit" and the signal SIGKILL is the rough equivalent of `TerminateThread()`.

This idea seemed hopeful because the C run-time library supports the standard signals such as SIGABRT and SIGINT. Handlers for the various signals can be set with the `signal()` C run-time call.

I rapidly ran into a dead end with this approach. There is no C run-time call named `kill()`, which is how signals are sent in Unix. There is a call named `raise()`, but that only sends a signal within the current thread.

After looking at the sources to the run-time library, I discovered that signals are simulated using Win32 exceptions, and there is no native support in Win32 for signals. So this approach did not work either.

Throwing Exceptions Across Threads

What I really wanted to do was to cause an exception in the target thread. The exception could be caught by the target thread if need be to clean things up; otherwise the target thread would just exit.

After spending hours doing research, I can tell you with certainty that there is no standard supported way in the Win32 API to throw an exception into another thread. It is unfortunate because the effect would be exactly what is needed.

FOR THE
EXPERTS
There has been a great deal of discussion on Usenet about ways of simulating throwing an exception in another thread. One technique was to use the debugging APIs to write an illegal instruction at the current address in the thread. Another technique was to change a frequently used pointer to point at an illegal address, thereby forcing the code to generate an exception. Both of these approaches have drawbacks and aren't for the faint of heart, but they may be workable if all else fails.

Setting a Flag

When all else fails, use the simple and obvious. The approved way in Win32 to cause a thread to terminate is to set a flag in your code that asks the thread to terminate itself.

This technique has the obvious advantage that the target thread can guarantee that it is in a safe and consistent state before it exits. The obvious problem, though, is that the thread needs some sort of polling mechanism to check and see if it should exit. By now you should shudder when you hear the word "polling." We do *not* want to write a busy loop to check the state of the flag. Instead, we will use a manual-reset event object. The worker thread can check the state of the object or wait on it depending on the circumstance.

Shutting down a thread sounds easy, but the shutdown sequence must be timed just right to prevent race conditions. Getting the sequence right is especially important when the application is exiting. Exiting the application is like demolishing a building. You want to make very sure that everyone has safely exited the building before you bulldoze it! Exiting an application is similar because any currently running threads will be forcibly terminated regardless of what they may be working on.

Let's look at a simple example of how this might work. In the example THRDTERM in Listing 5-1 we will start two threads, which will periodically check an event object to see if it is time to exit. The code is very similar to the BUSY2 example in Chapter 3.

Listing 5-1. THRDTERM—Cleanly shut down a thread

```
/*
 * ThrdTerm.c
 *
 * Demonstrates how to request threads to exit.
 *
 * Build command: cl /MD ThrdTerm.c
 */
```

Listing 5-1 (continued)

```c
#include <stdio.h>
#include <stdlib.h>
#include <windows.h>
#include <time.h>
#include "MtVerify.h"

DWORD WINAPI ThreadFunc(LPVOID);

HANDLE hRequestExitEvent = FALSE;

int main()
{
    HANDLE hThreads[2];
    DWORD dwThreadId;
    DWORD dwExitCode = 0;
    int i;

    hRequestExitEvent = CreateEvent(
        NULL, TRUE, FALSE, NULL);

    for (i=0; i<2; i++)
        MTVERIFY( hThreads[i] = CreateThread(NULL,
            0,
            ThreadFunc,
            (LPVOID)i,
            0,
            &dwThreadId )
        );

    // Wait around for awhile, make
    // sure the thread is running.
    Sleep(1000);

    SetEvent(hRequestExitEvent);
    WaitForMultipleObjects(2, hThreads, TRUE, INFINITE);

    for (i=0; i<2; i++)
        MTVERIFY( CloseHandle(hThreads[i]) );

    return EXIT_SUCCESS;
}
```

Listing 5-1 (continued)

```c
DWORD WINAPI ThreadFunc(LPVOID p)
{
    int i;
    int inside = 0;

    UNREFERENCED_PARAMETER(p);

    /* Seed the random-number generator */
    srand( (unsigned)time( NULL ) );

    for (i=0; i<1000000; i++)
    {
        double x = (double)(rand())/RAND_MAX;
        double y = (double)(rand())/RAND_MAX;
        if ( (x*x + y*y) <= 1.0 )
            inside++;
        if (WaitForSingleObject(hRequestExitEvent, 0) != WAIT_TIMEOUT)
        {
            printf("Received request to terminate\n");
            return (DWORD)-1;
        }
    }
    printf("PI = %.4g\n", (double)inside / i * 4);
    return 0;
}
```

First of all, notice that an event object is being used instead of a simple global variable. This example does not require the use of an event object, but by using an event object we allow the worker threads to be able to wait on it if necessary. For example, a worker thread could use the event object to wait on either an Internet socket to connect *or* for the user to request an exit. In the worker thread, this would be a simple change from `WaitForSingle-Object()` to `WaitForMultipleObjects()`.

The next thing to notice is that there is only one event object, which all worker threads use. If the application is trying to exit, there is no need to create a separate notification mechanism for each thread because all threads need to be notified at once. Other situations may require finer control.

Finally, notice that the primary thread, in `main()`, does a `WaitFor-MultipleObjects()` on all of the thread handles. Waiting for the thread handles to become signaled is the only way of guaranteeing that the threads have actually exited safely. Although this example uses an INFINITE timeout, a commercial application would probably want to set an upper limit, such as 15 or 30 seconds, in case one of the threads has stopped responding.

Thread Priority

Have you ever been in your car, very late to get to where you are going, desperately wishing that you could tell everyone around you that it is terribly important for you to get where you are going, and would they please get out of your way? Unfortunately, roads are not built to accommodate high-priority traffic. Wouldn't it be nice if there was an on-ramp to the "very important" traffic lane where you could get around everyone else?

In Win32 there is a concept called **priority** that determines what thread gets to run next. A high-priority thread will get to use most of the available CPU time. The entire discussion of priority is actually quite complex. You can get your application in a lot of trouble by using priority indiscriminately, but judicious use of priority allows you to tune how your application runs. For example, you can set your GUI thread to be more responsive to the user, or change worker threads so they operate only during system idle time.

The priority in Win32 is a number that is calculated based on the process's **priority class**, the **priority level** of the thread, and the **dynamic boost** currently being applied by the operating system. All of these are put together to arrive at a single number between 0 and 31. The thread with the highest number runs next. If you have a bunch of worker threads all of whom have the same priority class and priority level, they will each take turns running. This is **round robin** scheduling. If you get a single worker thread with a higher priority, it will always be scheduled to run next and it can prevent all other threads from running. This is why thread priority must be used judiciously.

Priority Class

A priority class is an attribute of a process. The priority class represents how important this process is compared to other processes in the system. There are four priority classes in Win32, each of which corresponds to a base priority level, which is the integral number that the priority level and the dynamic boost modify. The four priority classes are shown in Table 5-1.

Table 5-1.   Priority classes

Priority Class	Base Priority Level
HIGH_PRIORITY_CLASS	13
IDLE_PRIORITY_CLASS	4
NORMAL_PRIORITY_CLASS	7 or 8
REALTIME_PRIORITY_CLASS	24

Most applications run with NORMAL_PRIORITY_CLASS. There are only a few cases where you would want to use anything else. For example, the Task Manager runs in HIGH_PRIORITY_CLASS so that it will always be responsive even if your other applications are very busy.

There is a good example in Windows NT of a place where a priority class should have been used and was not. The OpenGL screen savers make intensive use of all available CPU time. If one of these screen savers starts up while you are trying to back up your system, the backup slows down to a snail's pace. If the screen saver was running at IDLE_PRIORITY_CLASS, then it would only run when the CPU had absolutely nothing else to do.

The final case is REALTIME_PRIORITY_CLASS. This priority class was added to Win32 to help solve problems with extremely time-sensitive processing. An example would be a user application that must respond to a device driver that is performing real-time monitoring of a real-world experiment. A process set at this priority class will preempt even kernel processes and device drivers. There should never be a reason to use this priority class for a standard GUI application or even for the typical server application.

The priority class, which applies to processes, not threads, can be adjusted and examined with `SetPriorityClass()` and `GetPriority-Class()`. These calls will not be covered in this book.

Priority Level

The priority level of a thread is a modifier to the priority class of the process. The priority level allows you to adjust the relative importance of threads within a process without having to know the importance of the process as a whole. There are seven priority levels as shown in Table 5-2.

Table 5-2. Priority levels

Priority Level	Adjustment to Base
THREAD_PRIORITY_HIGHEST	+2
THREAD_PRIORITY_ABOVE_NORMAL	+1
THREAD_PRIORITY_NORMAL	0
THREAD_PRIORITY_BELOW_NORMAL	-1
THREAD_PRIORITY_LOWEST	-2
THREAD_PRIORITY_IDLE	set to 1
THREAD_PRIORITY_TIME_CRITICAL	set to 15

Note: The adjustments for REALTIME_PRIORITY_CLASS are somewhat different than those shown in this table.

Priority levels are modified with `SetThreadPriority()`.

BOOL SetThreadPriority(

    HANDLE hThread,
    int nPriority
    );

Parameters

hThread   Handle to the thread whose priority should be changed.

nPriority   A value as shown in Table 5-2.

Return Value

If the function succeeds it returns one of the thread priorities from Table 5-2. If it fails it returns FALSE, in which case `GetLastError()` can be used to find out why the call failed.

A thread's current priority level can be examined using `GetThread-Priority()`.

int GetThreadPriority(

    HANDLE hThread
    );

Parameters

hThread   Handle to the thread whose priority should be examined.

Return Value

If the function succeeds it returns TRUE. If it fails it returns THREAD_PRIORITY_ERROR_RETURN, in which case `GetLastError()` can be used to find out why the call failed.

Priority in KERNEL32.DLL

I used the Windows 95 version of PVIEW32 to look at the processes running on my system. The results are shown in Figure 5-1. I saw that the system process, KERNEL32.DLL, had eight threads running. The process itself was set at HIGH_PRIORITY_CLASS, so it had a base priority of 13. Examining the threads within the process showed that there were four threads with THREAD_PRIORITY_LOWEST and so had a priority of 11. Three threads were running at THREAD_PRIORITY_NORMAL and so had a priority of 13. One thread was running at THREAD_PRIORITY_TIME_CRITICAL, and so had a priority of 15. This thread would always be scheduled to run before any other non-real-time thread in the system.

```
Process Viewer Application                                          _ □ ×
File   Process   Help

📄 ×

Process       PID        Base Priority   Num. Threads   Type     Full Path
PVIEW95.EXE   FFFEF7...   8 (Normal)     1              32-Bit   \\MACAW\MAIN\MSDEV\BIN\WIN95\...
WINOLDAP      FFFE205F    8 (Normal)     1              16-Bit   C:\WINDOWS\SYSTEM\WINOA386.M...
SAGE.EXE      FFFFD187    8 (Normal)     2              32-Bit   C:\WINDOWS\SYSTEM\SAGE.EXE
ATIICON.EXE   FFFFE9...   8 (Normal)     1              32-Bit   C:\WINDOWS\SYSTEM\ATIICON.EXE
SYSTRAY.EXE   FFFE591F    8 (Normal)     1              32-Bit   C:\WINDOWS\SYSTEM\SYSTRAY.EXE
ATIKEY32.EXE  FFFE6B...   8 (Normal)     1              32-Bit   C:\WINDOWS\SYSTEM\ATIKEY32.EXE
EXPLORER.E... FFFE716B    8 (Normal)     3              32-Bit   C:\WINDOWS\EXPLORER.EXE
MMTASK        FFFFF37F    8 (Normal)     1              16-Bit   C:\WINDOWS\SYSTEM\mmtask.tsk
MPREXE.EXE    FFFFFAE...   8 (Normal)    1              32-Bit   C:\WINDOWS\SYSTEM\MPREXE.EXE
MSGSRV32      FFFFBE...   8 (Normal)     1              16-Bit   C:\WINDOWS\SYSTEM\MSGSRV32.E...
KERNEL32.DLL  FFCF65...   13 (High)      8              32-Bit   C:\WINDOWS\SYSTEM\KERNEL32.DLL

TID         Owning PID    Thread Priority
FFFFA42B    FFCF65BF      13 (Normal)
FFFFB397    FFCF65BF      15 (Time Critical)
FFFF4B7F    FFCF65BF      11 (Lowest)
FFFF4897    FFCF65BF      11 (Lowest)
FFFF4ECF    FFCF65BF      11 (Lowest)
FFFF4C4B    FFCF65BF      11 (Lowest)
FFFF583F    FFCF65BF      13 (Normal)
FFCF674B    FFCF65BF      13 (Normal)
```

Figure 5-1. PVIEW32 in Windows 95.

Dynamic Boost

The final piece that goes into determining a thread's actual priority is its current dynamic boost. The dynamic boost is an adjustment to current priority that the system applies to a thread on an as-needed basis to enhance the application's usability.

One of the most visible kinds of dynamic boost is applied by Windows NT to all threads in the foreground application. The Performance page in System Properties, shown in Figure 5-2, allows the user to specify how responsive the foreground application should be. You can get here by right-clicking on My Computer and bringing up Properties.

By default the performance boost is set to maximum, which causes a +2 dynamic boost to be applied to all threads in whichever process currently has the focus. This tweak means that the foreground application will get more CPU time than the background applications and will stay responsive even if the system is busy.

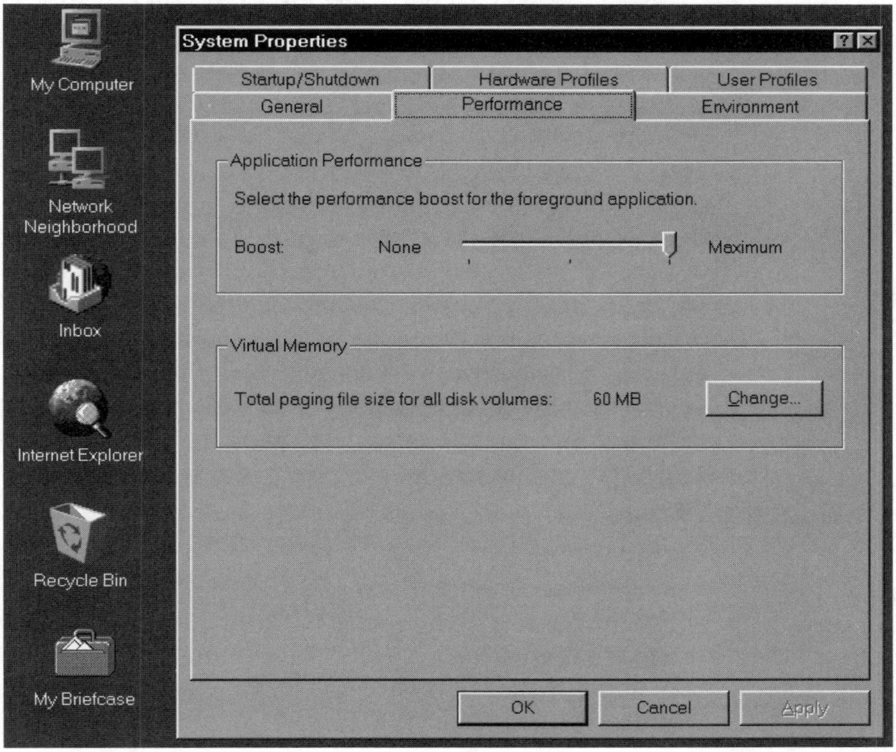

Figure 5-2. System Properties in Windows NT 4.0.

The second kind of priority boost is also applied to all threads in a process and happens in response to input from the user or from the disk. For example, a thread receives a +5 adjustment whenever there is keyboard input for the thread. This gives the thread an opportunity to process the input and provide immediate feedback to the user. Other things that cause a priority boost include mouse messages, timer messages, and disk input that has completed.

A final case where priority boosts are applied is on a per-thread basis when a wait condition is satisfied. For example, if a thread is waiting on a mutex, the thread will get a priority boost as it returns from the Wait…() function. This dynamic boost means that critical sections will be processed as fast as possible and waiting will be minimized.

More Busy Waiting Horrors

In Chapter 2 you saw how a busy loop could pull CPU time away from worker threads that the busy loop was monitoring. The problem is much worse when you start adjusting thread priorities. In the sample code for this chapter on the CD-ROM, there is a program call BUSYPRIO that runs the primary thread at THREAD_PRIORITY_HIGHEST while the worker thread runs at THREAD_PRIORITY_NORMAL.

If you run the program, you will see the somewhat unexpected result that the program never finishes. Why? The primary thread is constantly busy and so has constant need of the processor. Because it has a higher priority than the worker thread, the worker thread will never receive any time to run. This condition is called **starvation.**

BUSYPRIO shows how important it is to be very careful about how you set your thread priorities. Changing the priorities of threads in an application opens up a whole new class of things that can go wrong and potential situations for deadlock. Although the basics of priorities are quite simple, the practice can be quite complex. If your goal is to keep it simple, avoid priorities.

Initializing a Thread

A common problem when using threads is how to properly initialize the thread before it starts running. The most common reason to do this is to adjust a new thread's priority. Another reason would be to set a thread's preferred processor on SMP systems. We will see other reasons when we look at threads in MFC in Chapter 10.

The fundamental problem is that you need a handle to a thread to adjust the thread, but if you call `CreateThread()` in its default form then the new thread is already running and it is too late to do initial setup.

The solution is the fifth parameter of `CreateThread()`, which allows you to specify creation flags. At this time there is only a single flag defined called CREATE_SUSPENDED. This flag tells `CreateThread()` to set up a new thread and return its handle, but not to start it running.

Here is an example where we create a new thread and set its priority to idle.

```
HANDLE hThread;
DWORD threadId;

hThread = CreateThread(NULL,
        0,
        ThreadFunc,
        0,
        CREATE_SUSPENDED,
        &threadId );
SetThreadPriority(hThread, THREAD_PRIORITY_IDLE);
```

Once the thread is setup, you can start the thread running with `ResumeThread()`.

BOOL ResumeThread(
   HANDLE hThread
);

Parameters

hThread   Handle to the thread to restart.

Return Value

If the function succeeds it returns the previous suspend count of the thread. If it fails it returns 0xFFFFFFFF, in which case `GetLastError()` can be used to find out why.

Suspending Threads

There is a companion function to `ResumeThread()` called, not surprisingly, `SuspendThread()`. The function allows the caller to put a thread to sleep. The thread will not wake until someone calls `ResumeThread()`. Therefore it is impossible for the sleeping thread to wake itself. The call looks like this:

BOOL SuspendThread(

   HANDLE hThread,

);

Parameters

hThread   Handle to the thread to suspend.

Return Value

If the function succeeds it returns the current suspend count of the thread. If it fails it returns 0xFFFFFFFF, in which case `GetLastError()` can be used to find out why the call failed.

   `SuspendThread()` is another one of those calls with lots of hidden gotchas. Consider the case of a process running three threads, A, B, and C. Thread C is in a critical section and Thread B is waiting to get into the critical section. Then Thread A suspends Thread C. In this case, Thread C will never get out of the critical section and Thread B will deadlock.

   The biggest use for `SuspendThread()` is when writing debuggers where starting and stopping threads in a process is under the developer's control.

Summary

In this chapter you saw the approved way to shut down a thread. You saw how a thread's priority is defined and the effect of changing that priority. Finally you saw how to use CREATE_SUSPENDED to initialize a thread before it runs.

Chapter 6

Overlapped I/O, or Juggling Behind Your Back

This chapter describes how to use overlapped, or asynchronous, I/O. In some cases overlapped I/O can be used instead of threads. However, overlapped I/O with completion ports is designed to use multiple threads to get high performance out of an I/O bound application.

Now that we have spent several chapters talking about how and why you might want to use threads, I will spend this chapter talking about one place you can often avoiding using threads. Many application programs, such as terminal emulators, need to simultaneously handle reading and writing to multiple file handles at the same time. Using a feature in Win32 called overlapped I/O, you can set up all of these I/O operations to run concurrently and your program will be notified as each operation completes. Other operating systems call this nonblocking or asynchronous I/O.

You saw back in Chapters 2 and 3 how to create a thread that does background printing. In reality, the description "background printing" is a misnomer. What we really did in the background was to generate the printer data. The operating system took care of printing using the Print Manager, which spooled the data and slowly fed it to the printer at a speed the printer could handle.

The point of all this is that I/O devices are slow, regardless of whether they are printers, modems, or even hard disks. Sitting around waiting for I/O to complete is not a particularly good use of time for your program. Sometimes the actual data rates are surprising. Moving data off of your file server at Ethernet speeds can reasonably be expected to give speeds up to a megabyte per second. If you try and read 100K from the file server, it happens almost instantly from the user's point of view, but your thread executing the command might have lost 10 million cycles of processing.

Now imagine that this same file server is being accessed using Remote Access Services (RAS) over a dial-up connection. Now a 100K read will take anywhere from 15 seconds over ISDN to almost 2 minutes at 9600 bps! Even from a user's point of view, that is an awfully long time for an application's window to be unresponsive.

An obvious solution to this problem would be to use another thread to do the I/O. However, the related problems exist of coordinating the worker thread with the primary thread, setting up the synchronization mechanisms, handling errors, putting up dialogs, and all the other issues we have seen in this part of the book.

FAQ 21

What is overlapped I/O?

An easier solution to this problem is a technique in Win32 called **overlapped I/O,** where you can ask the operating system to transfer data for you and to notify you when it is finished. This arrangement leaves your application free to continue processing while the I/O is being performed. In point of fact, the implementation of overlapped I/O uses threads inside the kernel to do the work. You get all the benefits of threads with very little of the pain.

IMPORTANT!

FAQ 22

What are the limitations on overlapped I/O in Windows 95?

Support for overlapped I/O is limited in Windows 95 and can only be used for named pipes, mailslots, serial I/O, and sockets returned by `socket()` or `accept()`. Overlapped I/O is not supported for file operations on disk or CD-ROM. All of the examples in this chapter work only under Windows NT.

In this chapter we will walk through the use of overlapped I/O starting with the simplest usage and progressing to the most advanced.

- Signaled file handles
- Signaled event objects
- Asynchronous Procedure Calls (APCs)
- I/O completion ports

I/O completion ports are particularly important because they are the only mechanism that is suited for high-volume servers that must maintain many simultaneous connections. Completion ports help load-balance the servicing of I/O requests with a pool of available threads. This architecture is particularly suited for creating scaleable servers on SMP systems.

The Win32 File Calls

There are three basic calls for performing I/O in Win32. They are:

- `CreateFile()`
- `ReadFile()`
- `WriteFile()`

There is no distinct call for closing a file; you simply use `CloseHandle()`. This chapter will only cover the parts of these calls that relate to overlapped I/O. For a more detailed description of how file I/O works in Win32, see the Win32 Programmer's Reference.

`CreateFile()` can be used to open a wide variety of resources, including but not limited to:

- Files (hard disk, floppy disk, CD-ROM, and others)
- Serial and parallel ports
- Named pipes
- Console (see Chapter 8)

The prototype for `CreateFile()` looks like this:

```
HANDLE CreateFile(
    LPCTSTR lpFileName,       // pointer to name of the file
    DWORD dwDesiredAccess,  // access (read-write) mode
    DWORD dwShareMode,      //  share mode
    LPSECURITY_ATTRIBUTES lpSecurityAttributes, // ptr to security
    DWORD dwCreationDistribution, // how to create
    DWORD dwFlagsAndAttributes,   // file attributes
    HANDLE hTemplateFile // handle to file with attributes to copy
);
```

The sixth parameter to `CreateFile()`, *dwFlagsAndAttributes*, is the key to using overlapped I/O. Although this parameter can be set by combining a wide variety of values, the important one for this discussion is FILE_FLAG_OVERLAPPED. Specifying this parameter is an all-or-nothing proposition. You can either access a particular file handle using synchronous (traditional) calls, or with overlapped calls, but not both. In other words, if this flag is specified, then every operation on the file handle must be overlapped.

An unusual feature of overlapped I/O is that it can read and/or write from multiple parts of the file at the same time. The tricky part is that the operations all use the same file handle at the same time. Therefore there is no concept of "current file position" when you are using overlapped I/O. Every read or write call must include the file position.

If you issue multiple overlapped requests, then the order of execution is not guaranteed. Although you will rarely see the behavior if you are working with files on a single disk, you will frequently see the I/O requests complete out of order if you are working with multiple drives or with different kinds of devices, such as the network and the disk drives.

FAQ 23

Can I use overlapped I/O with the C run-time library?

There is no way to use overlapped I/O with the calls in *stdio.h* in the C run-time library. Therefore there is no easy way of doing overlapped text-based I/O. For example, `fgets()` in the run-time library allows you to read a line of text at a time. You cannot use `fgets()`, `fprintf()`, and other such calls with overlapped I/O.

The basic form of overlapped I/O is performed with `ReadFile()` and `WriteFile()`. Their prototypes look like this:

```
BOOL ReadFile(
    HANDLE hFile,                 // handle of file to read
    LPVOID lpBuffer,              // ptr to buffer that receives data
    DWORD nNumberOfBytesToRead,   // # of bytes to read
    LPDWORD lpNumberOfBytesRead,  // address of # of bytes read
    LPOVERLAPPED lpOverlapped     // ptr to overlapped info
);
BOOL WriteFile(
    HANDLE hFile,                  // handle to file to write to
    LPCVOID lpBuffer,              // ptr to data to write to file
    DWORD nNumberOfBytesToWrite,   // # of bytes to write
    LPDWORD lpNumberOfBytesWritten, // ptr to # of bytes written
    LPOVERLAPPED lpOverlapped      // ptr to overlapped info
);
```

Each of this calls is similar to `fread()` and `fwrite()` from the C run-time library except for the last parameter, *lpOverlapped*. You must supply a pointer to a valid OVERLAPPED structure if `CreateFile()` was called with FILE_FLAG_OVERLAPPED.

The OVERLAPPED Structure

The OVERLAPPED structure performs two important functions. First, it acts as a key that uniquely identifies each overlapped operation currently in progress. Second, it provides a shared area between you and the system where parameters can be passed in each direction.

The OVERLAPPED structure looks like this:

```
typedef struct _OVERLAPPED {
    DWORD   Internal;
    DWORD   InternalHigh;
    DWORD   Offset;
    DWORD   OffsetHigh;
    HANDLE  hEvent;
} OVERLAPPED;
```

Structure Members

Table 6-1 describes the structure members of the OVERLAPPED structure.

Table 6-1. Structure members of the OVERLAPPED structure

Member	Description
Internal	Normally reserved. However, when `GetOver-lappedResult()` returns FALSE and `GetLastError()` is not set to ERROR_IO_PENDING, this field contains a system-dependent status.
InternalHigh	Normally reserved. However, when `GetOver-lappedResult()` returns TRUE, this member contains the length of the data transferred.
Offset	Byte offset within the file to begin reading or writing. This offset is measured from the beginning of the file. This member is ignored for devices that do not support a file position, such as pipes.
OffsetHigh	High 32 bits of the 64-bit file offset to begin reading and writing. This member is ignored for devices that do not support a file position, such as pipes.
hEvent	Manual reset event object to signal upon completion of I/O operation. This field is ignored for `Read-FileEx()` and `WriteFileEx()` and may be used to pass a user pointer.

Because the lifetime of the OVERLAPPED structure extends beyond the call to `ReadFile()` or `WriteFile()`, it is important to put the structure in a safe place. Typically a local variable is not a safe place because it will go out of scope too soon. It is usually safest to allocate the OVERLAPPED structure on the heap.

Now that we have all the basic pieces, let's see how to use them.

Signaled File Handles

The simplest type of overlapped I/O operation uses the file handle itself as the synchronization mechanism. You begin by opening the file with FILE_FLAG_OVERLAPPED to tell Win32 that you do not want to use the default of synchronous I/O. Second, set up an OVERLAPPED structure that will contain the parameters for the I/O request and will uniquely identify the request until it completes. Next, call `ReadFile()` and pass the address of the OVERLAPPED structure. At this point Win32 is, in theory, processing your request in the background. Your program can safely go and do something else.

If you need to wait for the result as part of a call to `WaitForMultipleObjects()`, use the handle to the file in the handle array. The file handle, as a kernel object, will be signaled when the operation is complete. When you are ready to process the request, call `GetOverlappedResult()` to find out what happened.

`GetOverlappedResult()` returns the same thing you would have gotten if you had called `ReadFile()` or `WriteFile()` and not used overlapped I/O. This call exists because it is not possible to know for sure if the operation succeeded until it actually happens. Even under the "perfect" circumstances of reading a known disk file, it is possible for the hardware to fail, the server to go down, or any number of unexpected failures. Therefore it is always important to call `GetOverlappedResult()`.

`GetOverlappedResult()` looks like this:

BOOL GetOverlappedResult(
    HANDLE hFile,
    LPOVERLAPPED lpOverlapped,
    LPDWORD lpNumberOfBytesTransferred,
    BOOL bWait
);

Parameters

hFile	Handle to the file or device.
lpOverlapped	Pointer to an OVERLAPPED structure.
lpNumberOf-BytesTransferred	Pointer to a DWORD where the actual number of bytes transferred will be placed.
bWait	Flag indicates whether to wait for operation to complete. Waits if TRUE.

Return Value

If the overlapped operation succeeded this function returns TRUE. If the operation failed this function returns FALSE, in which case `GetLast-Error()` can be used to find out what failed. If *bWait* is FALSE and the overlapped operation still has not completed, `GetLastError()` returns ERROR_IO_INCOMPLETE.

The code shown in Listing 6-1 reads 300 bytes starting at location 1500 in the file C:\WINDOWS\WINFILE.EXE. This code is on the CD-ROM in the sample program IOBYFILE.

Listing 6-1. Excerpt from IOBYFILE.C—Overlapped I/O with a signaled file handle

```c
int ReadSomething()
{
    BOOL rc;
    HANDLE hFile;
    DWORD numread;
    OVERLAPPED overlap;
    char buf[512];

    // Open the file for overlapped reads
    hFile = CreateFile( "C:\\WINDOWS\\WINFILE.EXE",
                    GENERIC_READ,
                    FILE_SHARE_READ|FILE_SHARE_WRITE,
                    NULL,
                    OPEN_EXISTING,
                    FILE_FLAG_OVERLAPPED,
                    NULL
                );
    if (hFile == INVALID_HANDLE_VALUE)
        return -1;

    // Initialize the OVERLAPPED structure
    memset(overlap, 0, sizeof(overlap));
    overlap.Offset = 1500;

    // Request the data
    rc = ReadFile(
                hFile,
                buf,
                300,
```

Listing 6-1 (continued)

```
                    &numread,
                    &overlap
                );

    if (rc)
    {
        // The data was read successfully
    }
    else
    {
// Was the operation queued?
        if (GetLastError() == ERROR_IO_PENDING)
        {
            // We could do something else for awhile here...

            WaitForSingleObject(hFile, INFINITE);
            rc = GetOverlappedResult(
                                    hFile,
                                    &overlap,
                                    &numread,
                                    FALSE
                                );
        }
        else
        {
            // Something went wrong
        }
    }

    CloseHandle(hFile);

    return TRUE;
}
```

FAQ 24

Is over-lapped I/O always performed asynchronously?

There are several important things to notice from this code sample. First and foremost, just because you ask for an operation to be overlapped does not mean that it *will* be overlapped. If the data was already in the cache or if the operating system thinks it can get the data quickly, then the operation will be completed before `ReadFile()` returns and `ReadFile()` will return TRUE. If this happens, it does not mean you have to handle the request at that point. The file handle will still be signaled and the operation can be treated as if it really was overlapped.

The next thing to notice is that if you ask for an operation to be overlapped, and the operating system queues the request for execution, then `ReadFile()` and `WriteFile()` return FALSE to indicate failure. This behavior is not intuitive. You need to call `GetLastError()` and make sure that it returns ERROR_IO_PENDING, which simply means that the overlapped I/O is queued and waiting to happen. It is possible for `GetLastError()` to return other values, such as ERROR_HANDLE_EOF, which really *is* an error and must be treated as such.

Notice how overlapped I/O works around the problem of not having a current file pointer. The OVERLAPPED structure itself includes information about where this operation should start. It is worth noting that, although not shown in Listing 6-1, the OVERLAPPED structure is capable of handling 64-bit offsets for extremely large files.

To wait for the operation to complete, I passed the file's handle to `Wait-ForSingleObject()`. The file handle will become signaled when the overlapped operation completes. This example is oversimplified because a real-world application would probably wait for multiple handles at the same time in a central part of the program.

The call to `WaitForSingleObject()` is actually redundant in Listing 6-1 because `GetOverlappedResult()` can be told to wait until the overlapped operation completes. In practice, however, you would normally be using one of the `Wait…()` functions to wait for an overlapped operation to complete, and I wanted to demonstrate the usage.

Signaled Event Objects

An obvious limitation to using file handles as the signaling mechanism is that you cannot tell which operation has completed. This is not a problem when you only have a single operation pending per file handle, but as I mentioned earlier, it is possible to simultaneously queue up several operations, all of which use the same file handle. It is clear that calling `GetOver-lappedResult()` on each possible overlapped operation in progress is not a very efficient solution. Not surprisingly, Win32 provides a better way of handling this problem.

The final member of the OVERLAPPED structure is a handle to an event object. If you are using a signaled file handle, this member is set to NULL. When this member is set to an event object, the kernel will automatically signal the event object when the overlapped I/O operation is completed. Because every overlapped I/O operation has its own unique OVERLAPPED structure, each structure can have a unique event object to represent the operation.

FAQ 25

How should I create the event object for overlapped I/O?

It is very important that the event object you use be created as manual-reset and not as auto-reset. (See Chapter 4 for details on event objects.) If you use an auto-reset event, then a race condition arises because the kernel could signal the object before you have a chance to wait on it. Event objects do not "store up" the signaled condition, unlike semaphores, so the event would be lost and your wait would never return. When a manual reset event object is signaled, it stays signaled.

By using event objects and overlapped I/O, you can issue multiple reads and writes against the same file handle, each with its own event object, then do a `WaitForMultipleObjects()` to wait for one or all of them to finish.

The relevant code from the sample IOBYEVNT is shown in Listing 6-2. This routine takes care of queuing up a particular request given the offset in the file and the length of the data.

Listing 6-2. Excerpt from LOBYEVNT.C—Overlapped I/O with signaled events

```c
// Need to keep the events in their own array so we can wait on them.
HANDLE  ghEvents[MAX_REQUESTS];
// Keep track of each individual I/O operation
OVERLAPPED gOverlapped[MAX_REQUESTS];
// Handle to the file of interest.
HANDLE ghFile;
// Need a place to put all this data
char gBuffers[MAX_REQUESTS][READ_SIZE];

int QueueRequest(int nIndex, DWORD dwLocation, DWORD dwAmount)
{
    int i;
    BOOL rc;
    DWORD dwNumread;
    DWORD err;

    MTVERIFY(
        ghEvents[nIndex] = CreateEvent(
                    NULL,    // No security
                    TRUE,    // Manual reset - extremely important!
                    FALSE,   // Initially set Event to nonsignaled
                    NULL     // No name
                    )
    );
    gOverlapped[nIndex].hEvent = ghEvents[nIndex];
    gOverlapped[nIndex].Offset = dwLocation;
```

Listing 6-2 (continued)

```c
for (i=0; i<MAX_TRY_COUNT; i++)
{
    rc = ReadFile(
        ghFile,
        gBuffers[nIndex],
        dwAmount,
        &dwNumread,
        &gOverlapped[nIndex]
    );

    // Handle success
    if (rc)
    {
        printf("Read #%d completed immediately.\n", nIndex);
        return TRUE;
    }

    err = GetLastError();

    // Handle the error that isn't an error. rc is zero here.
    if (err == ERROR_IO_PENDING)
    {
        // asynchronous i/o is still in progress
        printf("Read #%d queued for overlapped I/O.\n", nIndex);
        return TRUE;
    }

    // Handle recoverable error
    if ( err == ERROR_INVALID_USER_BUFFER ||
         err == ERROR_NOT_ENOUGH_QUOTA ||
         err == ERROR_NOT_ENOUGH_MEMORY )
    {
        Sleep(50);  // Wait around and try later
        continue;
    }

    // Give up on fatal error.
    break;
}

printf("ReadFile failed.\n");
return -1;
}
```

You will notice that this block of code creates a new event object for *each* overlapped I/O request. The handle to the event object gets stored in the OVERLAPPED structure and in a global array that can be used by `WaitForMultipleObjects()`.

You will again see that a particular request can sometimes be returned immediately. For example, here are the results from a sample run:

OUTPUT FROM IOBYEVNT:

```
Read #0 queued for overlapped I/O.
Read #1 completed immediately.
Read #2 completed immediately.
Read #3 completed immediately.
Read #4 completed immediately.
QUEUED!!
Read #0 returned 1. 512 bytes were read.
Read #1 returned 1. 512 bytes were read.
Read #2 returned 1. 512 bytes were read.
Read #3 returned 1. 512 bytes were read.
Read #4 returned 1. 512 bytes were read.
```

In this case, Windows NT did predictive read-ahead after the first request and subsequent requests were able to be returned immediately.

You will also see that the call to `ReadFile()` is inside of a loop. Because of the way the operating system works, the buffer you specify for overlapped I/O must be locked into memory. If too many buffers in the system or the program are locked at the same time, it can cause a dramatic drop in performance. Therefore the system sometimes needs to throttle back the running programs. Instead of blocking, which would defeat the purpose of overlapped I/O, Win32 returns an error such as ERROR_INVALID_USER_BUFFER to indicate that there are insufficient resources at the moment to process the request. This problem could also have occurred in the IOBYFILE example, but the error processing was left out for the sake of clarity.

In our problem at the beginning of the chapter, in which the RAS connection to the server took 2 minutes instead of two-tenths of a second to finish moving the data, we could have queued the operation as overlapped I/O and then used `MsgWaitForMultipleObjects()` in the main message loop to respond once the data was received.

Asynchronous Procedure Calls (APCs)

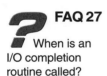

FAQ 26

What is the advantage of `ReadFileEx()` and `Write-FileEx()`?

There are two fundamental problems with using overlapped I/O in combination with event objects. First, using `WaitForMultipleObjects()` you can only wait on up to MAXIMUM_WAIT_OBJECTS, which was set to 64 in the Win32 SDK that came with Windows NT 3.x and 4.0. Waiting on more than 64 objects is problematic. In a client-server operation, you would be limited to 64 simultaneous connections. The second problem is that you are constantly trying to figure out how to react based on which handle was signaled. You need to have some dispatch table that is tied into the position of a handle in the array that is passed to `WaitForMultipleObjects()`.

Both of these problems can be solved using a mechanism called the **Asynchronous Procedure Call (APC).** You invoke this mechanism by using the "Ex" versions of `ReadFile()` and `WriteFile()`. These functions, `ReadFileEx()` and `WriteFileEx()`, take an additional parameter that specifies a callback routine that the system should call when an overlapped I/O operation finishes. This callback routine is called the **I/O completion routine** because the system calls it when a particular overlapped I/O operation is complete.

FAQ 27

When is an I/O completion routine called?

However, Windows will not interrupt your program in the middle of whatever it is doing just to call your completion routine. Windows will only call the completion routine when the thread says that it is in a safe state. In Windows parlance, your thread must be in an **alertable** state. If an I/O operation completes and the thread is not in an alertable state, the call to the I/O completion routine will be queued up. Therefore, when a thread finally enters an alertable state, there may be a large backlog of APCs waiting to be serviced.

A thread is in an alertable state if it is waiting in one of these five functions with the alertable flag set to TRUE:

- `SleepEx()`
- `WaitForSingleObjectEx()`
- `WaitForMultipleObjectsEx()`
- `MsgWaitForMultipleObjectsEx()`
- `SignalObjectAndWait()`

The concept that APCs can only be called when the application is in an alertable state is important. The result is that the completion routine will not be called while your application is in the middle of calculating pi to 10,000 digits, nor will another thread be used if the original thread is busy repainting the screen.

**FOR THE
EXPERTS**

The APCs used for overlapped I/O are user-mode APCs. Windows NT also has kernel-mode APCs. Kernel-mode APCs are internally queued up like user-mode APCs, but a kernel mode APC is called at the beginning of the next timeslice. In other words, a kernel-mode APC will be called no matter what a thread may be doing. Kernel-mode APCs handle operating system functionality and are not under program control.

The I/O completion routine is a routine that you supply that looks like this:

VOID WINAPI FileIOCompletionRoutine(
   DWORD dwErrorCode,
   DWORD dwNumberOfBytesTransferred,
   LPOVERLAPPED lpOverlapped
   );

Parameters

dwErrorCode	This parameter contains one of these values: zero if the operation was successful; ERROR_HANDLE_EOF if the operation would have read past the end of the file.
dwNumberOf-BytesTransferred	Actual number of bytes that were transferred.
lpOverlapped	Pointer to the OVERLAPPED structure that was supplied by the function that started the overlapped I/O operation.

FAQ 28

How do I pass user-defined data to an I/O completion routine?

The I/O completion routine needs to have some way to understand its context. If it does not know what I/O operation completed, then it is hard to decide what to do with the data. When using APCs, the *hEvent* member of the OVERLAPPED structure does not need to be used to hold an event object handle. The Win32 documentation states that *hEvent* can be used by the developer. It is most useful to allocate a structure that describes to your program where the data came from or what to do with the data, then set *hEvent* to point at the structure.

The usage of overlapped I/O with APCs is shown in Listing 6-3. This listing contains the complete source to the sample IOBYAPC.

Listing 6-3. IOBYAPC.C—Overlapped I/O with APCs

```c
/*
 * IoByAPC.c
 *
 * Sample code for Multithreading Applications in Win32
 *
 * Demonstrates how to use APCs (asynchronous
 * procedure calls) instead of signaled objects
 * to service multiple outstanding overlapped
 * operations on a file.
 */

#define WIN32_LEAN_AND_MEAN
#include <windows.h>
#include <stdio.h>
#include <stdlib.h>
#include "MtVerify.h"

#define MAX_REQUESTS    5
#define READ_SIZE       512
#define MAX_TRY_COUNT   5

// Need a single event object so we know when all I/O is finished
HANDLE  ghEvent;
// Keep track of each individual I/O operation
OVERLAPPED gOverlapped[MAX_REQUESTS];
// Handle to the file of interest.
HANDLE ghFile;
// Need a place to put all this data
char gBuffers[MAX_REQUESTS][READ_SIZE];
int nCompletionCount;

/*
 * I/O Completion routine gets called
 * when app is alertable (in WaitForSingleObjectEx)
 * and an overlapped I/O operation has completed.
 */
VOID WINAPI FileIOCompletionRoutine(
    DWORD dwErrorCode,  // completion code
    DWORD dwNumberOfBytesTransfered,    // number of bytes transferred
    LPOVERLAPPED lpOverlapped   // ptr to structure with I/O info
    )
{
    // The event handle is really the user-defined data
    int nIndex = (int)(lpOverlapped->hEvent);
    printf("Read #%d returned %d. %d bytes were read.\n",
```

Listing 6-3 (continued)

```
            nIndex,
            dwErrorCode,
            dwNumberOfBytesTransfered);

    if (++nCompletionCount == MAX_REQUESTS)
        SetEvent(ghEvent);  // Cause the wait to terminate
}

/*
 * Queue up a single overlapped request.
 */
int QueueRequest(int nIndex, DWORD dwLocation, DWORD dwAmount)
{
    int i;
    BOOL rc;
    DWORD err;

    gOverlapped[nIndex].hEvent = (HANDLE)nIndex;
    gOverlapped[nIndex].Offset = dwLocation;

    for (i=0; i<MAX_TRY_COUNT; i++)
    {
        rc = ReadFileEx(
            ghFile,
            gBuffers[nIndex],
            dwAmount,
            &gOverlapped[nIndex],
            FileIOCompletionRoutine
        );

        // Handle success
        if (rc)
        {
            // asynchronous i/o is still in progress
            printf("Read #%d queued for overlapped I/O.\n", nIndex);
            return TRUE;
        }

        err = GetLastError();

        // Handle recoverable error
        if ( err == ERROR_INVALID_USER_BUFFER ||
             err == ERROR_NOT_ENOUGH_QUOTA ||
             err == ERROR_NOT_ENOUGH_MEMORY )
```

Listing 6-3 (continued)

```
        {
            Sleep(50);   // Wait around and try later
            continue;
        }

        // Give up on fatal error.
        break;
    }

    printf("ReadFileEx failed.\n");
    return -1;
}

int main()
{
    int i;

    // Need to know when to stop
    MTVERIFY(
        ghEvent = CreateEvent(
                    NULL,    // No security
                    TRUE,    // Manual reset - extremely important!
                    FALSE,   // Initially set Event to nonsignaled
                    NULL     // No name
                    )
    );

    // Open the file for overlapped reads
    ghFile = CreateFile( "C:\\WINDOWS\\WINFILE.EXE",
                    GENERIC_READ,
                    FILE_SHARE_READ|FILE_SHARE_WRITE,
                    NULL,
                    OPEN_EXISTING,
                    FILE_FLAG_OVERLAPPED,
                    NULL
                );
    if (ghFile == INVALID_HANDLE_VALUE)
    {
        printf("Could not open C:\\WINDOWS\\WINFILE.EXE\n");
        return -1;
    }

    // Queue up a few requests
    for (i=0; i<MAX_REQUESTS; i++)
```

Listing 6-3 (continued)

```
{
    // Read some bytes every few K
    QueueRequest(i, i*16384, READ_SIZE);
}

printf("QUEUED!!\n");

// Wait for all the operations to complete.
for (;;)
{
    DWORD rc;
    rc = WaitForSingleObjectEx(ghEvent, INFINITE, TRUE );
    if (rc == WAIT_OBJECT_0)
        break;
    MTVERIFY(rc == WAIT_IO_COMPLETION);
}

CloseHandle(ghFile);

return TRUE;
}
```

The QueueRequest() routine in this sample is very similar to the routine of the same name in IOBYEVNT. The big difference is that there is no separation between "returned immediately" versus "not complete." You can see that this routine also has to handle the case of the system being out of resources.

A new addition to this sample is the routine FileIOCompletion-Routine(). This is the callback that the system calls when an overlapped I/O request completes. Notice that the routine is passed all the information that would normally be obtained from GetOverlappedResult().

Finally, notice that main() is calling WaitForSingleObjectEx() so that the APCs will be processed. We have to stay in a loop because WaitForSingleObjectEx() returns WAIT_IO_COMPLETION after processing the APCs.

Creating Completion Routines in C++

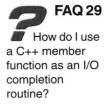

FAQ 29

How do I use a C++ member function as an I/O completion routine?

A C++ member function cannot be used as an I/O completion routine unless it is static. If it is static, it has no *this* pointer, and so cannot directly call other member functions that require a *this* pointer.

The solution is to store a pointer to the object in the user-defined data, then call a member function through this pointer. Because a static member function is part of the class, you can still call private member functions. This problem is very similar to the problem of starting a thread in a C++ member function. I describe the solution to this problem in detail in Chapter 9.

APC Wrap-up

Given the existence of APCs, I see very little use for waiting on either file handles or event objects for `ReadFile()` and `WriteFile()` operations. If you use either of these techniques, you would have to figure out the meaning of the signaled handle and then dispatch to your own routine. By and large, this would be a waste of time since the system can handle all of the grunt work for you.

Drawbacks of Overlapped I/O with Files

As part of writing this book, I did extensive testing on the performance benefits of using overlapped I/O. What I discovered was very unexpected. It appears that Windows NT decides whether or not to queue an operation based on the size of the request. For example, if you ask for an 8K block of data, then Windows NT will block your thread and get the data immediately instead of queuing the operation.

The problem with this approach is that, for disk transfers less than about 64K, the average time to move the head is greater than the time to transfer the data. Assuming an actual transfer rate of 5MB/sec (typical of a PCI bus mastering SCSI controller driving a SCSI-II drive where the data is not in the cache on the host or on the drive), it will take an average of 10 ms to seek the head but only 1.8 ms to transfer the 8K of data! This time does not include SCSI bus setup time and other more nitty-gritty driver issues.

Because the operating system chose to block for this "quick" transfer of data, your process will lose at least 12 ms (on average) of potential processing time. On the other hand, if you try and move 1MB of data, then the I/O operation will in fact be queued and your thread can continue processing.

My testing showed that for a series of requests less than 32K, using overlapped I/O took 15 percent longer than making blocking calls to `ReadFile()`.

In an environment such as a Web server where most requests are small, using overlapped I/O to talk to the disk would actually decrease overall performance without freeing your program to do background processing.

A reasonable alternative would be to have a small pool of threads doing all I/O to the hard drive, and then queuing up requests for this pool of threads. This is the approximate model that using I/O completion ports yields. Testing shows that this configuration would have an overall performance better than overlapped and nonoverlapped operations.

It is possible to bypass the virtual memory manager and go directly to the file system by using the flag FILE_FLAG_NO_BUFFERING in the call to `CreateFile()`. However, doing so also bypasses the cache manager and can potentially cause a dramatic *decrease* in performance if not done properly. A discussion of the relevant issues is beyond the scope of this book. An excellent discussion of the Windows NT file system can be found in the July, 1995 issue of *Microsoft Systems Journal* in the article, "Design and Implementation of the Windows NT Virtual Block Cache Manager," by Helen Custer.

Finally, there are two situations where overlapped I/O will always be performed synchronously, even if FILE_FLAG_NO_BUFFERING is specified. The first is if you are doing a write operation that causes a file to be extended. The second is if you are reading or writing a compressed file.

I/O Completion Ports

Although APCs are a very handy way of doing overlapped I/O, they do have their drawbacks. The biggest problem is that there are several I/O APIs that do not have a version that supports APCs. Two examples are `listen()`, for sockets being connected, and `WaitCommEvent()`, for events on the comm ports. The other problem with APCs is that only the thread that started the overlapped request can service the callback. In a scalable system it is preferable that any available thread would be able to service events.

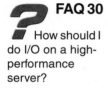

FAQ 30

How should I do I/O on a high-performance server?

In Windows NT 3.5 a fourth kind of overlapped I/O was created called **I/O completion ports.** Completion ports were designed to more easily build scalable servers by allowing a pool of threads to service a pool of events.

In spite of the similarity in names, I/O completion ports have absolutely nothing to do with the I/O completion functions used with APCs.

Completion ports solve all of the problems we have seen so far:

- Unlike `WaitForMultipleObjects()`, there is no limit to the number of handles that can be used with an I/O completion port.

- I/O completion ports allow one thread to queue a request and another thread to service it.
- I/O completion ports implicitly support scalable architectures.

Server Threading Models

There are three basic ways of deciding how many threads to use in a server:

- **One Single Thread**. In a file server or simple Web server, a single thread can move data around just by issuing overlapped I/O. This thread could keep the processor and the disks as busy as possible. However, the entire server would bog down if the thread had to do any processing.
- **One Thread per Client**. If you assign each client its own thread, then theoretically everyone will share in an equally good (or bad) response time because processing power will be equally divided. In reality, system resources are finite and a dramatic decrease in performance will occur at some point. If there are 2,000 clients, running 2,000 separate threads is not an option.
- **One Active Thread per Processor**. This approach would keep each processor as busy as possible without oversaturating any particular processor. This method is difficult to implement with event objects or APCs because they are tightly bound to a particular thread. The solution to this problem is a special synchronization object called the I/O completion port.

An I/O completion port is a very special kind of kernel object that coordinates how a pool of threads services overlapped requests, even across multiple processors. The completion port can automatically compensate for growing servers and for heavy loads.

What Completion Ports Do

So far in this chapter we have seen how the completion of an overlapped I/O operation can be communicated to an interested thread using a signaled file handle, signaled event object, or APC. The way an I/O completion port works is radically different from any of these.

The goal we are seeking is for any one of several threads to be able to service a completed overlapped I/O request. With the other kinds of overlapped I/O mechanisms, you are locked in to having a particular thread service a particular I/O request. The I/O completion port allows you to decouple the thread that starts an overlapped request from the thread that services it.

To use an I/O completion port, your application creates a bunch of threads that all wait on the I/O completion port. These threads become the "pool" of threads that can take care of completed overlapped I/O requests. A thread implicitly becomes part of the pool by waiting on the I/O completion port.

Every time a new file is opened for overlapped I/O, you associate its file handle with the I/O completion port. Once this association is established, any file operation that completes successfully will cause an **I/O completion packet** to be sent to the completion port. This happens inside the operating system and is transparent to the program.

In response to the I/O completion packet, the completion port releases one of the waiting threads in the pool. The completion port does not create new threads if no threads are currently waiting.

The released thread is given enough information to be able to identify the context of the completed overlapped I/O operation. The thread can then go off and handle the request as necessary, but it remains in the pool of threads that is assigned to the completion port. The difference is that the thread becomes an active thread and not a waiting thread. When the thread is done handling the overlapped I/O request, it should wait on the I/O completion port again.

FAQ 31

Why are I/O completion ports so special?

Based on this overview, I can broadly describe a completion port as a mechanism that manages how a pool of threads services completed overlapped I/O requests. However, the completion port is much more than a simple dispatcher that gives threads work to do. The I/O completion port also functions as a valve that keeps the processor or processors as busy as possible, but also keeps them from being overwhelmed by having too many threads running. The I/O completion port tries to keep the number of concurrently running threads hovering around a particular number. Typically you want to keep all processors busy, so by default the number of concurrent threads is the number of processors.

The fascinating part of how the I/O completion port works is that it will notice when one of the running threads blocks and release another thread! For example, suppose there are two threads waiting on an I/O completion port in a single processor system. Thread 1 is woken up by the completion port and is given a packet of data from the network. To service the packet, Thread 1 must read from a file on the disk and so calls `CreateFile()` and `ReadFile()`, but not in overlapped mode.

The completion port will notice that Thread 1 blocked on disk I/O and will release Thread 2 to bring the count of currently running threads back up to the requested number.

The ramification of this is that when Thread 1 returns from the disk operation, there may now be a total of two threads that are running, even though the requested number of concurrent threads was one (because there is one processor in the system). This behavior is surprising, but correct. The completion port will not release another thread until the number of running threads drops below one again.

Overview of Operation

The quick summary of how to use a completion port is as follows. In the following sections I will go over each point in detail.

1. Create the I/O completion port.
2. Associate file handles with it.
3. Create a pool of threads.
4. Make each thread wait on the completion port.
5. Start issuing overlapped I/O requests with the file handles.

As new files are opened, they can also be associated with the I/O completion port at any time. Threads that have waited on the completion port should not be used for tasks other than servicing the completion port because those threads will stay a part of the thread pool that the I/O completion port keeps track of.

Creating an I/O Completion Port

The I/O completion port is a kernel object. Create an I/O completion port using the call `CreateIoCompletionPort()`.

HANDLE CreateIoCompletionPort (

> **HANDLE** FileHandle,
> **HANDLE** ExistingCompletionPort,
> **DWORD** CompletionKey,
> **DWORD** NumberOfConcurrentThreads
>);

Parameters

FileHandle	Handle to the file or device that should become associated with the completion port. In NT 3.51 or later, this value may be set to INVALID_HANDLE_VALUE to create a port without associating a file handle with it.
ExistingCompletionPort	If this parameter is given, the FileHandle will be added to this port instead of a new port being created. Use NULL to create a new port.

| *CompletionKey* | User-defined value that will be passed to the thread that services a request. This key is associated with *FileHandle*. |
| *NumberOfConcurrentThreads* | Number of threads associated with this I/O completion port that are allowed to execute concurrently. If zero, then this value will be set to the number of processors in the system. |

Return Value

If this function succeeds it returns a handle to the I/O completion port. If this function fails it returns FALSE, in which case `GetLastError()` can be used to find out what failed.

Any file that is attached to an I/O completion port must have been opened with FILE_FLAG_OVERLAPPED. A file handle attached to an I/O completion port can no longer be used with `ReadFileEx()` or `WriteFileEx()`. You can safely close a file handle that has been associated with an I/O completion port.

Notice that a valid *FileHandle* must be given on Windows NT 3.5. On NT 3.51 or later, the value can be set to INVALID_HANDLE_VALUE. This problem is easy to work around by creating a temporary file and using that to create the completion port.

You will usually want to set *NumberOfConcurrentThreads* to be zero so that as many threads will run as there are processors in the system. This will keep each processor as busy as possible while reducing the overhead of excessive context switches.

Associating File Handles

`CreateIoCompletionPort()` is usually used by calling it once to create the port with *FileHandle* set to INVALID_HANDLE_VALUE and *ExistingCompletionPort* set to NULL, then calling `CreateIoCompletionPort()` again once for each new file handle to be associated. These subsequent calls should set *ExistingCompletionPort* to be the handle returned by the first call to `CreateIoCompletionPort()`. For example:

```
HANDLE hPort;
HANDLE hFiles[MAX_FILES];
int index;
// Create the completion port
hPort = CreateIoCompletionPort(
```

```
                    INVALID_HANDLE_VALUE,
                    NULL,
                    0,    // key
                    0     // default # of threads
        );
// Now associate each file handle
for (index=0; index<OPEN_FILES; index++)
{
    CreateIoCompletionPort(
                    hFiles[index],
                    hPort,
                    0,    // key
                    0     // default # of threads
    );
}
```

Notice that all of this is being done by a single thread. Typically the completion port is completely set up by a single thread. The worker threads do not have any work to do to initialize the completion port in their context.

Creating a Pool of Threads

Once the completion port is created, you set up the pool of threads that will wait on the port. The I/O completion port does not create threads itself, it only uses threads that you have created. Therefore you need to explicitly create each thread using `CreateThread()`, `_beginthreadex()` (see Chapter 8), or `AfxBeginThread()` (see Chapter 10).

When you first create the threads, all of them should wait on the completion port. As the threads start servicing requests, the makeup of the threads in the pool is described as follows:

	Threads currently running
+	Threads blocked (on disk I/O or a `Wait…()` call)
+	Threads waiting on the completion port
=	Number of threads in pool

Because of this, you want to create *more* threads than there are processors. For example, if there was one processor in the system and you created just one thread, then that thread could block and cause the processor to become idle. Because there are no other threads in the pool, the completion port would not be able to service any more packets, even though there was processing power to spare.

FAQ 32

How many threads should wait on an I/O completion port?

A reasonable number of threads to create is twice the number of processors plus two. There is no reason you cannot create more; just remember that threads are not free and that creating 100 worker threads to wait on the completion port would probably not be doing anything to speed the system up.

Waiting on an I/O Completion Port

After each thread initializes itself it should call `GetQueuedCompletion-Status()`. This call acts like a combination of `WaitForSingleObject()` and `GetOverlappedResult()`. The call looks like this:

BOOL GetQueuedCompletionStatus(
    HANDLE CompletionPort,
    LPDWORD lpNumberOfBytesTransferred,
    LPDWORD lpCompletionKey,
    LPOVERLAPPED *lpOverlapped,
    DWORD dwMilliseconds
    );

Parameters

CompletionPort — Handle to the completion port on which to wait.

lpNumberOf-BytesTransferred — Pointer to DWORD that will receive the number of bytes transferred.

lpCompletionKey — Pointer to DWORD that will receive the completion key that was defined when `CreateIoCompletionPort()` was called.

lpOverlapped — This variable is misnamed. It should really be *lplpOverlapped*. You should pass the address of a pointer that the system will fill in with a pointer to the overlapped structure that initiated the I/O operation.

dwMilliseconds — Maximum number of milliseconds to wait. If the call times out, *lpOverlapped* will be set to NULL and the function returns FALSE.

Return Value

If this function successfully dequeues a completion packet for a successful operation, the function returns TRUE and fills in the variables pointed at by *lpNumberOfBytesTransferred*, *lpCompletionKey*, and *lpOverlapped*.

If a completion packet for an unsuccessful operation is dequeued, the function returns FALSE and sets *lpOverlapped* to the operation that failed. Call GetLastError() to find out why the I/O operation failed.

If this function fails it returns FALSE and sets *lpOverlapped* to NULL, in which case GetLastError() can be used to find out why the call failed.

Unlike other kernel objects, such as semaphores and mutexes, threads waiting on a completion port are serviced in first-in, last-out (FILO) ordering. There is no reason to worry about fairness of ordering because all the threads do exactly the same thing. By using FILO, a running thread that calls GetQueuedCompletionStatus() can get the next request and keep running without ever blocking. This is very efficient. Also, threads that have been waiting for a long time are more likely to have been paged out. By running threads that have run recently, it is much more likely that they are in memory and will be able to run without having to be paged in.

Issuing Overlapped I/O Requests

The following calls can start I/O operations that can be handled by an I/O completion port.

- ConnectNamedPipe()
- DeviceIoControl()
- LockFileEx()
- ReadFile()
- TransactNamedPipe()
- WaitCommEvent()
- WriteFile()

To use the completion port, the primary thread (or any other) can do a read, a write, or any of the other above operations to one of the file handles associated with the completion port. There is no need for that thread to ever call WaitForMultipleObjects() because each individual thread in the pool has called GetQueuedCompletionStatus(). When the I/O operation finishes, one of the waiting threads will automatically be released to service the operation.

Preventing Completion Packets

It commonly happens that you read or write to a file handle but you do not want the I/O completion port to be notified when the operation finishes. An example is a network server, where a thread reads a request from a file handle for a named pipe or socket, and then writes a response back to the same file handle. The problem is that the file handle was opened for overlapped I/O, so the write operation will be overlapped and the I/O completion port will receive a packet when the write operation finishes. If the result of the write operation is not important, then the server would spend a lot of time processing completion packets that were not important. The ideal would be to turn off completion port notification on a per-operation basis.

It is possible to do an I/O operation that does not result in an I/O completion packet being sent to the completion port and instead uses the old signaled event object mechanism. To do so, set up an OVERLAPPED structure with a valid *hEvent* manual-reset event object, then set the low-order bit of the handle to 1. Although it sounds like a hack, this is the documented way to do it. For example:

```
OVERLAPPED overlap;
HANDLE hFile;          // Set somewhere else
char buffer[128];
DWORD dwBytesWritten;

memset(&overlap, 0, sizeof(OVERLAPPED));
overlap.hEvent = CreateEvent(NULL, TRUE, FALSE, NULL);
overlap.hEvent = (HANDLE)((DWORD)hEvent | 0x1);

WriteFile(hFile, buffer, 128, dwBytesWritten, &overlap);
```

Using Overlapped I/O with Sockets

The sample ECHO on the CD-ROM demonstrates using an I/O completion port to do the equivalent of standard TCP port 7, which echoes back everything that is written to it. This sample consists of two executables. ECHOSRV is a server that listens on TCP port 5554 (a completely arbitrary number) and writes everything it reads from a socket back to the same socket. ECHOCLI is the client that takes whatever you type, sends it to the server, and then prints out the response that it receives from the server.

ECHOSRV and ECHOCLI are Winsock applications that use TCP/IP. You must have TCP/IP installed on your machine to run either of them. Because ECHOSRV uses completion ports, it will only run under Windows NT 3.51 or later. The client will run under Windows 95 if you modify the IP address that it uses to be a Windows NT machine. Currently both the client and server are hard coded to talk to address 127.0.0.1, which is an alias for the local machine.

The server can handle numerous simultaneous requests. Because it is hard to type into several windows at the same time, I have provided a batch file on the CD-ROM called TESTME.BAT that launches several windows, all of which read from a text file instead of from the keyboard.

FAQ 33

Why shouldn't I use select()?

Completion ports are the *only* way to obtain high throughput on a Windows NT machine talking to the network. Although Windows NT supports the `select()` call that is the standard way of supporting multiple simultaneous connections, the `select()` call does not scale across multiple processors.

David Treadwell, one of the developers of Windows Sockets, says in his article "Developing Transport-Independent Applications Using the Windows Sockets Interface" (on the *Microsoft Developer's Network* CD-ROM) that the performance of programs using `select()` "... can suffer because every network I/O call passes through `select()` which incurs significant CPU overhead for each I/O. This is acceptable when CPU use is not an issue, but presents a problem when the service requires high performance."

When you call `CreateIoCompletionPort()` to associate a handle with a completion port, you also pass in a key. The key is nothing more than a user-defined value. In ECHOSRV, I allocate a structure called ContextKey that keeps track of what has been read or written for the current handle. The structure looks like this:

```
struct ContextKey
{
    SOCKET   sock;
    // Input
    char       InBuffer[4];
    OVERLAPPED ovIn;
    // Output
    int        nOutBufIndex;
    char       OutBuffer[MAXLINE];
    OVERLAPPED ovOut;
    DWORD      dwWritten;
};
```

InBuffer is used for overlapped reads. *OutBuffer* is used for overlapped writes. As characters are read one at a time into *InBuffer*, they are accumulated in *OutBuffer* and then written back to the socket when a complete line is received.

The function `main()` from ECHOSRV is shown in Listing 6-4. It opens the socket, creates the I/O completion port, starts the worker threads, and goes into a loop waiting for connections. It is written just as outlined in the five steps given earlier. One key point is that a SOCKET can be passed where ever a HANDLE is expected.

Listing 6-4. main() from ECHOSRV.C—Setting up an I/O completion port

```c
int main(int argc, char *argv[])
{
    SOCKET  listener;
    SOCKET  newsocket;
    WSADATA WsaData;
    struct sockaddr_in serverAddress;
    struct sockaddr_in clientAddress;
    int     clientAddressLength;
    int     err;

    CheckOsVersion();

    err = WSAStartup (0x0101, &WsaData);
    if (err == SOCKET_ERROR)
    {
        FatalError("WSAStartup Failed");
        return EXIT_FAILURE;
    }

    /*
     * Open a TCP socket connection to the server
     * By default, a socket is always opened
     * for overlapped I/O.  Do NOT attach this
     * socket (listener) to the I/O completion
     * port!
     */
    listener = socket(AF_INET, SOCK_STREAM, 0);
    if (listener < 0)
    {
        FatalError("socket() failed");
        return EXIT_FAILURE;
    }

    /*
     * Bind our local address
     */
    memset(&serverAddress, 0, sizeof(serverAddress));
    serverAddress.sin_family      = AF_INET;
    serverAddress.sin_addr.s_addr = htonl(INADDR_ANY);
    serverAddress.sin_port        = htons(SERV_TCP_PORT);

    err = bind(listener,
            (struct sockaddr *)&serverAddress,
            sizeof(serverAddress)
          );
```

Listing 6-4 (continued)

```c
if (err < 0)
    FatalError("bind() failed");

ghCompletionPort = CreateIoCompletionPort(
        INVALID_HANDLE_VALUE,
        NULL,   // No prior port
        0,      // No key
        0       // Use default  # of threads
        );
if (ghCompletionPort == NULL)
    FatalError("CreateIoCompletionPort() failed");

CreateWorkerThreads(ghCompletionPort);

listen(listener, 5);

fprintf(stderr, "Echo Server with I/O Completion Ports\n");
fprintf(stderr, "Running on TCP port %d\n", SERV_TCP_PORT);
fprintf(stderr, "\nPress Ctrl+C to stop the server\n");

//
// Loop forever accepting requests new connections
// and starting reading from them.
//
for (;;)
{
    struct ContextKey *pKey;

    clientAddressLength = sizeof(clientAddress);
    newsocket = accept(listener,
                        (struct sockaddr *)&clientAddress,
                        &clientAddressLength);
    if (newsocket < 0)
    {
        FatalError("accept() Failed");
        return EXIT_FAILURE;
    }

    // Create a context key and initialize it.
    // calloc will zero the buffer
    pKey = calloc(1, sizeof(struct ContextKey));
    pKey->sock = newsocket;
    pKey->ovOut.hEvent = CreateEvent(NULL, TRUE, FALSE, NULL);
    // Set the event for writing so that packets
    // will not be sent to the completion port when
    // a write finishes.
```

Listing 6-4 (continued)

```
    pKey->ovOut.hEvent = (HANDLE)((DWORD)pKey->ovOut.hEvent | 0x1);

    // Associate the socket with the completion port
    CreateIoCompletionPort(
            (HANDLE)newsocket,
            ghCompletionPort,
            (DWORD)pKey,    // No key
            0               // Use default # of threads
        );

    // Kick off the first read
    IssueRead(pKey);
    }
    return 0;
}
```

The function `main()` calls `CreateWorkerThreads()`, which starts up the appropriate number of threads. No startup value is given to the threads because the completion port is a global variable to which everyone has access. `CreateWorkerThreads()` is shown in Listing 6-5.

Listing 6-5. CreateWorkerThreads() from ECHOSRV.C

```
void CreateWorkerThreads()
{
    SYSTEM_INFO    sysinfo;
    DWORD          dwThreadId;
    DWORD          dwThreads;
    DWORD          i;

    GetSystemInfo(&sysinfo);
    dwThreads = sysinfo.dwNumberOfProcessors * 2 + 2;
    for (i=0; i<dwThreads; i++)
    {
        HANDLE hThread;
        hThread = CreateThread(
            NULL, 0, ThreadFunc, NULL, 0, &dwThreadId
            );
        CloseHandle(hThread);
    }
}
```

The final routine of interest is `ThreadFunc()`, which is where the worker threads spend all of their time. As soon as a thread starts up, it loops forever on calling `GetQueuedCompletionStatus()`. As each completion packet is processed, we use the key returned by `GetQueuedCompletionStatus()` as the pointer to the ContextKey where we have state information about that file handle.

Back in `main()` we created the handle to the event object in the overlapped structure used for writing. We set the low bit in the handle to indicate that no packet should be sent to the completion ports when the write complete. This sample program does not check the result of the completed overlapped writes.

`ThreadFunc()` is shown in Listing 6-6. Notice how each of the various error state permutations of *bResult* and the *lpOverlapped* pointer are checked.

Listing 6-6. ThreadFunc() from ECHOSRV.C

```
DWORD WINAPI ThreadFunc(LPVOID pVoid)
{
    BOOL      bResult;
    DWORD     dwNumRead;
    struct ContextKey *pCntx;
    LPOVERLAPPED lpOverlapped;

    UNREFERENCED_PARAMETER(pVoid);

    // Loop forever on getting packets from
    // the I/O completion port.
    for (;;)
    {
        bResult = GetQueuedCompletionStatus(
                ghCompletionPort,
                &dwNumRead,
                &(DWORD)pCntx,
                &lpOverlapped,
                INFINITE
            );

        if (bResult == FALSE
            && lpOverlapped == NULL)
        {
            FatalError(
              "ThreadFunc - Illegal call to GetQueuedCompletionStatus");
        }

        else if (bResult == FALSE
```

Listing 6-6 (continued)

```
            && lpOverlapped != NULL)
        {
            // This happens occasionally instead of
            // end-of-file. Not sure why.
            closesocket(pCntx->sock);
            free(pCntx);
            fprintf(stderr,
                "ThreadFunc - I/O operation failed\n");
        }

        else if (dwNumRead == 0)
        {
            closesocket(pCntx->sock);
            free(pCntx);
            fprintf(stderr, "ThreadFunc - End of file.\n");
        }

        // Got a valid data block!
        // Save the data to our buffer and write it
        // all back out (echo it) if we have see a \n
        else
        {
            // Figure out where in the buffer to save the character
            char *pch = &pCntx->OutBuffer[pCntx->nOutBufIndex++];
            *pch++ = pCntx->InBuffer[0];
            *pch = '\0';    // For debugging, WriteFile doesn't care
            if (pCntx->InBuffer[0] == '\n')
            {
                WriteFile(
                        (HANDLE)(pCntx->sock),
                        pCntx->OutBuffer,
                        pCntx->nOutBufIndex,
                        &pCntx->dwWritten,
                        &pCntx->ovOut
                    );
                pCntx->nOutBufIndex = 0;
                fprintf(stderr, "Echo on socket %x.\n", pCntx->sock);
            }

            // Start a new read
            IssueRead(pCntx);
        }
    }

    return 0;
}
```

Although this server is not optimal because it reads one byte at a time, it is about as simple as an example can be that properly demonstrates I/O completion ports. Some of the helper routines from ECHOSRV are not shown in Listing 6-6, and the client listings are not shown. You can find them in the source files in the ECHO directory on the CD-ROM.

Summary

This chapter has provided a whirlwind tour of overlapped I/O, a technique for doing I/O asynchronously that often avoids the need for using multiple threads. Overlapped I/O can be done using signaled file handles, signaled event objects, asynchronous procedure calls (APCs), and I/O completion ports.

I/O completion ports are very important because they are the preferred mechanism for creating high-performance servers that are easily scalable. A server of this type was presented in the ECHO sample program that implements a Winsock application that uses an I/O completion port.

Part II

Multithreading Tools and Tricks

Chapter 7

Data Consistency

This chapter describes the use of the volatile *keyword and discusses the design and uses of a Readers/Writers lock.*

So far we have looked at a lot of small examples that are carefully designed to illustrate a point. In Chapters 2 and 3, we tried printing in the background, but we ignored the problem of sharing data between threads by prepackaging the data so only one thread would have to read it. In Chapter 4 we saw EVENTTST, which demonstrates how event objects work but does nothing to show them being applied. None of these examples really considers the fact that, in the real world, programs are not cut and dried and cannot be neatly partitioned to fit the optimum or simplest models.

This chapter looks at how you handle data in the real world, when multiple threads are reading and writing the same array, and threads are feeding each other data on the fly. This situation is obviously much more complex.

Understanding the *volatile* Keyword

Even after you have made every effort to properly write a multithreaded program, you might wonder if it is possible for the compiler to generate "unsafe" code in spite of your best efforts. The answer is yes! Sometimes you must tell the compiler that data is shared so that the proper code will be generated.

I am sure you have run into the problem of putting someone's name and phone number into your address book, then trying to call that person several months later and discovering that the phone number is out of date. The same thing can happen inside the code the compiler generates for your program.

The optimizer in the compiler tries to keep frequently used data in the processor's internal registers. These registers are akin to an address book. Data can be read from the registers much faster than from RAM, just as you can get information from your address book faster than from the big phone book. Of course, if another thread changes the original value in RAM, then the copy of the variable in the register will be out of date.

In a single-threaded program this situation would be impossible. The compiler can analyze everything your program does to make sure that values will be reloaded at the proper time. In a multithreaded program it is impossible to know what any of the other threads are doing, so the compiler must not be allowed to keep a copy of shared variables in a register.

FOR THE EXPERTS

You might have noticed the compiler flag /Oa to enable, "Assume no aliasing." This optimization is normally disabled. Aliasing happens when you create a pointer to a value instead of accessing the value directly. For example, the following line creates an alias:

```
int *pVal = &Contexts[j].buf[index];
```

It is very easy to confuse the compiler with aliasing, and so the compiler takes some steps to safeguard against it. These steps improve safety at a slight performance penalty.

Aliasing effectively causes the same problem that multiple threads do because the compiler cannot always be sure when a value changes.

There is a little-known keyword in both C and C++ that instructs the compiler how to behave on a variable-by-variable basis. The keyword is **volatile.** This keyword tells the compiler not to keep temporary copies of a variable. This keyword can be applied to a basic type such as an `int` or `long` as well as a structure or a C++ class, in which case all members of that structure or class will be considered volatile.

Using `volatile` does not negate the need for critical sections or mutexes. For example, if you say

```
a = a + 3
```

there is still a short amount of time that *a* will be kept in a register because arithmetic operations can only be performed on a value if it is in a register. Typically, the `volatile` keyword applies between lines, but not within a line.

Let's take a look at a very simple function and see how the assembly language that the compiler generates is flawed and how the `volatile` keyword fixes the problem. The sample routine is a busy loop, which I have already said you are not supposed to write, but it is the simplest example to illustrate this point. In this example, `WaitForKey()` waits for a character to show up at a certain position given by *pch*.

```
void WaitForKey(char *pch)
{
        while (*pch == 0)
                ;
}
```

When you compile this program with all compiler optimizations disabled you get the following result. The entry and exit code are removed for brevity, and comments are added for clarity. Lines in bold show the location of the lines from the source code above.

```
;       while (*pch == 0)
$L27:
        ; Load the address stored in pch
        mov     eax, DWORD PTR _pch$[ebp]
        ; Load the character into the EAX register
        movsx   eax, BYTE PTR [eax]
        ; Compare the value to zero
        test    eax, eax
        ; If not zero, exit loop
        jne     $L28
;       ;
        jmp     $L27
$L28:
;   }
```

This nonoptimized routine continually reloads the appropriate address, loads the contents of that address, and tests the result. Slow but sure. This version would work fine in a multithreaded program.

Now watch what happens when you turn on optimization.

```
;   {
            ; Load the address stored in pch
            mov     eax, DWORD PTR _pch$[esp-4]
            ; Load the character into the AL register
            mov     al, BYTE PTR [eax]
;       while (*pch == 0)
$L84:
            ; Compare the value in the AL register to zero
            test    al, al
            ; If still zero, try again
            je      SHORT $L84
;           ;
;   }
```

Much shorter! The optimizer appears to be doing its job. But notice that
the compiler has taken the MOV instruction and placed it outside of the
loop. This process is called loop-invariant removal. This would be a great
optimization in a single-threaded program, but in this case the loop will
never exit if another thread were to change the value. The value being tested
is kept permanently in a register. Obviously, that's a problem.

The solution is to rewrite WaitForKey() with the parameter *pch* declared
as volatile, like this:

```
void WaitForKey(volatile char *pch)
{
    while (*pch == 0)
        ;
}
```

This change has no impact on the nonoptimized version, but when you
look at the optimized version you get this:

```
;   {
            ; Load the address stored in pch
            mov     eax, DWORD PTR _pch$[esp-4]
;       while (*pch == 0)
$L84:
            ; Directly compare the value to zero
            cmp     BYTE PTR [eax], 0
            ; If still zero, try again
            je      SHORT $L84
;           ;
;   }
```

This version is perfect. The address never changes, so the calculation of the address is moved outside the loop. The contents of that address is volatile, so it is continually rechecked every time through the loop.

Curiously enough, it is legal to have a `const volatile` variable passed to a function. Such a declaration would mean that the function would not be allowed to change the variable, but the variable's value might be changed at any moment by another thread.

Both `const` and `volatile` are ANSI standard keywords that should be available in all C and C++ compilers.

Referential Integrity

Having seen how to deal with some of the problems that might arise at the assembly language level, let's move in the other direction and look at the problem of logical data integrity versus physical data integrity.

SQL Transactions

In the database world there exists the concept of a transaction. A **transaction** is a group of changes that are meaningful only if taken all together. For example, a point of sale database typically has one entry for a sales invoice and several other entries for each item the customer purchases. Obviously, these things are essentially meaningless without each other.

A developer needs some way of adding the invoice and the line items all at once. Otherwise the database would be logically inconsistent for a few moments in time. If another client read information from the database in that brief period, either some line items would be missing, or there would be line items without an invoice. Database lingo refers to this as "referential integrity."

The problem is that databases are just programs. They only do things in a step-by-step manner. You have to add the invoice and then individually add each line item. If the customer's credit card does not clear, then you have to backtrack and delete the entries one by one, too.

SQL databases solved this problem by introducing the concept of transactions. When you start a transaction, the database "saves up" your changes until you declare the transaction to be complete. At this point, all of the changes are made to the database together. The database engine makes sure that no client receives data that is part of this transaction while the transaction is being applied.

Multithreaded programs share the same problem. We saw a glimpse of this with the `SwapLists()` routine in Chapter 4 where a single change actually involved two separate data structures. Changing first one and then the other would have left the system momentarily in an inconsistent state.

A simpler example is appending to an array of data. To add an element to the end of an array (assuming the array is large enough), you typically have to write the data to the block and update the count. If you do not do the two operations atomically, then you risk overwriting the data or ending up with a wrong count.

The Case of the Deleted Shape

There are other even more insidious problems that can arise. Consider the case of a draw program that keeps a list of all of the shapes in the drawing. Thread 1 manages the user interface and Thread 2 takes care of rendering. There is an array that holds pointers to each of the shapes. The array is protected by a mutex to prevent corruption.

1. Thread 2 calls `GetShapePointer()` to get shape number 5.
2. `GetShapePointer()` waits on the array's mutex.
3. `GetShapePointer()` is granted ownership of the mutex.
4. `GetShapePointer()` retrieves the pointer to shape number 5.
5. `GetShapePointer()` releases the mutex and returns the pointer.
6. Meanwhile, Thread 1 had called `DeleteShape()`, which blocked on the mutex.
7. `DeleteShape()` is granted ownership of the mutex.
8. `DeleteShape()` frees the memory being used by the shape.
9. The pointer being used by Thread 2 now points to invalid memory.
10. Thread 2 crashes.

Since the program crashed, we can safely assume that there is a problem. The question is, what is the solution?

The obvious answer is that the shape should have had its own mutex. Well, that seems reasonable, but it may be problematic to implement. If a complex design has 10,000 parts, does that mean that there should be 10,000 mutexes? Somehow I think the overhead may be excessive. How about grouped or hierarchical shapes? Should the group have its own mutex?

To be safe, the only time the shape can be locked is while the linked list is locked. Otherwise there is a window for a race condition. In the scenario above, `GetShapePointer()` would have had to lock the shape before returning it. The caller would have had to know to unlock the shape.

The final problem is that this scenario introduces a gigantic opportunity for deadlock. If a shape is locked whenever you get a pointer to it, what happens if Thread A has locked 5 and needs 3, and Thread B has locked 3 and needs 5? Bingo! Deadlock and instant hang.

Protecting Data with Exclusive Locks

This problem can be solved by looking at your data as a tree that gets locked at the root. Once a lock is applied, all the data in the tree from the bottom to the top becomes locked. In the earlier scenario with `DeleteShape()`, the array of shape pointers is at the root of the tree and the shapes or groups of shapes are the limbs and leaves. If a thread locks the entire tree for the period that it has pointers to anything within the tree, then no other thread can do anything that is potentially damaging.

The `OpenFile()` call in Win16 supports sharing modes that illustrate this model. What I just described is roughly equivalent to the sharing mode OF_SHARE_EXCLUSIVE, which meant that all other applications would be denied read and write access to the file. In addition, if another application was already using the file when you made the call, then the call would fail. If you opened a file with OF_SHARE_EXCLUSIVE, you would be guaranteed that anything you did to the file would not be interfered with by another application.

We can look at our tree of data in the same theoretical light as this file. If we want to make a change in one thread to something in this tree, then it is not safe for any other thread to be reading or writing at the same time. It is not safe for another thread to be reading because of the problem of pointers being inconsistent while they are being updated. It is not safe for another thread to be writing because the two threads might walk on top of each other, as shown in the linked list in Figures 1-4 through 1-7 in Chapter 1.

Note that writing includes operations such as deleting, changing, updating, and rearranging. Reading means having any knowledge of anything inside the data structure, including having a pointer to anything inside the data structure. Therefore it would be illegal for `DeleteShape()` to delete a shape as long as another thread had a pointer to any shape within the structure.

In Chapter 4, when we needed to make a change to a data structure, we put a lock on that data structure inside each routine that acted on that structure. For example:

```
void AddLineItems(List *pList)
{
    Node node;
```

```
    while ( /* There are more line items */ )
    {
        GetLineItem(&node);
        AddHead(pList, &node);
    }
}

void AddHead(List *pList, Node *pNode)
{
    EnterCriticalSection(&pList->critical_sec);
    pNode->next = pList->head;
    pList->head = pNode;
    LeaveCriticalSection(&pList->critical_sec);
}
```

AddLineItems() updates the List of line items, by calling AddHead() once for each line. However, the List structure is only locked during AddHead(). This would mean that another thread would have ample opportunity to obtain its own lock between calls to AddHead().

Moving Locks to a Higher Level

If we obtain the lock from the calling routine instead, then we can safely add all the items before another thread can lock the structure. For example:

```
void AddLineItems(List *pList)
{
    Node node;
    EnterCriticalSection(&pList->critical_sec);
    while ( /* There are more line items */ )
    {
        GetLineItem(&Node);
        AddHead(pList, &Node);
    }
    LeaveCriticalSection(&pList->critical_sec);
}

void AddHead(List *pList, Node *pNode)
{
    pNode->next = pList->head;
    pList->head = pNode;
}
```

This model tends to work particularly well in Windows applications where threads are event driven and return frequently to the main message loop. Such an architecture provides obvious points to lock data structures, and the structures can be easily unlocked as the call stack unwinds again.

This model does impose some limitations. Other data structures may not point directly into any data structure that lives in the tree. If you had such a pointer you would be right back where you started because there would be no way to properly handle the case of an object being deleted when a pointer to it still exists somewhere. From previous experience, this is not a particularly onerous restriction, particularly in C++ where the separation between objects tends to be more defined.

The Readers/Writers Lock

Exclusive locks look great on paper, but I can already hear many of you muttering these three words:

- Performance
- Performance
- Performance

Performance is going to suffer if every thread has to stand in line to read a central data structure. The exclusive lock would force all access to be sequential, and the benefit of multithreading would be lost. In this case you might as well use just one thread because the other threads are going to spend most of their time being blocked.

FAQ 35

What is the Readers/Writers lock?

Let's go back to our `OpenFile()` analogy. If you look at the sharing modes in the `OpenFile()` call, there are two more sharing modes, OF_SHARE_DENY_READ and OF_SHARE_DENY_WRITE. These modes allow finer control than exclusive locks. In fact, there is nothing wrong with every thread in the application reading a data structure at the same time, as long as no other thread tries to change it. Comparing with `OpenFile()`, any thread that wants to read a file should open the file with OF_SHARE_DENY_WRITE.

On the other hand, we have already decided that if a thread is writing a data structure, other threads should be prevented from both reading and writing it. Continuing the `OpenFile()` analogy, any thread that needs to write to a file would call `OpenFile()` with both OF_SHARE_DENY_READ and OF_SHARE_DENY_WRITE. In this way no other thread could do anything to the file until this write finished.

It is possible to do exactly the same thing in multithreaded applications. The trick is to make it work properly. The solution I describe is derived from the article where it was introduced.[1] The pseudocode for this implementation is as follows. This design gives preference to readers, but other implementations exist that are fair-share or give preference to writers.

Lock for Reader:

```
Lock( ReaderMutex )
ReaderCount = ReaderCount + 1
if (ReaderCount == 1)
    Lock( DataSemaphore )
Unlock( ReaderMutex )
```

Unlock for Reader:

```
Lock( ReaderMutex )
ReaderCount = ReaderCount - 1
if (ReaderCount == 0)
    Unlock( DataSemaphore )
Unlock( ReaderMutex )
```

Lock for Writer:

```
Lock( DataSemaphore )
```

Unlock for Writer:

```
Unlock( DataSemaphore )
```

The design looks deceptively simple, but there is a lot to it. One common question is, "Why is *ReaderCount* needed? Why can't the semaphore do all the work? After all, semaphores are used for counting." The answer is that semaphores start at a maximum value and work down to zero. As long as the semaphore is non-zero, locks can still be acquired. The problem here is the exact opposite. We need the count to start at zero and count up.

Another common question is, "Why is the *ReaderMutex* needed? Won't the routine work without it?" The answer is no, because a race condition develops. Imagine if Thread 1 is the first thread to try to get a Read Lock. It starts by incrementing *ReaderCount,* then gets preempted by a context switch. *ReaderCount* is now equal to one. Thread 2 also tries to get a Read Lock, and it also increments *ReaderCount. ReaderCount* is now equal to

---

[1] Courtois, P.J., Heymans, F., and Parnas, D.L.: "Concurrent Control with Readers and Writers," *Communications of the ACM,* vol. 10, pp. 667-668, Oct. 1971.

two. Thread 2 gets preempted, and Thread 1 starts running again. It checks the value of *ReaderCount,* which is now equal to two. The condition fails and the database never gets locked even though there are now two readers that think they have the database locked.

When designing a solution such as the Reader/Writer algorithm, one of the hardest parts is remembering that there is no thread that has central control over the Readers/Writers lock. You must make sure that no wake-up events ever get lost because of race conditions. In writing this chapter I surveyed several other implementations that I found on the Internet. Most of the implementations were wrong and would either crash or deadlock. Typically the problem was that the author failed to analyze the potential interactions of the acquire and release routines. Without the application of formal methods, performing such analysis is very difficult.

I think that the only way to really understand all of this is to try coding it yourself. In spite of the short length of this algorithm, it took me several hours to get it running successfully. The problems involved translating the calls into the appropriate Win32 objects and putting into place proper error handling.

Here is the data structure I eventually came up with to represent a Readers/Writers lock:

```
typedef struct _RWLock
{
    // Handle to a mutex that allows
    // a single reader at a time access
    // to the reader counter.
    HANDLE   hMutex;

    // Handle to a semaphore that keeps
    // the data locked for either the
    // readers or the writers.
    HANDLE   hDataLock;

    // The count of the number of readers.
    // Can legally be zero or one while
    // a writer has the data locked.
    int          nReaderCount;
} RWLock;
```

Looks obvious, doesn't it? The big gotcha was *hDataLock*. When I originally implemented it, I used a mutex because the data was either locked or it wasn't. However, I started getting errors all over the place. The problem is that the first reader to get the lock is not necessarily the last reader to leave.

Therefore one thread would lock the mutex and another thread would try to release it. With Win32 mutexes, this is illegal. I changed the implementation to make *hDataLock* a semaphore instead because semaphores can be locked and released by any thread. The semaphore has a maximum count of one and an initial value of one, meaning that it starts out unowned and a grand total of one thread can lock it. The function `InitRWLock()` is shown in Listing 7-1.

Listing 7-1. Excerpt from READWRIT, InitRWLock()

```
BOOL InitRWLock(RWLock *pLock)
{
    pLock->nReaderCount = 0;
    pLock->hDataLock = CreateSemaphore(NULL, 1, 1, NULL);
    if (pLock->hDataLock == NULL)
        return FALSE;
    pLock->hMutex = CreateMutex(NULL, FALSE, NULL);
    if (pLock->hMutex == NULL)
    {
        CloseHandle(pLock->hDataLock);
        return FALSE;
    }
    return TRUE;
}
```

The next problem I faced was adding error checking. For example, I created a routine called `MyWaitForSingleObject()` that looks like this:

```
BOOL MyWaitForSingleObject(HANDLE hObject)
{
    int result;

    result = WaitForSingleObject(hObject, MAXIMUM_TIMEOUT);
    // Comment this out if you want this to be non-fatal
    if (result != WAIT_OBJECT_0)
        FatalError("MyWaitForSingleObject - "
          "Wait failed, you probably forgot to call
    release!");
    return (result == WAIT_OBJECT_0);
}
```

This routine always checks the return value and issues an error if there is a problem. The value of MAXIMUM_TIMEOUT in this example is set for 2 seconds. In any real application, if a structure stays locked for more than

2 seconds then an analysis needs to be made of whether a severe bottleneck is being created.

You will see that I return whether the result was a successful lock (`result == WAIT_OBJECT_0`) right after I issue a fatal error if it wasn't. There is method to my madness here. In a typical application I would use MTVERIFY, MTASSERT, or one of the equivalents in C or MFC. However, the error checking in these macros disappears when you switch from a debug build to a release build. As you saw in the beginning of this chapter, a release build turns on optimizations that have a much higher chance of failing in a multithreaded program than in a single-threaded program. Therefore I want to use an error-checking method that will still work in release builds. Once the program is thoroughly debugged, the `FatalError()` routine can be changed to simply return FALSE instead of writing out an error and exiting.

I also put in numerous other error checks. For example, I wrote two routines, `ReadOK()` and `WriteOK()`, that are called by every function that makes changes to the protected data. They are shown in Listing 7-2.

Listing 7-2. Excerpt from READWRIT, ReadOK() and WriteOK()

```
BOOL ReadOK(RWLock *pLock)
{
    // This check is not perfect, because we
    // do not know for sure if we are one of
    // the readers.
    return (pLock->nReaderCount > 0);
}

BOOL WriteOK(RWLock *pLock)
{
    int result;

    // The first reader may be waiting in the mutex,
    // but any more than that is an error.
    if (pLock->nReaderCount > 1)
        return FALSE;

    // This check is not perfect, because we
    // do not know for sure if this thread was
    // the one that had the semaphore locked.
    result = WaitForSingleObject(pLock->hDataLock, 0);
    if (result == WAIT_TIMEOUT)
        return TRUE;
```

Listing 7-2 (continued)

```
    // a count is kept, which was incremented in Wait.
    ReleaseSemaphore(pLock->hDataLock, 1, NULL);
    return FALSE;
}
```

If you look through the comments, you can see some of the problems I ran into. For example, you would think that if the read-count were nonzero, then you would not be allowed to write. Not true! It is possible for one reader to be inside the mutex and waiting on the *hDataLock* semaphore that the current writer has already locked. Therefore the validity check fails only if there is more than one reader.

Another problem is determining the current value of the semaphore to see if it is locked. There is no way to read a semaphore's current value. If you try to call `ReleaseSemaphore()` with a count of zero just to get the *Previous-Count* value, the call fails. The solution used here was to make sure that the lock fails because the semaphore should already be locked. If the lock succeeds then it is not okay to write and the lock must be unlocked again to restore its value.

Ideally these two routines should have an exact list of what threads have locked the tree for reading or for writing. Otherwise one thread could lock for writing and another thread with a coding bug could try to write and still think it is okay. This list would probably be kept using the current thread ID. Note that using `GetCurrentThread()` to obtain a handle to the thread does not provide a useful, unique ID because the handle returned is merely a special identifier that is interpreted as the current thread.

Acquiring and Releasing Locks

The routines that take care of acquiring and releasing the lock are shown in Listing 7-3. Again, note that errors are carefully checked and returned. These routines are essentially the same thing you saw in the pseudocode above. As I said in Chapter 3, I think the biggest hurdle to understanding is the terminology. Calling `MyWaitForSingleObject()` does the lock and calling `ReleaseMutex()` or `ReleaseSemaphore()` does the unlock.

Listing 7-3. Excerpt from READWRIT, acquiring and releasing locks

```
BOOL AcquireReadLock(RWLock *pLock)
{
    BOOL result = TRUE;

    if (!MyWaitForSingleObject(pLock->hMutex))
        return FALSE;

    if (++pLock->nReaderCount == 1)
        result = MyWaitForSingleObject(pLock->hDataLock);

    ReleaseMutex(pLock->hMutex);
    return result;
}

BOOL ReleaseReadLock(RWLock *pLock)
{
    int result;
    LONG lPrevCount;

    if (!MyWaitForSingleObject(pLock->hMutex))
        return FALSE;

    if (--pLock->nReaderCount == 0)
        result = ReleaseSemaphore(pLock->hDataLock, 1, &lPrevCount);

    ReleaseMutex(pLock->hMutex);
    return result;
}

BOOL AcquireWriteLock(RWLock *pLock)
{
    return MyWaitForSingleObject(pLock->hDataLock);
}

BOOL ReleaseWriteLock(RWLock *pLock)
{
    int result;
    LONG lPrevCount;

    result = ReleaseSemaphore(pLock->hDataLock, 1, &lPrevCount);
    if (lPrevCount != 0)
        FatalError("ReleaseWriteLock - Semaphore was not locked!");
    return result;
}
```

Running the Sample

The Readers/Writers routines are contained and demonstrated in the sample READWRIT on the CD-ROM. The files READWRIT.C and READWRIT.H contain the full source for the routines presented above. The file LIST.C contains a minimal implementation of a linked list that uses the Readers/Writers lock, as well as a test program that kicks off four threads that simultaneously load, read, and tear down the linked list.

If you look at a routine such as `DeleteHead()`, it no longer tries to lock the list itself; the parent routine is expected to do that to enforce logical consistency. Instead, `DeleteHead()` calls `WriteOK()` to try to verify that the caller did the correct thing. For example:

```
BOOL DeleteHead(List *pList)
{
    Node *pNode;

    if (!WriteOK(&pList->lock))
        return FatalError("AddHead - not allowed to write!");

    if (pList->pHead == NULL)
        return FALSE;

    pNode = pList->pHead->pNext;
    GlobalFree(pList->pHead);
    pList->pHead = pNode;
    return TRUE;
}
```

In the test routines, one of the four threads calls this routine and deletes linked list entries in batches of three.

```
DWORD WINAPI DeleteThreadFunc(LPVOID n)
{
    int i;

    for (i=0; i<100; i++)
    {
        Sleep(1);
        AcquireWriteLock(&gpList->lock);
        DeleteHead(gpList);
        DeleteHead(gpList);
        DeleteHead(gpList);
        ReleaseWriteLock(&gpList->lock);
    }

    return 0;
}
```

Running this sample just prints out the results of the two search threads, as well as any errors that may happen. It is somewhat more instructive to set breakpoints in the acquire and release routines and watch what happens as the threads interact.

Do I Need Locking?

Many people have difficulty in deciding whether or not data needs to be protected. Using synchronization mechanisms can slow down a program and they are tedious to use, but under some circumstances there is no alternative. Here are a few guidelines:

- If you are not sure, then you probably need a lock.
- If you use a piece of data from more than one thread, then you must protect it. In general this means reading, comparing against, writing, updating, changing, or any other operation that mentions the variable's name.
- If a fundamental type of size 32 bits or less, such as a DWORD or int, stands alone (in other words, there is no problem of logical consistency), then you may read from it or compare against it. If you need to change it, use the `Interlocked...()` calls. You should also declare the variable to be `volatile`.
- If you have a lot of data, consider using a database manager that is already designed for multiuser and multithreaded access. These systems are designed to handle complex locking situations, including managing logical consistency and referential integrity.

Another mechanism that may work for you is to limit access to a data structure to a single thread, and then use that thread as a sort of "miniserver" for other threads in order to read and write the data. This mechanism removes some of the self-discipline required to use locking because there is no way to access the data without going through the server thread. The concept is somewhat similar to `private` member data in C++.

Lock Granularity

FAQ 36

How much data should I lock at a time?

My example of locking 10,000 separate CAD shapes was one extreme. It illustrates **fine granularity** locking. On the other hand, locking an entire tree of data with the Readers/Writers lock is an example of **coarse granularity** locking. Both of these situations are extreme. Here are the tradeoffs:

Coarse Granularity	*Fine Granularity*
• Simple to work with	• Very easy to deadlock
• Low risk of deadlock	• Relieves bottlenecks
• Potential bottleneck	• Time spent locking objects may incur high overhead

Obviously, a program does not have to use just fine or just coarse locking; it can be a combination as needed. My only warning is that fine granularity locking can be a nightmare to debug because of the complex dependencies that can arise. If you decide to use fine granularity locking, put deadlock resolution code into your program to help you find the problems. You can find such code in many operating systems textbooks. If you are looking for a place to start, the Banker's algorithm is discussed in *Operating Systems, Design and Implementation,* by Andrew S. Tanenbaum (New Jersey: Prentice-Hall, 1987).

My recommendation for building your application is to start with as few locks as possible, and then break pieces out with their own locks as you start finding bottlenecks. It is very important to go about this slowly, step by step, with thorough testing between each step. Otherwise deadlocks become substantially more difficult to track down because there could be several changes that might have caused the problem. In the worst scenario, the problem could be caused by a combination of the changes and not by any single change.

Summary

You have seen how to use the `volatile` keyword to instruct the compiler not to keep temporary copies of variables. You have also seen a detailed discussion of how the implementation of the Readers/Writers lock was developed and how to use it. You now have a better appreciation for the complex issues that can arise in multithreaded development. My recommendation continues to be to avoid sharing data between threads if at all possible.

Chapter 8

Using the C Run-time Library

This chapter describes why you should use _beginthreadex() instead of CreateThread(), and discusses the few situations when you might not need to. It also looks at how you can avoid using the C run-time stdio functions by using the Win32 Console API.

IMPORTANT!

If are using MFC, most of this chapter is superseded by information in Chapter 9. Do not use `_beginthreadex()` or `CreateThread()` in an MFC program.

There is a dire warning in the Microsoft *Programming Techniques* documentation in the online help that reads as follows:

Warning   If you are going to call C run-time routines from a program built with LIBCMT.LIB, you must start your threads with the `_beginthread()` function. Do not use the Win32 functions `ExitThread()` and `CreateThread()`.

There are several problems with this warning. The first problem is that `_beginthread()` has a race condition that makes its use unreliable. The second problem is that the documentation does not say anything about *why* you should be concerned.

I will start out this chapter by talking about _beginthreadex(), not _beginthread(). The function _beginthreadex() replaces _beginthread() and it corrects several problems with _beginthread(). I will talk about _beginthread() at the end of the chapter.

Here is my own warning that is somewhat more precise and much more up to date:

IMPORTANT!

FAQ 37

When should I use the multithreaded C run-time library?

> If you are writing a multithreaded program without MFC, always link with the multithreaded C run-time library, and always use _beginthreadex() and _endthreadex() instead of CreateThread() and Exit-Thread(). The function _beginthreadex() takes the same arguments as CreateThread() and takes care of properly initializing the C run-time library.

Although there are serious problems with _beginthread() that make following Microsoft's warning difficult, the problems have been solved with _beginthreadex(). As long as you call _beginthreadex() instead of CreateThread(), you can safely call any function in the C run-time library from any thread.

In this chapter we will look at what the multithreaded C run-time library is, why you need to use it, and how to use _beginthreadex() and _endthreadex(). We will also look at the few circumstances under which you could write a multithreaded program that uses the single-threaded C run-time library.

What Is the Multithreaded C Run-time Library?

There is a serious problem with the original implementation of the C run-time library that makes it unusable for multithreaded programs. When the C run-time library was created in the 1970s, memory sizes were still very small and multitasking was still a novel idea, much less multithreading.

The C run-time library uses several global variables and static data areas that can conflict with each other in a multithreaded program. The best known is the variable *errno,* which gets set when an error occurs within the run-time library, particularly within the file functions. Consider what would happen if two threads were each doing file I/O with the FILE* functions, and both of them set *errno.* Obviously, there would be a race condition and one of the threads would get the wrong result.

Another example is the string call `strtok()`, which maintains a pointer to the current working string between calls. The contents of the per-thread data structure that the C run-time library maintains is shown in Chapter 15.

There are also data structures within the library that must be made thread-safe. For example, `fopen()` returns FILE*, which is typically a pointer into a descriptor table within the run-time library. This descriptor table must be protected with a synchronization mechanism to prevent corruption. It is also possible that the run-time library does its own memory allocation, in which case the memory handling routines need to be protected, too.

Using the synchronization mechanisms described in earlier chapters, it is possible to create a library that supports multithreading. The problem is that adding this support incurs a slight size and performance penalty for the over-head of performing the synchronization, even if there is only one thread running.

In Visual C++, a compromise was made by creating two versions of the C run-time library. One version is for single-threaded programs and one ver-sion is for multithreaded programs. The multithreaded version of the library has two significant differences from the single-threaded version. First, vari-ables such as *errno* are kept on a per-thread basis in the multithreaded version. Second, structures within the multithreaded run-time library are protected with synchronization mechanisms.

IMPORTANT!   MFC applications *must* use the multithreaded library, or you will get "unde-fined function" errors when you try to link.

Selecting a Multithreaded C Run-time Library

FAQ 38

How do I choose which version of the C run-time library I am using?

There are several different versions of the C run-time library, and if you choose the wrong one your program may not build. It is often difficult to fig-ure out how to change which version you are using, so in the next two sections I will describe how to choose a version of the C run-time library in the Visual C++ IDE and from the command line.

Visual C++ 4.x IDE

In Visual C++ 4.x, you can choose which version of the library to use by fol-lowing these steps:

1. Choose Settings from the Build menu.
2. Choose the C/C++ tab.

3. Choose Code Generation in the Category combo box.
4. Open the combo box "Use run-time library."

There are three variations to choose from:

*   Single-Threaded (static)
*   Multithreaded (static)
*   Multithreaded DLL

There is also a Debug version of each of these three libraries.

When you make this change in the C/C++ tab, the Link tab will automatically select the proper library to link.

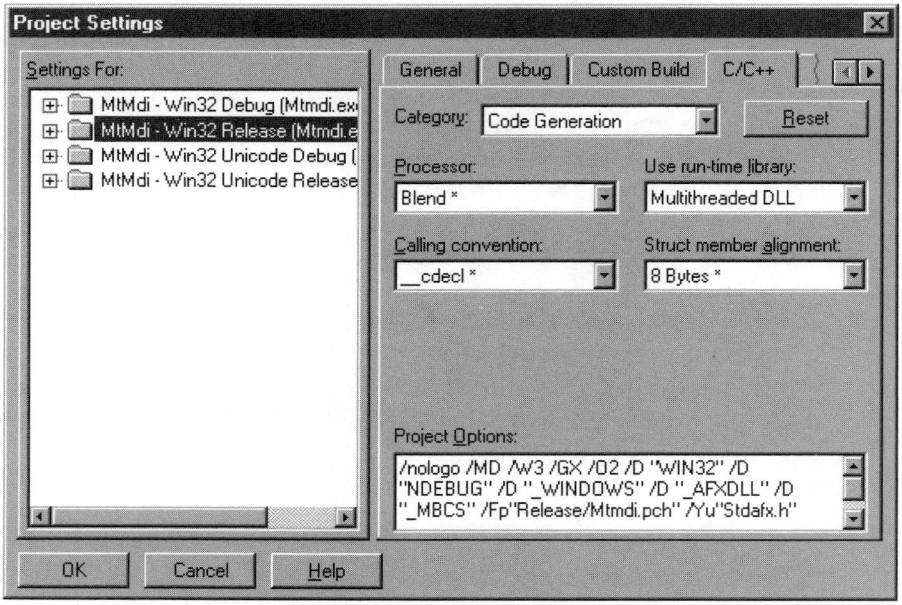

Figure 8-1. Visual C++ 4.x build settings.

The default run-time library version when you create a new Application project is Single-Threaded. The default when you use AppWizard and MFC is Multithreaded. For MFC applications only, the DLL is used for Debug and the static library is used for Release.

IMPORTANT!

> If you receive the error message "_beginthreadex is undefined" while linking, it means that you are linking with the single-threaded library and you need to change to the multithreaded library.

From the Command Line

If you are running the Visual C++ compiler from the command line or from an external makefile, you can select the type of library with the following options:

/ML	Single-Threaded
/MT	Multithreaded
/MD	Multithreaded DLL
/MLd	Debug Single-Threaded
/MTd	Debug Multithreaded
/MDd	Debug Multithreaded DLL

For example, to choose the Debug Multithreaded DLL, you would use:

```
cl /MDd srcfile.c
```

To use the Single-Threaded statically linked library you would use:

```
cl /ML srcfile.c
```

You would also get this same library if you use the default:

```
cl srcfile.c
```

Starting Threads with the C Run-time Library

FAQ 39

How do I use _beginthreadex() and _endthreadex()?

In order to be thread-safe, the run-time library must do some bookkeeping for each thread that starts up and shuts down. Without this bookkeeping, the run-time library would not know to allocate a new block of thread-local data for each new thread. Therefore, there is a wrapper for `CreateThread()` called `_beginthreadex()` that takes care of this additional bookkeeping.

IMPORTANT!

The parameters to `_beginthreadex()` are identical to those for `Create-Thread()`, although they have been sanitized to remove any trace of Win32 types. This is unfortunate because it prevents the compiler from performing type checking.

The sanitized parameters were supposed to make the call portable to other operating systems. In theory, by avoiding Win32 types, the call could be implemented on other platforms because there is no need to know about *windows.h*. Unfortunately, the need to call `CloseHandle()` means you still need to include *windows.h*. The whole situation appears to be the result of a good idea that did not work out.

In the description of `_beginthreadex()`, I have included the actual Win32 types in the description of each parameter. It has been my experience that the indirection confuses more people than it helps, so it appears that this call is most easily understood if you treat it as a funny-looking version of `CreateThread()`.

unsigned long _beginthreadex (

```
void *security,
unsigned stack_size,
unsigned ( __stdcall *start_address )( void * ),
void *arglist,
unsigned initflag,
unsigned* thrdaddr
);
```

Parameters

security	Security attributes as used by CreateThread(). Use NULL to get the default security attributes. Ignored on Windows 95. The actual Win32 type is LPSECURITY_ATTRIBUTES.
stack_size	Size of stack in bytes for the new thread. The actual Win32 type is DWORD.
start_address	Function that will be used to start the thread. The actual Win32 type is LPTHREAD_START_ROUTINE.
arglist	Pointer that the new thread will receive. The pointer is simply passed through; the run-time library does *not* make a copy of the data being pointed at. The actual Win32 type is LPVOID.

initflag	Startup state flag. The actual Win32 type is DWORD.
thrdaddr	Location to receive ID of the new thread. The actual Win32 type is LPDWORD.

Return Value

`_beginthreadex()` returns the handle to the thread. The return value must be cast to a Win32 HANDLE to be used. This function returns zero if it fails, and the reason for failure is in *errno* and *doserrno*.

Note the leading underscore. It must be there because this function is not part of the ANSI standard C run-time library. You will not find this function on Unix or OS/2 compilers, for example.

Although it is not obvious from the declaration of `_beginthreadex()`, the *unsigned long* that it returns is a Win32 HANDLE to the new thread or zero if the creation failed. In other words, the return values are the same as for `CreateThread()`, except that `_beginthreadex()` also sets *errno* and *doserrno*.

The simplest version of a program that uses these calls looks something like this:

```
#include <windows.h>
#include <process.h>
unsigned __stdcall myfunc(void* p);

void main()
{
    unsigned long thd;
    unsigned tid;

    thd = _beginthreadex(NULL,
                         0,
                         myfunc,
                         0,
                         0,
                         &tid );
    if (thd != NULL)
    {
            CloseHandle(thd);
    }
}
```

```
unsigned __stdcall myfunc(void* p)
{
    // ...
}
```

IMPORTANT!   Because _beginthreadex() calls CreateThread(), you must call CloseHandle() on the return value from _beginthreadex(). See the discussion on kernel objects in Chapter 3 for more information.

There is also a C run-time function that corresponds to ExitThread() called _endthreadex(). It looks like this:

```
void _endthreadex ( unsigned );
```

Like ExitThread(), _endthreadex() can be called by a thread at any time, and it takes as a parameter the exit code for the thread. In fact, _endthreadex() will be called by the run-time library automatically if your thread startup function returns.

IMPORTANT!   You should never call ExitThread() in a thread that was started with _beginthreadex() because the C run-time library will not have a chance to free resources allocated for that thread.

CreateThread() or _beginthreadex()?

As you have seen so far, if you write a multithreaded program that uses the C run-time library, you must use:

1. The multithreaded C run-time library
2. _beginthreadex()/_endthreadex()

FAQ 40

When should I use _begin-threadex() as opposed to Create-Thread()?

Therefore, an application that uses multiple threads *without* calling the run-time library from any of the worker threads should be able to link to the single-threaded run-time library and therefore be able to use CreateThread() instead of _beginthreadex(). However, writing in C without calling anything from the run-time library is almost impossible. In fact, under the hood, the compiler frequently calls helper functions in the run-time library, and it is not possible to stop this from happening. Given all of this, can you ever avoid the multithreaded C run-time library and use `CreateThread()`?

I want to preface this discussion by saying that you should consider very seriously whether you really want to do this. The C run-time library provides some significant advantages, and it can be very hard to prevent people on your project from using run-time functions without even thinking about it. Because the startup code and utility functions *must* come from the C run-time library, it is not possible to leave it out of the link command.

The only circumstance I can think of where I would want to avoid the C run-time library is if I had extremely precise synchronization conditions and using the C run-time could cause deadlocks because of its internal locking mechanism.

The quick answer is that there is a subset of the C run-time library that *is* safe to call, and many of the run-time functions that you cannot call have Win32 equivalents. However, there are also some very useful things, such as stream I/O and `printf()`, which the C run-time provides and for which there is no Win32 equivalent.

Here are some general rules. You should always use the multithreaded C run-time library, along with `_beginthreadex()`/`_endthreadex()`, if any thread other than the primary thread does any of the following:

- Uses `malloc()` or `free()` in C, or `new` or `delete` in C++.
- Calls anything in *stdio.h* or in *io.h*. This includes functions such as `fopen()` and `open()`, `getchar()`, `write()`, and `printf()`. All of these functions use shared data structures as well as *errno*. You can use `wsprintf()` to do string formatting without using *stdio.h*. (You may need to link with USER32.LIB if the linker can't find `wsprintf()`.)
- Uses floating point variables or functions.
- Calls any run-time functions that use a static buffer, such as `asctime()`, `strtok()`, or `rand()`.

Therefore, it is *usually* safe to use the single-threaded run-time library as well as `CreateThread()` if the worker threads only use functions not on the list above.

Here are a couple of examples. In this first example, shown in Listing 8-1, worker threads are searching files for a string. The request buffer area is being allocated in the primary thread with `calloc()`, and then cleaned up in the worker thread with `free()`. Also, the worker thread uses `fopen()` and other file operations. Therefore this example must use the multithreaded library and `_beginthreadex()`.

Listing 8-1. SRCHCRT.C—Application that requires _beginthreadex()

```c
/*
 * SrchCrt.c
 *
 * Uses multiple threads to search the files
 * "*.c" in the current directory for the string
 * given on the command line.
 *
 * This example uses the multithreaded version of
 * the C run-time library so as to be able to use
 * the FILE functions as well as calloc and free.
 *
 * Build this file with the command line: cl /MD SrchCrt.c
 *
 */

#include <windows.h>
#include <process.h>     /* _beginthreadex, _endthreadex */
#include <stddef.h>
#include <stdio.h>
#include <stdlib.h>
#include "MtVerify.h"

DWORD WINAPI SearchProc( void *arg );

#define MAX_THREADS 3

HANDLE hThreadLimitSemaphore;
char szSearchFor[1024];

int main(int argc, char *argv[])
{
    WIN32_FIND_DATA *lpFindData;
    HANDLE hFindFile;
    HANDLE hThread;
    DWORD dummy;
    int i;

    if (argc != 2)
    {
        printf("Usage: %s <search-string>\n", argv[0]);
        return EXIT_FAILURE;
    }

    /* Put search string where everyone can see it */
    strcpy(szSearchFor, argv[1]);
```

Listing 8-1 (continued)

```
/* Each thread will be given its own results buffer */
lpFindData = calloc( 1, sizeof(WIN32_FIND_DATA) );

/* Semaphore prevents too many threads from running */
MTVERIFY( hThreadLimitSemaphore = CreateSemaphore(
        NULL,    /* Security */
        MAX_THREADS,    /* Make all of them available */
        MAX_THREADS,    /* No more than MAX_THREADS */
        NULL )          /* Unnamed */
    );

hFindFile = FindFirstFile( "*.c", lpFindData );

if (hFindFile == INVALID_HANDLE_VALUE)
    return EXIT_FAILURE;

do {
    WaitForSingleObject( hThreadLimitSemaphore,
        INFINITE );

    MTVERIFY(
        hThread = (HANDLE)_beginthreadex(NULL,
                    0,
                    SearchProc,
                    lpFindData,
                    0,
                    &dummy
            )
    );
    MTVERIFY( CloseHandle( hThread ) );

    lpFindData = calloc( 1, sizeof(WIN32_FIND_DATA) );

} while ( FindNextFile( hFindFile, lpFindData ));

FindClose( hFindFile );

for (i=0; i<MAX_THREADS; i++)
    WaitForSingleObject(
                hThreadLimitSemaphore,
                INFINITE );
MTVERIFY( CloseHandle( hThreadLimitSemaphore ) );

return EXIT_SUCCESS;
}
```

Listing 8-1 (continued)

```
DWORD __stdcall SearchProc( void *arg )
{
    WIN32_FIND_DATA *lpFindData = (WIN32_FIND_DATA *)arg;
    char buf[1024];
    FILE* fp;

    fp = fopen(lpFindData->cFileName, "r");
    if (!fp)
        return EXIT_FAILURE;

    while (fgets(buf, sizeof(buf), fp))
    {
        /* Inefficient search strategy, but it's easy */
        if (strstr(buf, szSearchFor))
            printf("%s: %s", lpFindData->cFileName, buf);
    }

    fclose(fp);
    free(lpFindData);

    MTVERIFY( ReleaseSemaphore( hThreadLimitSemaphore,
                1,            // Add one to the count
                NULL ) );     // Do not need the old value
}
```

In the second example, shown in Listing 8-2, most references to the C run-time library have been removed. There are two significant disadvantages for this application. The first is that we have to do our own locking to make sure that the output of the various threads does not get intermingled. In contrast, in the multithreaded C run-time library, a mutex is placed around any operations involving a file handle. This prevents the output from getting mixed up, as we saw in Chapter 2.

The second disadvantage is that Win32 does not provide buffered stream I/O, so I created a simple routine called `GetLine()` to read byte by byte from the file stream. `GetLine()`'s implementation is not optimal, but it is a necessary workaround to not having the buffered I/O C run-time functions. Clearly, this version of the program is much more complex than the version that used the run-time library, because it has to duplicate functionality found in the run-time library.

Listing 8-2. SRCHWIN.C—Application that safely uses CreateThread()

```c
/*
 * SrchWin.c
 *
 * Uses multiple threads to search the files
 * "*.c" in the current directory for the string
 * given on the command line.
 *
 * This example avoids most C run-time functions so that
 * it can use the single threaded C libraries.
 *
 * It is necessary to use a critical section to
 * divvy up output to the screen or the various
 * threads end up with their output intermingled.
 * Normally the multithreaded C run-time does this
 * automatically if you use printf.
 *
 */

#include <windows.h>
#include <process.h>      /* _beginthreadex, _endthreadex */
#include <stdlib.h>
#include "MtVerify.h"

DWORD WINAPI SearchProc( void *arg );
BOOL GetLine( HANDLE hFile, LPSTR buf, DWORD size );

#define MAX_THREADS 3

HANDLE hThreadLimitSemaphore;    /* Counting semaphore */
HANDLE hConsoleOut;              /* Console output */
CRITICAL_SECTION ScreenCritical; /* Lock screen updates */

char szSearchFor[1024];

int main(int argc, char *argv[])
{
    WIN32_FIND_DATA *lpFindData;
    HANDLE hFindFile;
    HANDLE hThread;
    DWORD dummy;
    int i;

    hConsoleOut = GetStdHandle( STD_OUTPUT_HANDLE );
```

Listing 8-2 (continued)

```c
if (argc != 2)
{
    char errbuf[512];
    wsprintf(errbuf,
        "Usage: %s <search-string>\n",
        argv[0]);
    WriteFile( hConsoleOut,
        errbuf,
        strlen(errbuf),
        &dummy,
        FALSE );
    return EXIT_FAILURE;
}

/* Put search string where everyone can see it */
strcpy(szSearchFor, argv[1]);

/* Allocate a find buffer to be handed
 * to the first thread */
lpFindData = HeapAlloc( GetProcessHeap(),
        HEAP_ZERO_MEMORY,
        sizeof(WIN32_FIND_DATA) );

/* Semaphore prevents too many threads from running */
MTVERIFY( hThreadLimitSemaphore = CreateSemaphore(
        NULL,    /* Security */
        MAX_THREADS,     /* Make all of them available */
        MAX_THREADS,     /* Allow a total of MAX_THREADS */
        NULL )           /* Unnamed */
    );

InitializeCriticalSection(&ScreenCritical);

hFindFile = FindFirstFile( "*.c", lpFindData );

if (hFindFile == INVALID_HANDLE_VALUE)
    return EXIT_FAILURE;

do {
    WaitForSingleObject( hThreadLimitSemaphore,
                    INFINITE );

    MTVERIFY( hThread = CreateThread(NULL,
                    0,
                    SearchProc,
```

Listing 8-2 (continued)

```
                            lpFindData, // arglist
                            0,
                            &dummy )
            );

        MTVERIFY( CloseHandle( hThread ) );

        lpFindData = HeapAlloc( GetProcessHeap(),
                        HEAP_ZERO_MEMORY,
                        sizeof(WIN32_FIND_DATA) );

    } while ( FindNextFile( hFindFile, lpFindData ));

    FindClose( hFindFile );
    hFindFile = INVALID_HANDLE_VALUE;

    for (i=0; i<MAX_THREADS; i++)
        WaitForSingleObject( hThreadLimitSemaphore,
                        INFINITE );

    MTVERIFY( CloseHandle( hThreadLimitSemaphore ) );

    return EXIT_SUCCESS;
}


DWORD WINAPI SearchProc( void *arg )
{
    WIN32_FIND_DATA *lpFindData = (WIN32_FIND_DATA *)arg;
    char buf[1024];
    HANDLE hFile;
    DWORD dummy;

    hFile = CreateFile(lpFindData->cFileName,
                    GENERIC_READ,
                    FILE_SHARE_READ,
                    NULL,
                    OPEN_EXISTING,
                    FILE_FLAG_SEQUENTIAL_SCAN,
                    NULL
                );
    if (!hFile)
        return 1;    /* Silently ignore problem files */
```

Listing 8-2 (continued)

```c
    while (GetLine(hFile, buf, sizeof(buf)))
    {
        /* Inefficient search strategy, but it's easy */
        if (strstr(buf, szSearchFor))
        {
            /* Make sure that this thread is the
             * only one writing to this handle */
            EnterCriticalSection( &ScreenCritical );

            WriteFile( hConsoleOut,
                lpFindData->cFileName,
                strlen(lpFindData->cFileName),
                &dummy,
                FALSE );
            WriteFile( hConsoleOut,
                ": ", 2, &dummy, FALSE );
            WriteFile( hConsoleOut,
                buf, strlen(buf), &dummy, FALSE );
            WriteFile( hConsoleOut,
                "\r\n", 2, &dummy, FALSE );

            LeaveCriticalSection( &ScreenCritical );
        }
    }

    CloseHandle(hFile);
    HeapFree( GetProcessHeap(), 0, lpFindData);

    MTVERIFY( ReleaseSemaphore( hThreadLimitSemaphore,
                                    1,
                                    NULL ) );
}

/*
 * Unlike fgets(), this routine throws away CR/LF
 * automatically.  Calling ReadFile() one character
 * at a time is slow, but this illustrates the
 * advantages of using stdio under some conditions
 * (because buffering the stream yourself is difficult)
 */
BOOL GetLine(HANDLE hFile, LPSTR buf, DWORD size)
{
    DWORD total = 0;
    DWORD numread;
    int state = 0;   /* 0 = Looking for non-newline */
                     /* 1 = Stop after first newline */
```

Listing 8-2 (continued)

```
for (;;)
{
    if (total == size-1)
    {
        buf[size-1] = '\0';
        return TRUE;
    }
    if (!ReadFile(hFile, buf+total, 1, &numread, 0)
            || numread == 0)
    {
        buf[total] = '\0';
        return total != 0;
    }
    if (buf[total] == '\r' || buf[total] == '\n')
    {
        if (state == 0)
            continue;
        buf[total] = '\0';
        return TRUE;
    }
    state = 1;
    total++;
}
}
```

Avoiding *stdio.h*

In many cases, staying away from using functions in the C run-time library is not very difficult. Win32 provides equivalent functions for such things as file handling and memory management. The one place that everyone seems to get stuck is how to do screen I/O without *stdio.h*.

There are three separate problems that must be addressed in order to avoid *stdio.h*. The first problem is formatting output. This is solved by using a version of sprintf() built into Windows called wsprintf() (actually _wsprintfA() and _wsprintfW() to handle ANSI and Unicode). This function is part of the kernel, not part of the C run-time library. It will do most of what the C run-time sprintf() does with the exception of handling floating point variables.

The second problem is finding a replacement for *stdin* and *stdout,* which are predefined handles in the C run-time library for reading and writing the standard input and the standard output. These file handles go to the screen by default, but they can also refer to a file if the user types a command that uses redirection, such as:

```
sort <oldfile >newfile
```

The Win32 API normally uses the functions `CreateFile()`, `Read-File()`, `WriteFile()`, and `CloseHandle()` for its basic I/O operations. The last three functions take a handle returned by `CreateFile()`. The Win32 has exact equivalents for *stdin, stdout,* and *stderr* that are accessed with the API function `GetStdHandle()`. It looks like this:

HANDLE GetStdHandle(
   DWORD nStdHandle
   );

Parameter

nStdHandle   Determines the type of handle to return. Must be equal to one of the following constants:

STD_INPUT_HANDLE

STD_OUTPUT_HANDLE

STD_ERROR_HANDLE

You can use the handles returned by this function in calls to `ReadFile()` and `WriteFile()`. You will see examples of this function being used in the SRCHWIN sample program in Listing 8-2 and the BANNER sample program soon to come.

The last problem that must be addressed is direct control of the screen. Under MS-DOS you can do this in one of four ways:

1. The BIOS screen handler interrupts
2. Direct video writes
3. The C run-time *conio.h* functions
4. The C run-time *stdio.h* functions

Although options 3 and 4 are both available in Win32, they are part of the C run-time and should not be called in a multithreaded program without the multithreaded C run-time library.

The native alternative on both Windows NT and Windows 95 is a portion of the Win32 API called the **Console API.** The Console API is strictly for reading and writing to the screen. It provides control over cursor location, character attributes, the title bar, and the mouse. It even allows screen rectangles to be moved in blocks!

Using the Console API is not difficult. The sample program BANNER in the next section demonstrates many of its common operations.

UNIX

> A common concern among Unix developers moving to Windows NT is the loss of *curses*, the terminal management package. Although there are implementations of *curses* that exist on Windows NT, you should consider the Console API as the more appropriate replacement. Unlike *curses*, the Console API does not have to worry about a multiplicity of terminal types, and terminals with slow connections and slow update speeds.

A Run-time-Safe Multithreaded Program

FAQ 41

How do I use the Console API instead of *stdio.h?*

The example in Listing 8-3, BANNER, demonstrates several important points. It uses the Win32 Console API instead of common *stdio* functions, including alternatives to cursor handling and `gets()`. Also:

- The primary thread allocates memory with `HeapAlloc()` and the worker thread frees the memory with `HeapFree()`. The memory management functions in the C run-time library are not safe to call without the multithreaded library.
- All of the random numbers are generated in the primary thread. The run-time function `rand()` must maintain state between calls.
- An event object is used to simultaneously signal all threads when it is time to shut down.
- The sample program does not link with the multithreaded run-time library, nor does it need to.

Notice that the worker threads may safely use string handling functions such as `strcpy()` because these functions operate entirely on the stack.

Listing 8-3. BANNER.C—Console I/O with CreateThread()

```
/*
 * Banner.c
 *
 * Demonstrates how to write a program that can use
 * CreateThread instead of calling _beginthreadex.
 * This program does not need the multithreaded library.
```

Listing 8-3 (continued)

```
 *
 * This program could use ReadConsole and WriteConsole.
 * There are minor but significant differences between
 * these functions and ReadFile and WriteFile.
 *
 * This program is ANSI only; it will not compile
 * for Unicode.
 */

#include <windows.h>
#include <stdlib.h>
#include <time.h>          /* to init rand() */
#include "MtVerify.h"

/************************************************
 * Constants
 */
#define MAX_THREADS   256

#define INPUT_BUF_SIZE       80
#define BANNER_SIZE          12
#define OUTPUT_TEXT_COLOR    BACKGROUND_BLUE | \
          FOREGROUND_RED|FOREGROUND_GREEN|FOREGROUND_BLUE

/************************************************
 * Function Prototypes
 */
void MainLoop( void  );
void ClearScreen( void );
void ShutDownThreads( void );
void Prompt( LPCSTR str );     /* Display title bar info */
int StripCr( LPSTR buf );

/* Thread startup function */
DWORD WINAPI BannerProc( LPVOID pParam );

/************************************************
 * Global Variables
 */
HANDLE  hConsoleIn;           /* Console input  */
HANDLE  hConsoleOut;          /* Console output */
HANDLE  hRunObject;           /* "Keep Running" event object */
HANDLE  ThreadHandles[MAX_THREADS];
int     nThreads;             /* Number of threads started */
```

Listing 8-3 (continued)

```c
CONSOLE_SCREEN_BUFFER_INFO csbiInfo;

/***********************************************
 * Stucture passed to thread on startup
 */
typedef struct {
    TCHAR buf[INPUT_BUF_SIZE];
    SHORT x;
    SHORT y;
} DataBlock;


/***********************************************
 * Primary thread enters here
 */
int main()
{
    /* Get display screen information & clear the screen.*/
    hConsoleIn = GetStdHandle( STD_INPUT_HANDLE );
    hConsoleOut = GetStdHandle( STD_OUTPUT_HANDLE );
    GetConsoleScreenBufferInfo( hConsoleOut, &csbiInfo );

    ClearScreen();

    /* Create the event object that keeps threads running. */
    MTVERIFY( hRunObject = CreateEvent(
            NULL,               /* Security */
            TRUE,               /* Manual event */
            0,                  /* Clear on creation */
            NULL)               /* Name of object */
    );

    /* Start waiting for keyboard input to
     * dispatch threads or exit. */
    MainLoop();

    ShutDownThreads();

    ClearScreen();

    CloseHandle( hRunObject );
    CloseHandle( hConsoleIn );
    CloseHandle( hConsoleOut );
```

Listing 8-3 (continued)

```c
        return EXIT_SUCCESS;
}

void ShutDownThreads( void )
{
    if (nThreads > 0)
    {
        /* Since this is a manual event, all
         * threads will be woken up at once. */
        MTVERIFY( SetEvent(hRunObject) );
        MTVERIFY( WaitForMultipleObjects(
                    nThreads,
                    ThreadHandles,
                    TRUE, INFINITE
                ) != WAIT_FAILED
        );
        while (--nThreads)
            MTVERIFY( CloseHandle(
                    ThreadHandles[nThreads] ) );
    }
}

/* Dispatch and count threads. */
void MainLoop( void )
{
    TCHAR buf[INPUT_BUF_SIZE];
    DWORD bytesRead;
    DataBlock *data_block;
    DWORD thread_id;

    srand(time(NULL));
    for (;;)
    {
        Prompt(
            "Type string to display or ENTER to exit: "
        );
        MTVERIFY( ReadFile( hConsoleIn,
                    buf,
                    INPUT_BUF_SIZE-1,
                    &bytesRead,
                    NULL)
        );
        /* ReadFile is binary, not line oriented,
         * so terminate the string. */
        buf[bytesRead] = '\0';
```

Listing 8-3 (continued)

```
MTVERIFY( FlushConsoleInputBuffer( hConsoleIn ) );
if (StripCr( buf ) == 0)
    break;

if (nThreads < MAX_THREADS)
{
    /*
     * Use the Win32 HeapAlloc() instead of
     * malloc() because we would need the
     * multithread library if the worker
     * thread had to call free().
     */
    data_block = HeapAlloc(
                    GetProcessHeap(),
                    HEAP_ZERO_MEMORY,
                    sizeof(DataBlock) );
    strcpy(data_block->buf, buf);

    /*
     * Pick a random place on the screen to put
     * this banner. You may not call rand in the
     * worker thread because it is one of the
     * functions that must maintain state
     * between calls.
     */
    data_block->x = rand()
        * (csbiInfo.dwSize.X - BANNER_SIZE)
        / RAND_MAX;
    data_block->y = rand()
        * (csbiInfo.dwSize.Y - 1)
        / RAND_MAX + 1;

    MTVERIFY(
        ThreadHandles[nThreads++] = CreateThread(
                NULL,
                0,
                BannerProc,
                data_block,
                0,
                &thread_id )
    );
}
}
}
```

Listing 8-3 (continued)

```c
int StripCr( LPSTR buf )
{
    int len = strlen(buf);
    for (;;)
    {
        if (len <= 0) return 0;
        else if (buf[--len] == '\r' )
            buf[len] = ' ';
        else if (buf[len] == '\n' )
            buf[len] = ' ';
        else break;
    }
    return len;
}


void ClearScreen( void )
{
    DWORD     dummy;
    COORD     Home = { 0, 0 };
    FillConsoleOutputAttribute( hConsoleOut,
            csbiInfo.wAttributes,
            csbiInfo.dwSize.X * csbiInfo.dwSize.Y,
            Home,
            &dummy );
    FillConsoleOutputCharacter( hConsoleOut,
            ' ',
            csbiInfo.dwSize.X * csbiInfo.dwSize.Y,
            Home,
            &dummy );
}


void Prompt( LPCSTR str )
{
    COORD     Home = { 0, 0 };
    DWORD     dummy;
    int len = strlen(str);

    SetConsoleCursorPosition( hConsoleOut, Home );
    WriteFile( hConsoleOut, str, len, &dummy, FALSE );
    Home.X = len;
    FillConsoleOutputCharacter( hConsoleOut,
            ' ',
            csbiInfo.dwSize.X-len,
```

Listing 8-3 (continued)

```
            Home,
            &dummy );
}

/************************************************************
 * Routines from here down are used only by worker threads
 */

DWORD WINAPI BannerProc( LPVOID pParam )
{
    DataBlock *thread_data_block = pParam;
    COORD     TopLeft = {0,0};
    COORD     Size = {BANNER_SIZE ,1};
    int       i, j;
    int       len;
    int       ScrollPosition = 0;
    TCHAR     OutputBuf[INPUT_BUF_SIZE+BANNER_SIZE];
    CHAR_INFO CharBuf[INPUT_BUF_SIZE+BANNER_SIZE];
    SMALL_RECT rect;

    rect.Left   = thread_data_block->x;
    rect.Right  = rect.Left  + BANNER_SIZE;
    rect.Top    = thread_data_block->y;
    rect.Bottom = rect.Top;

    /* Set up the string so the output routine
     * does not have figure out wrapping. */
    strcpy(OutputBuf, thread_data_block->buf);
    len = strlen(OutputBuf);
    for (i=len; i<BANNER_SIZE; i++)
        OutputBuf[i] = ' ';
    if (len<BANNER_SIZE) len = BANNER_SIZE;
    strncpy(OutputBuf+len, OutputBuf, BANNER_SIZE);
    OutputBuf[len+BANNER_SIZE-1] = '\0';

    MTVERIFY( HeapFree( GetProcessHeap(), 0, pParam ) );

    do
    {
        for (i=ScrollPosition++, j=0;
                j<BANNER_SIZE;
                i++, j++)
        {
            CharBuf[j].Char.AsciiChar = OutputBuf[i];
            CharBuf[j].Attributes = OUTPUT_TEXT_COLOR;
        }
```

Listing 8-3 (continued)

```
        if (ScrollPosition == len)
            ScrollPosition = 0;

        MTVERIFY( WriteConsoleOutput(
                        hConsoleOut,
                        CharBuf,
                        Size,
                        TopLeft,
                        &rect)
        );

    /*
     * This next statement has the dual purpose of
     * being a choke on how often the banner is updated
     * (because the timeout forces the thread to wait for
     * awhile) as well as causing the thread to exit
     * when the event object is signaled.
     */
    } while ( WaitForSingleObject(
                        hRunObject,
                        125L
            ) == WAIT_TIMEOUT );

    return 0;
}
```

Exiting the Process

To properly clean up the structures in the C run-time library, you should use one of two techniques to exit an application that uses _beginthread() or _beginthreadex():

1. Call the C run-time function exit().
2. Return from main().

In either of these cases, the run-time library will automatically clean up properly and then eventually call ExitProcess(). Using either of these techniques will *not* wait for threads to exit. Any running threads will automatically be terminated. If you need to wait for other threads to exit, you should use one of the Win32 synchronization mechanisms discussed in Chapter 4.

Under extreme error conditions, you can also call abort() from any thread. This call should be used only as a last resort because no exit handlers are called and file buffers are not flushed.

Why You Should Avoid _beginthread()

FAQ 42

Why shouldn't I use _begin thread()?

The function _beginthreadex() is a fairly recent addition to the Microsoft C run-time library. For a long time, the only function that could be used to properly initialize the library when using multiple threads was _beginthread(), which has some significant differences compared to _beginthreadex(). Here is the declaration of _beginthread():

unsigned long _beginthread (
    void (__cdecl *start_address **)(void *),**
    unsigned stack_size,
    void *arglist
);

Parameters

start_address	Function that will be used to start the thread.
stack_size	Size of stack in bytes for the new thread. Like CreateThread(), this value can be zero to use the default size.
arglist	Pointer to data that the new thread will receive. The pointer is simply passed through; the run-time library does *not* make a copy of the data being pointed at.

Return Value

_beginthread() returns −1 if it fails. Otherwise it returns an *unsigned long,* which is really a HANDLE to the new thread. This handle may or may not be valid; it cannot safely be used by the caller.

The function _beginthread() was supposed to be the "no-brainer" thread call. However, there are several fundamental problems with it. First, _beginthread() does not take all the parameters that CreateThread() does. Therefore it is not possible to do things like create the thread in a suspended state so its priority can be adjusted or its data can be initialized.

Second, and most important, the first thing that the thread created by
_beginthread() does is to close the handle to the thread. This was done to
try to hide the Win32 implementation details. Therefore, the handle may be
invalid by the time _beginthread() returns, and there is an unavoidable
race condition if you try to use the handle returned by _beginthread().
Without this handle, there is no way to wait on the thread, change its parameters, or even to get an exit code.

If you remember from Chapter 2, the thread startup function called by
CreateThread() must be of type WINAPI (which is actually _stdcall). On
the other hand, _beginthread() takes a pointer to a normal C style function (calling convention _cdecl) that returns *void*. Here is the bare outline of
a thread startup that uses _beginthread():

```
void MyFunc(LPVOID);

void main()
{
    unsigned long htd;

    htd = _beginthread(
                    MyFunc,
                    0,    // stack size
                    0 );  // argument
    if (htd == -1)
      {
            // thread creation failed
      }
}

void MyFunc(LPVOID arg)
{
    // ...
}
```

There is also a C run-time function that corresponds to ExitThread()
called _endthread(). It looks like this:

```
void _endthread ( void );
```

You can see that _endthread() does not take an exit status. Therefore it
is not meaningful for the thread that called _beginthread() to call

GetExitCodeThread( ), nor is there anything in the run-time library that lets a thread created with _beginthread( ) return an exit code.

If you read the warning at the beginning of this chapter, it clearly stated that you had to use _beginthread( ) if you wanted to use the run-time library. Of course, if you needed to change the security attributes or create the thread suspended, as CreateThread( ) allows you to do, you were pretty much stuck. Therefore _beginthreadex( ) was created. You can still find _beginthread( ) in the library, but I would discourage its use.

Summary

In this chapter you saw the difference between _beginthreadex( ) and CreateThread( ). You saw when you have to use the multithreaded C run-time library and how you can use the single-threaded version under some conditions. You saw how to use the Console API instead of *stdio*. Finally, you saw the problems with _beginthread( ) and why you should use _beginthreadex( ).

Chapter 9

Using C++

This chapter describes how to create multiple threads with C++ classes. It shows how C++ can make multithreaded programming significantly easier and safer.

Up to this point, all of our examples have been in C. Now we will start using C++. C++ provides significant benefits to writing multithreaded programs because you can guarantee how objects are accessed and synchronized.

I will assume you have a basic understanding of C++, including classes, virtual functions, constructors, and destructors. If you do not already understand these terms, there are hundreds of books on C++ where you can learn about them.

Handling the Buggy Prototype for _beginthreadex()

Before I go any further, I want to point out the there is a bug in the prototype for _beginthreadex() in the C run-time library in Visual C++ 4.x. The problem does not show up in C, but C++ uses much stricter type checking. The problem stems from the prototype for _beginthreadex():

```
unsigned long _beginthreadex(
                  void *security,
                  unsigned stack_size,
```

```
        unsigned ( * start_address ) (void *),
        void *arglist,
        unsigned initflag,
        unsigned *thrdaddr );
```

The third and sixth parameters, *start_address* and *thrdaddr,* are both defined with *unsigned,* or more formally, *unsigned int.* If you look at the declaration for `CreateThread()`, these parameters are defined with *DWORD,* which is really *unsigned long.* Bit-wise, these two types are identical in a 32-bit compiler, so the C compiler ignores the difference. However, the stricter type checking for C++ in Visual C++ 4.x does notice the difference. If you declare *thrdaddr* to be DWORD and try to pass its address, you receive this error:

```
BadClass.cpp(30) : error C2664: '_beginthreadex' : cannot
convert parameter 6 from 'unsigned long *' to 'unsigned
int *' (new behavior; please see help)
```

The last part about "new behavior" explains why this problem did not show up in Visual C++ 2.x, which is when _beginthreadex() was introduced.

There are two workarounds for this problem. The first is to declare your variables *unsigned,* which is the way _beginthreadex() wants them. This solution has the advantage of simplicity, but if the prototype is ever fixed, then it would be necessary to go back and change all the variable types. This change could potentially ripple out and affect other parts of the code.

The second workaround is to declare the variables the way `Create-Thread()` wants them and cast the variables when passing them to _beginthreadex(). I will use this method because the cast can be buried in a typedef that can easily be updated if the prototype changes.

The updated version of the skeleton for using _beginthreadex() is shown in the Listing 9-1. The type PBEGINTHREADEX_THREADFUNC provides a way to cast the thread startup function, and the type PBEGINTHREADEX_THREADID provides a cast for the thread ID. I will use these prototypes throughout the book.

Listing 9-1. CPPSKEL.CPP—Minimal thread startup code

```
/*
 * CppSkel.cpp
 *
 * Show how to cast the parameters to _beginthreadex
 * so that they will work in Visual C++ 4.x with
 * the new stricter type checking.
```

Listing 9-1 (continued)

```
 *
 * Build this file with the command line:
 *
 *     cl /MD CppSkel.cpp
 *
 */

#include <stdio.h>
#include <windows.h>
#include <process.h>

typedef unsigned (WINAPI *PBEGINTHREADEX_THREADFUNC)(
    LPVOID lpThreadParameter
    );
typedef unsigned *PBEGINTHREADEX_THREADID;

DWORD WINAPI ThreadFunc(LPVOID);

int main()
{
    HANDLE hThread;
    DWORD threadId;
    int i;

    hThread = (HANDLE)_beginthreadex(NULL,
            0,
            (PBEGINTHREADEX_THREADFUNC)ThreadFunc,
            (LPVOID)i,
            0,
            (PBEGINTHREADEX_THREADID)&threadId
        );
    if (hThread) {
        WaitForSingleObject(hThread, INFINITE);
        CloseHandle(hThread);
    }
    return EXIT_SUCCESS;
}

DWORD WINAPI ThreadFunc(LPVOID n)
{
    // Do something ...

    return 0;
}
```

Starting a New Thread with an Object

The hidden *this* pointer in C++ creates some problems when trying to start a thread. Here are the wrong way and the right way to fix it.

The Wrong Way

FAQ 43

How do I start a thread with a C++ member function?

When most people try to write their first multithreaded C++ function, they come up with the idea of starting an object in its own thread. Typically they have two member functions, one function that can be called to start the new thread and one function where the new thread begins. This example class *ThreadObject* is typical:

```
class ThreadObject
{
public:
    void StartThread();
    virtual DWORD WINAPI ThreadFunc(LPVOID param);
private:
    HANDLE  m_hThread;
    DWORD m_ThreadId;
};
```

ThreadObject encapsulates the thread startup and remembers information about the thread once it has started up. *ThreadObject* is a base class that can be subclassed by any object that needs to work in a new thread. The derived class overrides the virtual function `ThreadFunc()` and then gets the thread startup functionality "for free." Listing 9-2 is a short sample program that shows the class being used.

Listing 9-2. BADCLASS.CPP—How not to start a thread with an object

```
/*
 * BadClass.cpp
 *
 * Shows the wrong way to try to start a thread
 * based on a class member function.
 *
 * Build this file with the command line:
 *
 *    cl /MD BadClass.cpp
 *
 */
```

Listing 9-2 (continued)

```c
#include <windows.h>
#include <stdio.h>
#include <process.h>

typedef unsigned (WINAPI *PBEGINTHREADEX_THREADFUNC)(
    LPVOID lpThreadParameter
    );
typedef unsigned *PBEGINTHREADEX_THREADID;


class ThreadObject
{
public:
    ThreadObject();
    void StartThread();
    virtual DWORD WINAPI ThreadFunc(LPVOID param);
    void WaitForExit();
private:
    HANDLE  m_hThread;
    DWORD m_ThreadId;
};

ThreadObject::ThreadObject()
{
    m_hThread = NULL;
    m_ThreadId = 0;
}

void ThreadObject::StartThread()
{
    m_hThread = (HANDLE)_beginthreadex(NULL,
                0,
                (PBEGINTHREADEX_THREADFUNC)ThreadFunc,
                0,
                0,
                (PBEGINTHREADEX_THREADID)&m_ThreadId );
    if (m_hThread) {
        printf("Thread launched\n");
    }
}

void ThreadObject::WaitForExit()
{
    WaitForSingleObject(m_hThread, INFINITE);
    CloseHandle(m_hThread);
}
```

Listing 9-2 (continued)

```
DWORD WINAPI ThreadObject::ThreadFunc(LPVOID param)
{
    // Do something useful ...

    return 0;
}

void main()
{
    ThreadObject obj;

    obj.StartThread();
    obj.WaitForExit();
}
```

There is only one small problem with this program. It does not compile. If you try to compile it, you get this somewhat cryptic error with Visual C++ 4.1:

```
BadClass.cpp(48) : error C2643: illegal cast from pointer to member
```

The problem is even worse if you used the first workaround to the _begin-threadex bug and declared the ThreadFunc() to be *unsigned* instead of DWORD. In this case, you would not need the cast and the function call would look like this:

```
    m_hThread = (HANDLE)_beginthreadex(NULL,
        0,
        ThreadFunc,
        0,
        0,
        &m_ThreadId );
```

This version of the program actually compiles and links successfully. (It should not, this is a bug in the compiler.) The code, correctly, crashes as soon as you run it.

The screen prints out "Thread launched," so the call to _begin-threadex() worked, but the call stack in the debugger shows these calls:

```
`vcall'() + 4 bytes
BaseThreadStart@8 + 97 bytes
```

Apparently the thread itself crashed during startup, but there is no clear reason why.

Dissecting a C++ Member Function

To understand why the code in Listing 9-1 does not work, it is necessary to take a short refresher in how member functions actually work. A non-static class member function actually has a hidden parameter that gets passed on the stack. The compiler uses it whenever it accesses a member variable or whenever you explicitly use the *this* pointer inside a member function. Therefore, the function `ThreadObject::ThreadFunc(LPVOID param)` really has *two* parameters, the *this* pointer and *param*.

When the operating system starts a new thread, it also creates a new stack for the new thread. The operating system must recreate the function call to your thread startup function on this new stack. That is why it is so important that the calling convention, __cdecl or WINAPI (or __stdcall, which is the same as WINAPI), matches properly.

The reason that BADCLASS crashed is that `ThreadObject::Wait-ForExit()` expected a *this* pointer, but the operating system only knew to push *param* onto the new stack. Abracadabra: instant crash.

The Right Way

FAQ 44

How do I start a thread with a member function?

To start an object with a member function, use either a static member function or a C-style function, either of which then calls the proper member function. Essentially, these techniques just introduce a helper function that correctly builds the stack for calling a member function. Internally, the two methods are equivalent, but a static member function has the added advantage of having access to the class's private and protected member data.

Listing 9-3 gives an example that uses a static member function.

Listing 9-3. MEMBER.CPP—Starting a thread with a member function

```
/*
 * Member.cpp
 *
 * Shows how to start a thread based on a
 * class member function using either a static
 * member function or a C-style function.
 *
 * Build this file with the command line:
 *
```

Listing 9-3 (continued)

```
 *      cl /MD Member.cpp
 *
 */

#include <windows.h>
#include <stdio.h>
#include <process.h>

typedef unsigned (WINAPI *PBEGINTHREADEX_THREADFUNC)(
    LPVOID lpThreadParameter
    );
typedef unsigned *PBEGINTHREADEX_THREADID;


class ThreadObject
{
public:
    ThreadObject();
    void StartThread();
    static DWORD WINAPI ThreadFunc(LPVOID param);
    void WaitForExit();

protected:
    virtual DWORD ThreadMemberFunc();

    HANDLE   m_hThread;
    DWORD    m_ThreadId;
};

ThreadObject::ThreadObject()
{
    m_hThread = NULL;
    m_ThreadId = 0;
}

void ThreadObject::StartThread()
{
    m_hThread = (HANDLE)_beginthreadex(NULL,
        0,
        (PBEGINTHREADEX_THREADFUNC) ThreadFunc,
        (LPVOID) this,
        0,
        (PBEGINTHREADEX_THREADID) &m_ThreadId );
```

Listing 9-3 (continued)

```cpp
    if (m_hThread) {
        printf("Thread launched\n");
    }
}

void ThreadObject::WaitForExit()
{
    WaitForSingleObject(m_hThread, INFINITE);
    CloseHandle(m_hThread);
}

//
// This is a static member function.  Unlike
// C static functions, you only place the static
// declaration on the function declaration in the
// class, not on its implementation.
//
// Static member functions have no "this" pointer,
// but do have access rights.
//
DWORD WINAPI ThreadObject::ThreadFunc(LPVOID param)
{
    // Use the param as the address of the object
    ThreadObject* pto = (ThreadObject*)param;
    // Call the member function. Since we have a
    // proper object pointer, even virtual functions
    // will be called properly.
    return pto->ThreadMemberFunc();
}

DWORD ThreadObject::ThreadMemberFunc()
{
    // Do something useful ...
    return 0;
}


void main()
{
    ThreadObject obj;

    obj.StartThread();
    obj.WaitForExit();
}
```

To change the code to start up with a C-style function instead of a static member function, you need only to make a few minor changes to the code. You must declare `ThreadFunc()` with a C-style prototype, you must move the thread startup member function into the public section of the class, and you must take the class name off the member function. The complete program is on the CD-ROM in MEMBER2.CPP. Only the changes are shown here:

```
DWORD WINAPI ThreadFunc(LPVOID param);

class ThreadObject
{
public:
    // . . .

    // Thread member function must be public
    // or the C-style function will not have
    // access rights.
    virtual DWORD ThreadMemberFunc();

protected:
    // . . .
};

DWORD WINAPI ThreadFunc(LPVOID param)
{
    ThreadObject* pto = (ThreadObject*)param;
    return pto->ThreadMemberFunc();
}
```

Building Safer Critical Sections

There are so many advantages to doing multithreading with C++, when compared to C, it is hard to know where to begin talking about them. Over the next few sections, I will show how to write safer multithreaded code by relying on constructors and destructors, then show how to make the locking mechanisms interchangeable by using virtual functions and polymorphism.

Let's start by creating a simple class that embodies a critical section. We will use two of the most basic features of C++, the constructor and the destructor, which will provide guaranteed initialization and cleanup.

Remember in Chapter 3 when you always had to worry about calling functions such as `InitializeCriticalSection()` and `DeleteCritical-Section()`? By using the constructor and destructor you know these will always be called properly.

Listing 9-4 shows a very simple example.

Listing 9-4. Encapsulating a critical section with a C++ class

```
class CriticalSection
{
public:
    CriticalSection();
    ~CriticalSection();
    void Enter();
    void Leave();
private:
    CRITICAL_SECTION m_CritSect;
};

CriticalSection::CriticalSection()
{
    InitializeCriticalSection(&m_CritSect);
}

CriticalSection::~CriticalSection()
{
    DeleteCriticalSection(&m_CritSect);
}

void CriticalSection::Enter()
{
    EnterCriticalSection(&m_CritSect);
}

void CriticalSection::Leave()
{
    LeaveCriticalSection(&m_CritSect);
}
```

At first this class seems downright boring, but it actually provides some powerful advantages to using just the straight API functions. To protect a string variable, we add a member which is a CriticalSection. Because C++ will automatically call the constructor and destructor, developers using the string class will not have to make any changes to their code to handle the critical section.

For example, Listing 9-5 shows a String class that uses the CriticalSection class.

Listing 9-5. Using CriticalSection in a String class

```cpp
class String
{
public:
    String();
    virtual ~String();
    virtual void Set(char* str);
    int GetLength();
private:
    CriticalSection m_Sync;
    char*           m_pData;
};

String::String()
{
    // The constructor for m_Sync will have
    // already been called automatically because
    // it is a member variable.
    m_pData = NULL;
}

String::~String()
{
    // Use the "array delete" operator.
    // Note: "delete" checks for NULL automatically.
    m_Sync.Enter();
    delete [] m_pData;
    m_Sync.Leave();
    // The destructor for m_Sync will be
    // called automatically.
}

void String::Set(char *str)
{
    m_Sync.Enter();
    delete [] m_pData;
    m_pData = new char[::strlen(str)+1];
    ::strcpy(m_pData, str);
    m_Sync.Leave();
}

int String::GetLength()
{
    if (m_pData == NULL)
        return 0;
```

Listing 9-5 (continued)

```
    m_Sync.Enter();
    int len = ::strlen(m_pData);
    m_Sync.Leave();
    return len;
}
```

You can declare a variable of type String and use it without ever realizing that the critical section exists and that synchronization is taking place. For example, this function would now work fine in a multithreaded application:

```
void SomeFunction(String& str)
{
    str.Set("Multithreading");
}
```

Building Safer Locks

Now that we have built a critical section that automatically cleans itself up, let's create another class that automatically cleans up the lock. If you try to write a function like `Truncate()` with class CriticalSection as it is currently defined, you end up having to do a lot of manual cleanup. For example, in order to return from the middle of this function, you need to call `Release()` at each point of return. (Obviously, this particular example could be "fixed" by structuring the logic a little differently, but allow me to use the example for illustration.)

```
void String::Truncate(int length)
{
    if (m_pData == NULL)
        return 0;
    m_Sync.Enter();
    if (length >= GetLength())
    {
        m_Sync.Leave();
        return;
    }
    m_pData[length] = '\0';
    m_Sync.Leave();
}
```

We can create another class, Lock, whose constructor and destructor are responsible for entering and leaving the critical section (Listing 9-6). The constructor for Lock takes a CriticalSection as its only argument. Internally, Lock keeps a pointer to the CriticalSection being locked.

Listing 9-6. Abstracting synchronization objects

```
class Lock
{
public:
    Lock(CriticalSection* pCritSect);
    ~Lock();
private:
    CriticalSection* m_pCritical;
};

Lock::Lock(CriticalSection* pCritSect)
{
    m_pCritical = pCritSect;
    EnterCriticalSection(m_pCritical);
}

Lock::~Lock()
{
    LeaveCriticalSection(m_ pCritical);
}
```

Just like class CriticalSection, class Lock does not do much by itself, but look how easy it is to rewrite `Truncate()` using Lock. The destructor will automatically be called and the critical section will be unlocked. It is impossible to "forget" to unlock the critical section.

```
void String::Truncate(int length)
{
    if (m_pData == NULL)
        return 0;
    // Declaring a "Lock" variable will call
    // the constructor automatically.
    Lock lock(&m_Sync);
    if (length >= GetLength())
    {
        // lock cleans itself up automatically
        return;
    }
```

```
    m_pData[length] = '\0';
    // lock cleans itself up automatically
}
```

In C++, when a variable goes out of scope, its destructor is called automatically. Whether the function goes out of scope because of a return in the middle of the function or because the function "falls off the end," the destructor for the variable *lock* will still be called.

Building Interchangeable Locks

Now we will use C++ virtual functions to build synchronization mechanisms that can be freely interchanged. In C++, an abstract base class (ABC) can be used to define an object with a standard interface. We will build an ABC called LockableObject that can be used to build concrete classes that implement particular kinds of synchronization mechanisms.

Here is LockableObject. The design is similar to the CriticalSection class, except that we will rename `Enter()` and `Leave()` to reflect the fact that this class will be used for objects other than just for critical sections.

```
class LockableObject
{
public:
    LockableObject() {}
    virtual ~LockableObject() {}
    virtual void Lock() = 0;
    virtual void Unlock() = 0;
};
```

Now we will create version 2 of CriticalSection as a class derived from LockableObject (Listing 9-7). It looks almost the same, except for the declaration itself. Each of the member functions except the constructor is declared to be virtual.

Listing 9-7. A CriticalSection as a LockableObject

```
class CriticalSectionV2 : public LockableObject
{
public:
    CriticalSectionV2();
    virtual ~CriticalSectionV2();
    virtual void Lock();
    virtual void Unlock();
```

Listing 9-7 (continued)

```
private:
    CRITICAL_SECTION m_CritSect;
};

CriticalSectionV2::CriticalSectionV2()
{
    InitializeCriticalSection(&m_CritSect);
}

CriticalSectionV2::~CriticalSectionV2()
{
    DeleteCriticalSection(&m_CritSect);
}

void CriticalSectionV2::Lock()
{
    EnterCriticalSection(&m_CritSect);
}

void CriticalSectionV2::Unlock()
{
    LeaveCriticalSection(&m_CritSect);
}
```

Now we can write version 2 of the Lock class to generically take a LockableObject instead of taking a specific kind of synchronization object. Notice how virtual functions are used to lock the object without having to know the exact type of the object (Listing 9-8).

Listing 9-8. Making locking foolproof

```
class LockV2
{
public:
    LockV2(LockableObject* pLockable);
    ~LockV2();

private:
    LockableObject* m_pLockable;
};

LockV2::LockV2(LockableObject* pLockable)
```

Listing 9-8 (continued)

```
{
    m_pLockable = pLockable;
    m_pLockable->Lock();
}

LockV2::~LockV2()
{
    m_pLockable->Unlock();
}
```

We now have the classes CriticalSectionV2 and LockV2, which work in concert with each other. By using the C++ classes instead of directly calling the Win32 API, it is possible to guarantee that initialization and cleanup are always done and will be performed correctly. Now let's write version 2 of the String class to use these new synchronization classes (Listing 9-9).

Listing 9-9. Rewriting the String class with foolproof locking

```
class StringV2
{
public:
    StringV2();
    virtual ~StringV2();
    virtual void Set(char *str);
    int GetLength();
private:
    CriticalSectionV2 m_Lockable;
    char*             m_pData;
};

StringV2::StringV2()
{
    m_pData = NULL;
}

StringV2::~StringV2()
{
    // The program must ensure that
    // it is safe to destroy the object.
    delete [] m_pData;
}
```

Listing 9-9 (continued)

```
void StringV2::Set(char *str)
{
    LockV2 localLock(&m_Lockable);
    delete [] m_pData;
    m_pData = NULL;// In case new throws an exception
    m_pData = new char[::strlen(str)+1];
    ::strcpy(m_pData, str);
}

int StringV2::GetLength()
{
    LockV2 localLock(&m_Lockable);
    if (m_pData == NULL)
        return 0;
    return ::strlen(m_pData);
}
```

Handling Exceptions

A final tremendous advantage to implementing synchronization mechanisms using classes is that they will work with exception handling. For this section, I will assume you are already familiar with how Win32 exceptions and C++ exceptions work.

The advantage to exception handling is that it works outside of the standard function call/return value paradigm. When an exception is thrown, Win32 works in combination with the C++ run-time library to unwind the stack and clean up all variables. Writing code that is safe for exception handling is substantially more difficult in C because you have to do all the bookkeeping yourself. In C++, with a little bit of foresight, you can let the compiler do all of the work.

By using classes like the Lock class we developed in this chapter, locked objects will automatically be destructed as the stack unwinds. The destructor will unlock the object. The net result is that locks will be cleaned up automatically.

Summary

As you have seen throughout this book, one of the keys to success in multi-threading is absolute diligence in handling your data. *Do not ever touch data that you cannot guarantee to be in a consistent state.*

The true beauty of C++ is that you can use the class definition to absolutely guarantee that the data is valid. By confining the data to only the `private` portion of the class definition, you can force users to only access the data with well-defined mechanisms in the public member functions. Although it can easily be argued that all of these things can be done in C, there is substantial benefit to having the compiler enforce your design needs. It takes just one developer on a team to create an obscure bug by deciding to "take a shortcut" by accessing data directly without a lock.

Chapter 10

Threads in MFC

This chapter describes the MFC classes that support worker threads and user interface threads, as well as the classes that encapsulate Win32 synchronization objects.

IMPORTANT!

If you are creating threads in an MFC application, you *must* use `AfxBegin-Thread()` or `CWinThread::CreateThread()` if the thread will be making any calls to MFC or using any MFC data types.

The Microsoft Foundation Classes, or MFC as they are called, have arguably been the greatest step taken by Microsoft in reducing the tedium and difficulty in writing Windows applications. MFC made creating dialogs simple. It made message dispatching, with all the pitfalls of WPARAM and LPARAM, a no-brainer. It transparently worked around a whole bunch of bugs and idiosyncrasies in Windows. MFC even pushed a lot of people into the age of C++.

In the fairly recent past, MFC also gained support for multithreading. In the typical MFC style, the multithreading support hides a tremendous amount of the work going on under the hood. MFC also tries to "improve" on some of the Win32 concepts of multiple threads. I think its success in this area is debatable, but we will look at the design ideas and the subsequent implementation.

You have now seen two "layers" when writing applications for Win32. The first layer was the Win32 API which has the calls `CreateThread()` and `EndThread()`. The second layer was the C run-time library, with the calls `_beginthreadex()` and `_endthreadex()` taking care of additional initialization required by the run-time library. These calls in the C run-time library look very similar to their Win32 counterparts and are about as easy to use. The MFC multithreading classes are a whole different story.

Starting Worker Threads in MFC

You have already seen the somewhat theoretical distinction between worker threads and GUI threads. Both of them normally start life using `Create-Thread()` or `_beginthreadex()`. If the thread then calls `GetMessage()`, `CreateWindow()`, or other similar functions, then a message queue is created for the thread and it becomes a GUI thread. The MFC documentation refers to a GUI thread as a user interface thread.

MFC makes a strong distinction between the two variations. Both types are started with `AfxBeginThread()`, but MFC uses function overloading in C++ to provide two different declarations for the function. The compiler will automatically choose the right one based on the arguments that you supply.

The first form of `AfxBeginThread()` starts a worker thread, and it looks like this. Notice that this function uses C++ optional parameters. You can call this function with just the first two parameters and the other parameters will be defaulted as shown in the prototype.

CWinThread* AfxBeginThread(

```
AFX_THREADPROC pfnThreadProc,
LPVOID pParam,
int nPriority = THREAD_PRIORITY_NORMAL,
UINT nStackSize = 0,
DWORD dwCreateFlags = 0,
LPSECURITY_ATTRIBUTES lpSecurityAttrs = NULL
);
```

Parameters

pfnThreadProc	Function that will be used to start the thread.
pParam	Arbitrary 4-byte value that will be passed to the new thread. The pointer is simply passed through, so it can be an int, a pointer, or just zero.

nPriority	Priority of the new thread. If zero (the default) the new thread will have the same priority as the current thread.
nStackSize	Size of stack in bytes for the new thread. Like `CreateThread()`, this value can be zero to use the default size.
dwCreateFlags	This flag must be either zero or CREATE_ SUSPENDED. If omitted, this flag will be zero to start the thread running immediately.
lpSecurityAttrs	Security attributes as used by `CreateThread()`. Ignored in Windows 95.

Return Value

`AfxBeginThread()` returns NULL if it fails. Otherwise it returns a pointer to a new `CWinThread` object.

The first thing you will notice is that `AfxBeginThread()` returns a pointer to a `CWinThread`, not a HANDLE. Like other MFC classes, `CWinThread` is a "wrapper" for many of the Win32 functions that work with threads. Member functions such as `ResumeThread()` and `SetThreadPriority()` should be familiar names, but you call them as members of the object.

`CWinThread` was carefully planned to cure many of the difficulties that we have seen so far with `CreateThread()` and `_beginthreadex()`. `CWinThread` even correctly handles the cleanup that `_beginthread()` was supposed to. Depending on your needs, `CWinThread` is flexible enough to be a one-line thread startup using `AfxBeginThread()` or to be as tightly controlled as a raw `CreateThread()` call.

Listing 10-1 is an example of `AfxBeginThread()` at its simplest. This sample program is identical in functionality to the NUMBERS sample from Chapter 2, but the code has been redone in MFC and C++.

Listing 10-1. NUMBERS.CPP—Creating worker threads with AfxBeginThread()

```
/*
 * Numbers.cpp
 *
 * Demonstrate basic thread startup in MFC
 * using AfxBeginThread.
 *
```

Listing 10-1 (continued)

```
 * Compile with the IDE or: nmake -f numbers.mak
 */

#include <afxwin.h>

CWinApp TheApp;

UINT ThreadFunc(LPVOID);

int main()
{
    for (int i=0; i<5; i++)
    {
        if (AfxBeginThread( ThreadFunc, (LPVOID)i ))
            printf("Thread launched %d\n", i);
    }

    // Wait for the threads to complete.
    Sleep(2000);

    return 0;
}


UINT ThreadFunc(LPVOID n)
{
    for (int i=0;i<10;i++)
        printf("%d%d%d%d%d%d%d%d\n",n,n,n,n,n,n,n,n);
    return 0;
}
```

Compared to the difficulty of writing this in C, this version is a breeze. We did not have to provide any of the more obscure parameters to `AfxBegin-Thread()`, we did not have to declare variables to store things like the thread ID, and, best of all, we did not have to worry about closing the handle! Let's look at how these things are accomplished.

- **Cleaning up the `CWinThread` object.**   By default, the `CWinThread` object will automatically be deleted when the thread terminates. This happens because MFC inserts its own thread startup function before yours that takes care of the cleanup. The good news is that things are simplified for the beginning developer. The bad news is that it now takes a little more work to make the `CWinThread` object stick around so that you can wait on it. I'll show how to do this shortly.

- **Closing the handle to the thread.**   The same cleanup routine that deletes the `CWinThread` object also closes the handle to the thread. The handle is closed when the thread finishes running.
- **Storing the handle and the thread ID.**   This information is stored as member variables of the `CWinThread` object. The handle is stored in *m_hThread* and the thread ID is stored in *m_nThreadID*. However, this information is not safe to access without further work. You will see how in a moment.

MFC has the additional advantage of being heavily asserted. Like the MTVERIFY macro we have used in prior chapters, MFC contains logic in debug builds that makes sure that parameters are correct and that calls are succeeding. For example, if you pass NULL as the address of the thread startup function, then MFC will assert in the debug build and warn you of the error. The code that does this check inside MFC will not be compiled into the release build. You get the benefits of safety in the debug build and speed in the release build. The assertion checking built into MFC is one of MFC's most useful properties.

Safely Using AfxBeginThread()'s Return Value

You probably saw immediately that I called `Sleep()` in Listing 10-1 instead of putting in a call to `WaitForMultipleObjects()`. The reason is that this default usage of `CWinThread` has the same "gotcha" as `_beginthread()`. If the time it takes for the thread to start and exit again is very short, the `CWinThread` object may already have been deleted by the time `AfxBeginThread()` returns. In this situation, just trying to dereference the pointer to get at the thread's handle will cause your application to crash. Fortunately the workaround is simple and built into `CWinThread`. The tradeoff is that managing the object takes slightly more work.

FAQ 45

How do I stop a CWinThread class from deleting itself?

There is a member variable in `CWinThread` called *m_bAutoDelete*. This parameter prevents the `CWinThread` object from being deleted automatically. In order to set this variable without creating a race condition, you need to create the thread in a suspended state. Listing 10-2 shows NUMBERS2, which properly handles this startup logic.

Listing 10-2. NUMBERS2.CPP—AfxBeginThread() with auto-delete disabled

```cpp
/*
 * Numbers2.cpp
 *
 * Demonstrate thread startup in MFC
 * using AfxBeginThread, but prevent
 * CWinThread from auto-deletion so that
 * we can wait on the thread.
 *
 * Compile with the IDE or: nmake -f numbers2.mak
 */

#include <afxwin.h>

CWinApp TheApp;

UINT ThreadFunc(LPVOID);

int main()
{
    CWinThread* pThreads[5];

    for (int i=0; i<5; i++)
    {
        pThreads[i] = AfxBeginThread(
                        ThreadFunc,
                        (LPVOID)i,
                        THREAD_PRIORITY_NORMAL,
                        0,
                        CREATE_SUSPENDED
                      );
        ASSERT(pThreads[i]);
        pThreads[i]->m_bAutoDelete = FALSE;
        pThreads[i]->ResumeThread();
        printf("Thread launched %d\n", i);
    }

    for (i=0; i<5; i++)
    {
        WaitForSingleObject(pThreads[i]->m_hThread, INFINITE);
        delete pThreads[i];
    }

    return 0;
}
```

Listing 10-2 (continued)

```
UINT ThreadFunc(LPVOID n)
{
    for (int i=0;i<10;i++)
        printf("%d%d%d%d%d%d%d%d\n",n,n,n,n,n,n,n,n);
    return 0;
}
```

The startup logic to properly initialize the values in the CWinThread object is as follows. You will see this again when we derive our own class from CWinThread that needs to be properly initialized.

1. Create the thread with the flag CREATE_SUSPENDED.
2. Set the members of the CWinThread object.
3. Call ResumeThread().

Obviously, if you set the object so it does not auto-delete then you need to take care of deleting it yourself. In NUMBERS2 the object is deleted with this code:

```
    delete pThreads[i];
```

Notice that NUMBERS2 does not call CloseHandle() on the thread handle. The destructor for CWinThread will take care of this automatically, regardless of whether *m_bAutoDelete* is set.

Also notice that we are using the MFC form of ResumeThread(), not the raw Win32 form. This MFC call does some assertion checking in the debug build, then calls the Win32 form of ResumeThread(). The call is implemented as an inline function, so there is no speed penalty for using it.

```
    pThreads[i]->ResumeThread();
```

Starting from Scratch

You can use CWinThread yourself to obtain even finer control than you would get from AfxBeginThread(). AfxBeginThread() is just a helper function that wraps the use of CWinThread. AfxBeginThread() goes through the following steps:

1. Allocates a new CWinThread object on the heap.
2. Calls CWinThread::CreateThread() and sets the thread to start suspended.

3. Sets the thread's priority.
4. Calls `CWinThread::ResumeThread()`.

Obviously, you could do this yourself very easily. Here is why you might want to. The `CWinThread` structure is an ideal place to store interthread communication information, not to mention thread startup information. Using `_beginthreadex()` or `CreateThread()`, you would allocate a structure of startup information and pass a pointer to this structure as the LPVOID startup parameter to the thread function.

To make this work, you start by subclassing `CWinThread` and adding your own data to it. As an additional benefit, we can set up the constructor of the thread to implicitly disable the auto-delete behavior when the object is created. Listing 10-3 is an example of creating your own class from a `CWinThread` called `CUserThread`. While we are at it, we can make the startup function a static member of the class as we saw in Chapter 9. The biggest advantage to doing this is that we reduce namespace pollution. We can have twenty functions all named `ThreadFunc()`, each of which is for a different kind of thread and which is identified by the class of which it is a member. In this case, the full name of the startup function is `CUserThread::ThreadFunc()`.

Listing 10-3. NUMCLASS.CPP—MFC worker threads without AfxBeginClass()

```
/*
 * NumClass.cpp
 *
 * Demonstrate worker thread startup in MFC
 * without AfxBeginThread.
 *
 * Compile with the IDE or: nmake -f NumClass.mak
 */

#include <afxwin.h>

CWinApp TheApp;


class CUserThread : public CWinThread
{
public:   // Member functions
    CUserThread(AFX_THREADPROC pfnThreadProc);

    static UINT ThreadFunc(LPVOID param);
```

Listing 10-3 (continued)

```
public:  // Member data
    int m_nStartCounter;

protected: // The "real" startup function
    virtual void Go();
};

CUserThread::CUserThread(AFX_THREADPROC pfnThreadProc)
 : CWinThread(pfnThreadProc, NULL)  // Undocumented constructor
{
    m_bAutoDelete = FALSE;

    // Set the pointer to the class to be the startup value.
    // m_pThreadParams is undocumented,
    // but there is no workaround.
    m_pThreadParams = this;
}


int main()
{
    CUserThread* pThreads[5];

    for (int i=0; i<5; i++)
    {
        // Pass our static member as the startup function
        pThreads[i] = new CUserThread( CUserThread::ThreadFunc );

        // Set the appropriate member variable
        pThreads[i]->m_nStartCounter = i;

        // Start the thread in motion
        VERIFY(
          pThreads[i]->CreateThread() );
        printf("Thread launched %d\n", i);
    }

    for (i=0; i<5; i++)
    {
        WaitForSingleObject(pThreads[i]->m_hThread, INFINITE);
        delete pThreads[i];
    }

    return 0;
}
```

Listing 10-3 (continued)

```
// static
UINT CUserThread::ThreadFunc(LPVOID n)
{
    CUserThread* pThread = (CUserThread*)n;
    pThread->Go();
    return 0;
}

void CUserThread::Go()
{
    int n = m_nStartCounter;
    for (int i=0;i<10;i++)
        printf("%d%d%d%d%d%d%d%d\n",n,n,n,n,n,n,n,n);
}
```

Writing the sample application in Listing 10-3 identified an interesting problem with MFC. `AfxBeginThread()` uses an undocumented constructor for `CWinThread` in order to set the startup function. The omission is curious because without that constructor it is impossible to customize `CWinThread` for non-GUI threads!

The undocumented constructor actually takes two arguments, the startup function and the startup parameter. The constructor for `CUserThread` uses an initializer list to call the nondefault constructor for `CWinThread`, which almost gives us the behavior we need. However, we need to set the (also undocumented) member variable *CWinThread::m_pThreadParam*, which will eventually become the startup parameter of the thread function.

After allocating the `CUserThread` structure, we initialize the member data that the thread will use while it runs, then call the member function `CreateThread()`. We'll use the default form with no parameters, which makes the function call very easy to write.

If you want to reuse this code, you can derive your own class from `CUserThread`, override the member function `Go()`, and you will be off and running.

Starting User Interface Threads in MFC

Starting user interface threads in MFC is very different than starting worker threads. You still use `CWinThread` and `AfxBeginThread()`, but they are both used very differently than you would for a worker thread. To begin with, MFC already does a lot of the things we just talked about in terms of abstracting the process of creating a thread.

AfxBeginThread(), Act II

Here is the function prototype for the second form of `AfxBeginThread()`.

CWinThread* AfxBeginThread(

CRuntimeClass* pThreadClass,
int nPriority = **THREAD_PRIORITY_NORMAL,**
UINT nStackSize = **0,**
DWORD dwCreateFlags = **0,**
LPSECURITY_ATTRIBUTES lpSecurityAttrs = **NULL**
);

Parameters

pThreadClass   Pointer to the runtime class you have created that derives from `CWinThread`.

nPriority   Priority of the new thread. If zero (the default) the new thread will have the same priority as the current thread.

nStackSize   Size of stack in bytes for the new thread. Like `CreateThread()`, this value can be zero to use the default size.

dwCreateFlags   This flag must be either zero or CREATE_ SUSPENDED. If omitted, this flag will be zero to start the thread running immediately.

lpSecurityAttrs   Security attributes as used by `Create-Thread()`. Ignored on Windows 95.

Return Value

`AfxBeginThread()` returns NULL if it fails. Otherwise it returns a pointer to a new `CWinThread` object.

When I took my first quick look at this function, it looked like a slight variation on `CreateThread()` and I thought, "No problem." When I went to put it into my code, I tried to put in the first argument and came up against a blank wall. I suddenly realized that the way this call worked was *very* different.

The user interface thread version of `AfxBeginThread()` expects to allocate a class that you specify according to *pThreadClass*. This class must be derived from `CWinThread`. `CWinThread` provides a variety of virtual functions that you can override to help with message processing, thread startup and shutdown, and even exception processing. These virtual functions are as follows:

* `InitInstance()`
* `ExitInstance()`
* `OnIdle()`
* `PreTranslateMessage()`
* `IsIdleMessage()`
* `ProcessWndProcException()`
* `ProcessMessageFilter()`
* `Run()`

It is not necessary to override any of these functions. By default, MFC will start a message loop as soon as `InitInstance()` has finished.

FAQ 46

What is the relationship between CWinApp and the primary thread?

Some of these function names should look familiar to you if you have done much MFC programming. `InitInstance()` and `ExitInstance()` are automatically generated by the AppWizard for every MFC program, and `PreTranslateMessage()` is a familiar sight to anyone who has tried to go around MFC's message routing. It turns out that the application object, which is contained in every MFC program, is actually derived from `CWinThread`! Therefore the primary thread integrates seamlessly and consistently with the application and with other threads.

Building an MFC User Interface Thread with ClassWizard

Back to the issue at hand. How do you set up your own `CWinThread`-derived object that you can give to `AfxBeginThread()`? The simplest way is to use the wizards that are built into Visual C++. In Visual C++ version 4.x, the procedure is as follows:

1. Open your project workspace. The project must be an MFC application.
2. Select ClassWizard from the View menu.
3. Click on the Add Class button.
4. Choose New… from the pop-up menu.
5. You will see the Create New Class dialog, which is shown in Figure 10-1.
6. Enter a name for the class, such as `CDemoThread`.
7. Here is the key: Select `CWinThread` in the Base Class combo box.
8. Click the Create button.

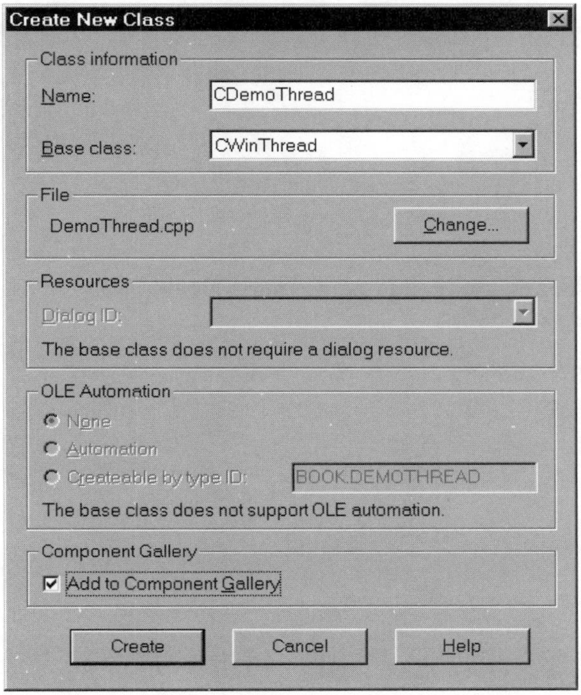

Figure 10-1. The Create New Class dialog.

In this example, the wizard would create two files, DemoThread.cpp and DemoThread.h, and add them to the project. In DemoThread.cpp, you will find that the wizard has already written skeletons for `InitInstance()` and `ExitInstance()` and created the top-level message map for this thread. How much easier could it be?

The declaration for `CDemoThread` that the wizard created is shown in Listing 10-4.

Listing 10-4. CDemoThread after being created by ClassWizard

```
class CDemoThread : public CWinThread
{
    DECLARE_DYNCREATE(CDemoThread)
protected:
    CDemoThread();   // protected constructor used by dynamic creation
```

Listing 10-4 (continued)

```
// Attributes
public:

// Operations
public:

// Overrides
    // ClassWizard generated virtual function overrides
    //{{AFX_VIRTUAL(CDemoThread)
    public:
    virtual BOOL InitInstance();
    virtual int ExitInstance();
    //}}AFX_VIRTUAL

// Implementation
protected:
    virtual ~CDemoThread();

    // Generated message map functions
    //{{AFX_MSG(CDemoThread)
    // NOTE - the ClassWizard will add and remove member functions here.
    //}}AFX_MSG

    DECLARE_MESSAGE_MAP()
};
```

At the beginning of the class declaration you will see the macro DECLARE_DYNCREATE used. This macro implements run-time typing and factory creation, and this is the key to making `CDemoThread` work with `AfxBeginThread()`. In `DemoThread.cpp` you would see the macro IMPLEMENT_DYNCREATE used. These two macros always go together.

Launching the User Interface Thread

FAQ 47

How do I use the *pThread-Class* parameter to `AfxBeginThread()`?

Once the wizard has created the thread class with the DYNCREATE macros, you are ready to use `AfxBeginThread()`. A suitable call for starting this thread would look like this:

```
CDemoThread* pThread = (CDemoThread*)AfxBeginThread(
                RUNTIME_CLASS(CDemoThread)
        );
```

What gets passed internally is a data structure that allows MFC to create an instance of the class at runtime. Just as with the worker thread, when you create a user interface thread with `AfxBeginThread()`, you let the function allocate the data structure and return it. Just as with worker threads, you can set *m_bAutoDelete* to FALSE in your constructor. In this case it is a little easier because you have already derived the class and the constructor will be called by `AfxBeginThread()`.

Once the thread has started, MFC will call your `InitInstance()` member function and enter the message loop. The message map for your `CWinThread`-derived class will be used for message dispatching.

Working with MFC Objects

There is one significant limitation to multithreading MFC applications that will affect almost everything you do. The mapping between MFC objects and Win32 handles is kept in thread local storage. Therefore, you cannot pass an MFC object from one thread to another, nor can you pass a pointer to an MFC object between threads. This list of objects includes, but is not limited to, `CWnd`, `CDC`, `CPen`, `CBrush`, `CFont`, `CBitmap`, and `CPalette`. This restriction exists to prevent the need for creating synchronization mechanisms around all of these objects, which would slow down MFC significantly.

There are some several ramifications to this restriction. If two threads each call `CWnd::GetDlgItem()` to retrieve a pointer to a dialog control such as an edit control, each thread would get a different pointer back, even if both asked for the same control. MFC often creates temporary objects when a request is made for a pointer to an object that has no permanent MFC structure. For example, `CWnd::GetDlgItem()` usually creates a temporary object when asked for a pointer to a `CEdit*` or a `CStatic*`. These objects are then cleaned up the next time the application enters an idle loop. If these objects were shared across threads, then MFC would not be able to predict their lifetime and could not perform cleanup. Therefore, MFC creates a new object for each thread that requests one.

The limitation on passing objects between threads means that you cannot put a pointer to a `CWnd` in a structure that is used by a worker thread, nor can you pass a pointer to a `CDialog` or `CView` to another thread. This restriction quickly becomes aggravating when you need to call a member function in the view or in the document, particularly functions such as `UpdateAllViews()`.

MFC checks for cross-thread usage in many places. Whenever MFC calls ASSERT_VALID on an object, it checks to make sure that the object is in the map kept in thread local storage. If you try to call a function such as `CWnd::UpdateAllViews()`, then `CWnd::AssertValid()` generates an assertion when the program is run. The following note comes right after this assert:

```
// Note: if either of the above asserts fire and you are
// writing a multithreaded application, it is likely that
// you have passed a C++ object from one thread to another
// and have used that object in a way that was not intended.
// (only simple inline wrapper functions should be used)
//
// In general, CWnd objects should be passed by HWND from
// one thread to another.  The receiving thread can wrap
// the HWND with a CWnd object by using CWnd::FromHandle.
//
// It is dangerous to pass C++ objects from one thread to
// another, unless the objects are designed to be used in
// such a manner.
```

The use of thread local storage explains why it is important to use `Afx-BeginThread()` to start a user-interface thread in MFC. If you were to use `CreateThread()` or `_beginthreadex()`, MFC would not be given an opportunity to create the structures necessary to maintain its handles.

There is a workaround to the problem of sharing objects between threads, but it is inconvenient. Instead of passing the MFC object, pass the handle to the object. You can get the handle to an object derived from `CGdiObject` with `GetSafeHandle()`. Such objects include `CPen` and `CPalette`. You can get the handle to an object derived from `CWnd`, such as a `CDialog`, using `GetSafeHWnd()`.

Once you pass the handle to the new thread, the thread can attach the handle to a new MFC object using `FromHandle()` to create a temporary object or `Attach()` for a permanent object. For example, if you pass an `HDC` to a thread, you could attach the `HDC` to a permanent `CDC` object with the following code:

```
HDC hOriginalDC = // ...
CDC dc;
dc.Attach(hOriginalDC);
```

Before exiting, the thread should call `Detach()` like this:

```
dc.Detach();
```

If the thread was going to use the value only briefly, it could create a temporary object like this:

```
CDC* pDC = CDC::FromHandle(hOriginalDC);
```

Not all MFC objects can easily be passed with this technique. `CView` is a good example. You can easily retrieve the window handle for a view and pass it to a new thread, but the best the new thread could do would be to attach the handle to a `CWnd`. There is no `CView::FromHandle()` function that will create a temporary view that mirrors the original. The original `CView` structure is not available, so all the related view information is not available, either.

Going back to the example of `UpdateAllViews()`, the pointers that this function works with are buried inside of the document and cannot be altered. Therefore there is no way that another thread will be able to call this function. The only way to work around this problem is to send a user-defined message back to the original thread to tell it to update its views.

The Microsoft MFC sample program MTGDI demonstrates the techniques discussed above. It comes with Visual C++.

Synchronization in MFC

In Chapter 9 we saw how to use C++ to simplify the locking and unlocking of synchronization objects. MFC has built-in classes for manipulating synchronization objects in this manner. For each of the standard Win32 synchronization objects (critical sections, events, mutexes, and semaphores), MFC provides a class to encapsulate its functionality, as shown in this chart:

Object name	*MFC class name*
Critical section	CCriticalSection
Event	CEvent
Semaphore	CSemaphore
Mutex	CMutex

Although each type has a different constructor that takes advantage of its particular functionality, there is a basic common interface for all of the classes. Each of these classes is derived from `CSyncObject`, which provides a minimally consistent interface to each object. In other words, no matter what kind of object you have, just call the `Lock()` or `Unlock()` member functions. A `CSyncObject` can also be passed to any Win32 function that expects a HANDLE to a synchronization object. I think this functionality makes the objects much easier to use than trying to remember the various API calls that are used to lock or unlock each kind of object.

Note: You must #include <afxmt.h> to use the MFC synchronization objects.

Writing the String Class with MFC

Let's rewrite the String class from Chapter 9 using the synchronization classes in MFC (see Listing 10-5). We'll call the class StringV3. About the only changes we need to make are to use CCriticalSection instead of CriticalSection and to call Lock() and Unlock() instead of Enter() and Leave().

*Warning: For performance reasons, the MFC string-handling class CString **does not** implement thread-safe locking. To make CString thread-safe you must write the support yourself.*

Listing 10-5. Writing a String class with MFC synchronization classes

```cpp
class StringV3
{
public:
    StringV3();
    virtual ~StringV3();
    virtual void Set(char *str);
    int GetLength();
private:
    CCriticalSection m_Sync;
    char*           m_pData;
};

StringV3::StringV3()
{
    // The constructor for m_Sync will have
    // already been called automatically because
    // it is a member variable.
    m_pData = NULL;
}

StringV3::~StringV3()
{
    // Use the "array delete" operator.
    // Note: "delete" checks for NULL automatically.
    m_Sync.Lock();
```

Listing 10-5 (continued)

```
    delete [] m_pData;
    m_Sync.Unlock();
    // The destructor for m_Sync will be
    // called automatically.
}

void StringV3::Set(char *str)
{
    m_Sync.Lock();
    delete [] m_pData;
    m_pData = new char[::strlen(str)+1];
    ::strcpy(m_pData, str);
    m_Sync.Unlock();
}

int StringV3::GetLength()
{
    if (m_pData == NULL)
        return 0;
    m_Sync.Lock();
    int len = ::strlen(m_pData);
    m_Sync.Unlock();
    return len;
}
```

Encapsulating the Lock Operation in MFC

The implementation of StringV3 in Listing 10-5 suffers from the same problem we had with our classes in Chapter 9. We have to be very careful to remember to always call `Unlock()` before returning, and the locks will not be cleaned up during C++ exception handling.

MFC offers two classes that fix this problem. The first, `CSingleLock`, is very similar to the Lock class we wrote in Chapter 9. Its use is shown in Listing 10-6. The second, `CMultiLock`, encapsulates the functionality of `WaitForMultipleObjects()`.

Listing 10-6. A better String class with CSingleLock

```
class StringV4
{
public:
    StringV4();
```

Listing 10-6 (continued)

```
    virtual ~StringV4();
    virtual void Set(char* str);
    inr GetLength();
private:
    CSyncObject* m_pLockable;
    char*        m_pData;
};

StringV4::StringV4()
{
    m_pData = NULL;
    m_pLockable = new CMutex;
}

StringV4::~StringV4()
{
    delete [] m_pData;

    delete m_pLockable;
}

void StringV4::Set(char *str)
{
    CSingleLock localLock(m_pLockable, TRUE);
    delete [] m_pData;
    m_pData = NULL;// In case new throws an exception
    m_pData = new char[::strlen(str)+1];
    ::strcpy(m_pData, str);
}

int StringV4::GetLength()
{
    CSingleLock localLock(m_pLockable, TRUE);
    if (m_pData == NULL)
        return 0;
    return ::strlen(m_pData);
}
```

Limitations of MFC Synchronization

Although the synchronization classes in MFC are very useful for basic structure locking, they fall short for more complex tasks. For example, there is no support for the alertable forms of WaitForSingleObject() and WaitFor-MultipleObjects(), so overlapped I/O with APCs will not be serviced.

Also, objects that may stay locked for several seconds will typically require the application to return to the main message loop and then use `MsgWait-ForMultipleObjects()`. The MFC classes do not allow for this behavior.

Supporting MsgWaitForMultipleObjects() in MFC

Earlier in the book we saw how to modify a main message loop to support `MsgWaitForMultipleObjects()` so that the application could efficiently wait on either messages or on kernel objects. Doing this in MFC is a little bit trickier because MFC runs the message loop.

There are two possible solutions. The first is to create another thread that does the waiting, and then send a message to the primary thread when an object becomes signaled. This has the advantage of being fairly easy to implement, but has a much higher overhead because of the context switching and message processing that must happen.

The alternative is to rewrite MFC's message loop. Fortunately the message loop resides in virtual functions that you can override. It lives in `CWinThread::Run()` and `CWinThread::PumpMessage()`, the sources for which are in THRDCORE.CPP in MFC\SRC.

The downside to this solution is that `PumpMessage()` is an undocumented call, and the logic in `Run()` to properly handle idle calls is somewhat obscure. If either of these member functions were to be changed in future versions of MFC, you would have to manually propagate the changes to your own version of these functions.

The code to override these functions is not presented here because it is very dependent on the version of MFC and is tightly tied to the structure of your application.

Summary

In this chapter you saw how to create worker threads and user interface threads in MFC, either with a single call to `AfxBeginThread()` or with a lower-level call to `CWinThread::CreateThread()`. You also saw how to derive a class from `CWinThread` that could be passed to `AfxBegin-Thread()` for user interface threads. Finally, we went over the basics of how MFC encapsulates the Win32 synchronization objects.

Chapter 11

GDI/Window Management

This chapter describes how message queues and threads work together and why you should not *use one thread per window in an MDI application.*

You know those "word association" psychological tests that TV shows are so fond of parodying? The doctor says one word, and the patient has to say the first word that comes to mind. Try saying the word "multithread" to a Win16 developer. You'll discover that "MDI" (multiple document interface) comes up over and over again.

MDI would seem to be the perfect place to start multithreading your application. Each MDI window acts like its own mini-application, so you can let the GUI thread of one MDI window print its contents while another GUI thread in another window takes care of editing.

Before we go any further, let me save you a lot of aggravation and give you a warning about using a separate user interface thread for each MDI window:

Don't do it!

Over the next few sections I will explain the architecture of message queues in Windows, why it leads to my recommendation, and how to design your application to get the desired effect.

Thread Message Queues

Let's take a moment and compare how message queues are set up in Win16 and Win32. In Win16, all windows share the same message queue. If one application stops processing its entries in the message queue, then all windows stop responding. This was a significant problem in Windows 3.x and one of the biggest reasons the system would lock up and stop responding.

In Win32, each thread has its own message queue. This does *not* mean that each window has its own message queue, because one thread can create many windows. If a thread stops responding or gets stuck in a long computation, then any windows created by that thread will stop responding, but other windows in the system will continue working.

There is a very basic rule that governs how threads, messages, and windows interact in Win32:

The thread that creates a window will process all messages sent to that window.

The ramifications of this statement are far-reaching. Remember that everything that happens to a window is controlled with messages and message passing. This fact is often obscured with the use of MFC and the message crackers in WINDOWSX.H. For example, if you put new text in an edit control using `SetWindowText()`, the control is updated by sending WM_SETTEXT to the edit control's window procedure.

Anything you do to a window will eventually be handled by the window procedure for that window and therefore by the thread that created that window. This architecture may lead to counterintuitive behavior in your code. For example, I wanted to use a separate thread to fill a list box that held thousands of items. I expected that I would be able to process the list box events in the thread where I was filling the list box.

What happened was that every time I added an item, the message was sent to my primary thread. My primary thread had created the control, and was therefore responsible for processing the control's messages. Each control on a dialog is a separate window and has its own window procedure.

From the perspective of Windows, there are many more windows on the screen than those that have a title bar and a menu. Remember that every control on the screen is a separate window with a separate window procedure. This means that a single dialog can be made of up of many windows. For example, the standard File Open dialog in Windows 95 is shown in Figure 11-1.

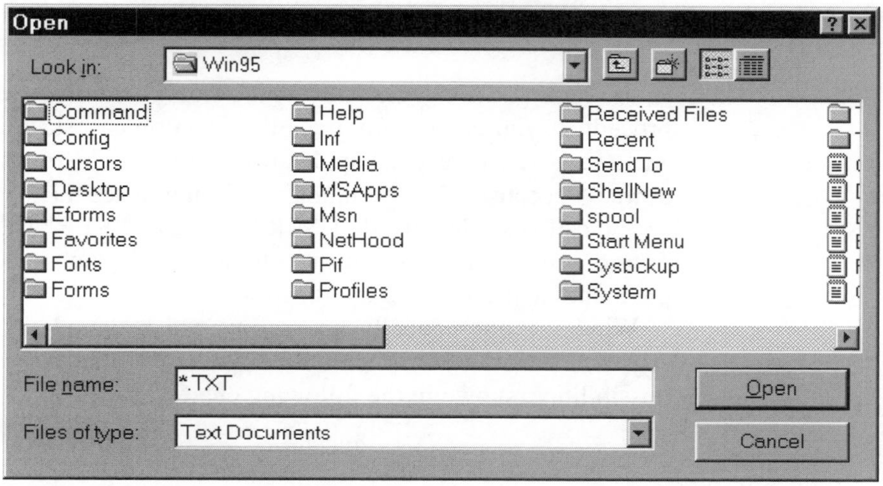

Figure 11-1. The File / Open dialog.

The results of running SPY++ on this window are shown in Figure 11-2. Each individual control is a separate window. Each of these windows has its own window procedure and has a thread designated to process all of its messages.

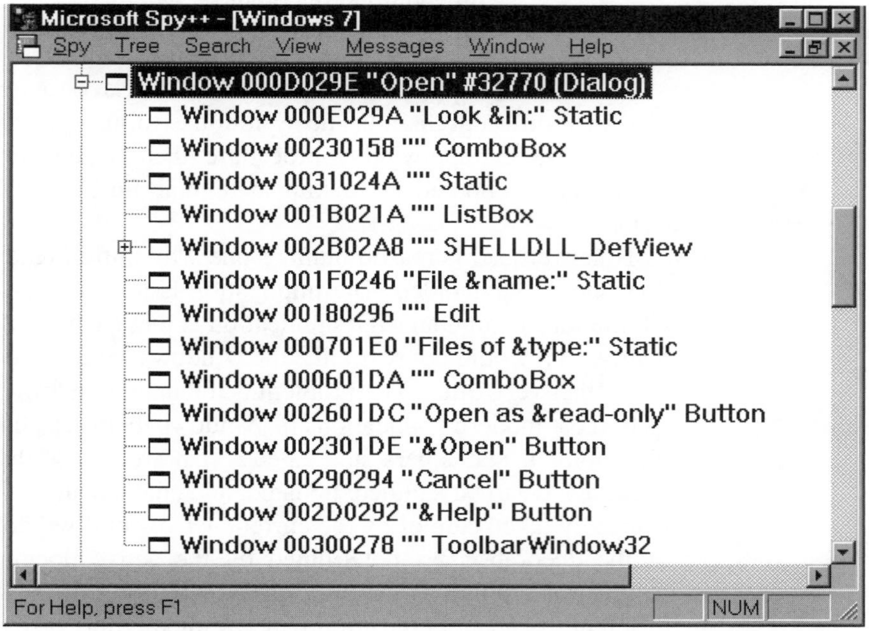

Figure 11-2. Dialog window list in SPY++.

How Messages Travel

If you look at the call stack in Windows NT when you are inside a window procedure, you can usually trace the function call stack all the way back to `WinMain()`, where your application started. (This does not work in Windows 95 because of 16-bit thunking.) You will see that some of the functions on the call stack live inside USER32.DLL and KERNEL.DLL. These functions are responsible for figuring out how to dispatch a message to a window procedure and setting up the function call.

Windows automatically figures out which thread should receive a message and how the thread should be notified of that message. There are four possibilities, shown in the following chart.

	SendMessage()	*PostMessage()*
Same thread	Call window procedure with a function call.	Place message in queue and return immediately.
Different Thread	Switch to new thread and call window procedure with a function call. `SendMessage()` will not return until the window procedure in the other thread returns.	`PostMessage()` returns immediately. Message is placed in the other thread's message queue.

Notice what happens when you send a message to a window that is handled by a different thread. The system has to make a context switch to that other thread, call the window procedure, then make a context switch back to the caller. Compared to making a regular function call, the overhead is tremendous.

This overhead is reason number one why multithreading each MDI window should be avoided. The implication is not immediately obvious. After all, the idea behind an MDI application is that each window works independently, so it would not seem like the windows would be communicating with each other very often. The problem is the main window.

In most modern applications in Windows there are all sorts of decorations like toolbars, status bars, and palettes that are part of the main window. All of these have to be handled, updated, and enabled and disabled. This process is usually taken care of by the current active child window because the state of the decorations is determined by the active document. In MFC, this behavior is typified by the `OnUpdate()` routines. If the decorations live in a different thread from the child window, then it may take hundreds of context switches to update all of the decorations. The result is a severe impact on performance.

Sleepwalking Threads

It is very important to understand that your thread is put to sleep when you send a message to another thread. This behavior gives the appearance that `SendMessage()` is a typical function call.

While your thread is waiting for `SendMessage()` to return, it will still process any `SendMessage()` calls to windows that it owns. This happens even though the thread is not in its main message loop where it can call `GetMessage()` or `DispatchMessage()`. If Windows did not do this, then any windows that the thread owned would stop responding and would not be able to answer `SendMessage()` calls.

Although the waiting thread will process messages from `SendMessage()`, it will not process other kinds of messages, such as those on the message queue. This could cause a problem if the destination thread put up a dialog box or entered a message loop without returning from the `SendMessage()`. To work around the problem, the waiting thread is automatically woken up if the destination thread calls any of the following functions:

```
DialogBox()
DialogBoxIndirect()
DialogBoxIndirectParam()
DialogBoxParam()
GetMessage()
MessageBox()
PeekMessage()
```

It is also possible to determine that a thread is inside a `SendMessage()` call and explicitly wake up the caller. This could be useful if you needed to start a long computation for which the caller does not need the results.

The function `InSendMessage()` returns TRUE if a thread is processing a message that was sent by another thread. `InSendMessage()` takes no arguments.

To allow the calling thread to continue, call `ReplyMessage()`.

BOOL ReplyMessage(
LRESULT lResult
);

Parameters

lResult	This value will be returned to the caller by `SendMessage()`. Its meaning is message-dependent.

Return Value

Returns TRUE if this thread was processing a message from another thread, otherwise FALSE.

Pitfalls with Interthread Messages

When Windows has to send a message across threads, regardless of whether the threads are in the same process, there is always the possibility that the destination thread will lock up or otherwise fail and the thread that sent the message will never wake up.

This is a problem particularly when you are sending messages across processes, where you may not be able to guarantee the behavior of the destination thread. Win32 provides two functions to help solve this problem.

The first function is `SendMessageTimeout()`. This function provides fine control over how the call behaves. It allows you to specify a timeout, after which the function will return regardless of whether the destination returns. It can also abort automatically if the destination thread appears to be hung.

The second function is `SendMessageCallback()`. This function returns immediately, but one of its parameters is a function that should be called when and if the `SendMessage()` call succeeds.

You can find details about these functions in the *Win32 Programmer's Reference*.

GUI Performance

The big question that has to be answered when analyzing whether to give each MDI window its own thread is, "What will I gain?" The usual answer to this question is that you can allow one window (and therefore one thread) to do calculations while the other windows are still responsive.

If you try running an application that runs like this, you discover that the window that is recalculating appears to become "dead." It no longer responds to paint messages, the cursor does not change over the window, and the menus and toolbars do not update properly. Because the thread is in the middle of recalculating, it cannot run the window's message loop and process messages. The application stays responsive, but the price is that a particular window may appear dead.

The other problem with having one thread per MDI child is that you may end up reducing performance on redraws. Even on a multiprocessor system, there is still usually only one graphics card, which becomes the bottleneck for all screen updates. No matter how many threads you have running, you will not be able to speed up the graphics card. Therefore, all of the context switching going on to handle the redrawing of each window is only going to *decrease* the redraw performance.

I can hear you saying "But, but, but..." even now. Bear with me and I will show you an alternative architecture that properly solves many of the problems that you wanted to solve with one thread per MDI child window.

Multithreading MDI with Worker Threads

The strategy that I recommend for efficiently using multiple threads in an MDI application is to have a single thread that handles all user input and all user interface management, and use worker threads for calculation and for printing. You may also have other threads that are handling your disk or network I/O.

No matter how you divide up the workload among threads, it is very important that the primary thread that runs the frame window always stays responsive and is not bogged down with calculations. Later you will see the CANCEL example that demonstrates the problems of doing calculations in a thread with a message loop.

Rendering

Ideally your primary thread should do all the painting, or the physical moving of the data to the screen. You can still multithread this process by using worker threads to calculate what to display, then painting with the primary thread. One way to do this would be to have one background rendering thread for each MDI window. Each thread would render to its own memory device context and so would be completely separated from other rendering threads. Because the threads would be rendering to an off-screen device context, they would not be conflicting with the primary thread. When the background threads complete, they could notify the primary thread, which could blit the memory device context to the screen.

Some of the Microsoft sample code recommends using a separate thread for graphics. With certain exceptions, I disagree with this approach for two reasons. The first is what I mentioned above, that there is only one graphics card and that can be the bottleneck. Second, using separate threads for painting the window can cause some thorny problems. For example, you will have to figure out what is and is not displayed so that the user can click and select what is on the screen while it is drawing. You also have paint messages coming in from the primary thread even while your window is painting. Remember that the system does not stop, and the user could be moving windows around and destroying what you have already painted.

There are a few cases where the time to move the data to the screen is dwarfed by the difficulty of calculating what to render. Examples of this include ray tracing, CAD applications, and fractal generation. In these cases, finding a way to use multiple threads for calculation will be a big win. However, the rendering must be carefully broken down among the various tasks.

Having all the threads draw into a single DC is almost always a bad idea because each thread will inevitably want to have its own pen, brush, or region selected. It is possible to protect the DC with a synchronization mechanism, but this reduces the efficiency of using multiple threads.

One possible solution is to break the area to be rendered into smaller squares, then have each thread render its square. This would work for ray tracing or fractals, where each pixel is independent of the rest.

In a CAD-type application, where you may be rendering entire objects at once, it may be best to have the threads create an intermediate data stream that a single thread interprets and renders into the DC. Using this technique, multiple threads can queue up their results to the drawing thread without interfering with each other.

Printing

Although painting the window and printing both use GDI, it is safe to do them at the same time because they typically work with completely different device contexts. They may share application data structures, which it would be necessary to protect with a synchronization mechanism, but there is no problem with different threads using different GDI objects at the same time.

Multiple Top-Level Windows

The limitations of using multiple threads to control different windows apply to MDI, dialogs, and other parent-child window relationships. In contrast, sometimes you use a different application model with multiple top-level windows. This is what Explorer does each time you open a new folder on the desktop. Even if a single program is controlling each of the windows, they are, to the user's mind, completely separate. Running each one with a separate thread is a reasonable thing to do because it provides each window with its own message loop and keyboard focus handling.

This model also provides some other benefits, particularly if a network is involved. Most applications are unresponsive while a File Open is in progress because there can be a lot of data that needs to be loaded, and finding convenient places to put `PeekMessage()` loops can be very difficult.

However, with multiple top-level windows it can be very disconcerting if all of the other windows hang while one window is opening a file. With Explorer, it can take a minute or two to connect to a network drive using Remote Access Services. While this is going on, other Explorer windows stay responsive. The one glitch in this is when you do an operation involving the desktop, in which case the desktop window will hang until the operation is complete.

Communicating Between Threads

After having spent the first part of the book talking about synchronization mechanisms and race conditions, let's look at a technique for communicating between threads that works around some of these problems.

It is frequently necessary for one thread to give information to another. A worker thread may need to acknowledge that an action has been completed. A GUI thread may need to give a worker thread a new task.

The API function `PostThreadMessage()` works like `PostMessage()`, except that it takes a thread ID instead of a window handle. An obvious limitation is that the receiving thread must have a message queue, but at least the operating system manages the queue and you do not have to.

BOOL PostThreadMessage(

> **DWORD** idThread,
> **UINT** Msg,
> **WPARAM** wParam,
> **LPARAM** lParam
>);

Parameters

idThread	Thread ID (not the thread HANDLE). Returned by `CreateThread()` and `GetCurrentThreadId()`.

Msg	Identifies which message this is.
wParam	Normal message wParam.
lParam	Normal message lParam.

Return Value

If the message is successfully posted, the return value is TRUE. If the return value is FALSE, use `GetLastError()` to find out what went wrong.

`PostThreadMessage()` posts a message to a thread without using a window handle. The receiving thread will get NULL if it tries to get the destination window handle, so the thread's message loop should have special handling to take care of the message outside of the window procedure.

Posting a message to communicate between threads has significant advantages over such standard techniques as using a global variable. If the destination thread is busy, the posting thread will not be put to sleep. In contrast, if you set a flag to say that data is ready, and then wait for another thread to read it, you might have to wait until the destination thread has time to acknowledge receipt of the data. Also, it is possible to post several messages without waiting for the destination thread to respond.

When used with threads in the same process, you can define a custom message, such as `WM_APP + 0x100`, allocate a structure that holds the desired information, then pass the structure pointer as the *lParam*. The receiving thread should deallocate the structure after processing the message.

IMPORTANT!

If you are using `PostThreadMessage()` to communicate between different processes, you must use WM_COPYDATA so that the information will be mapped from one address space into the other. This technique is discussed in Chapter 13.

The NT Shadow Thread

There is another incentive in Windows NT to avoid using one thread per MDI window. In Windows NT, the operating system creates another operating system thread for every one of your threads that has a message queue. This "shadow" thread services your calls to GDI. Therefore, you are actually creating two threads for each user interface thread that you create.

The reason this is done is that it protects other applications from possible malicious or mistaken behavior on the part of your thread. If you pass wildly out of range values, or something goes wrong while rendering in-range values, then the system thread may crash but the rest of the shadow threads in the system will be safe.

The Case of the Cancel Dialog

Sometimes it is not clear when the use of multithreading is appropriate for a user interface. There was one particular application I worked on that had a data import filter that could take a couple minutes to run. Reasonably enough, users wanted the progress dialog to have a Cancel button on it so they could give up if they decided they did not want to wait. Users also wanted the progress dialog to properly redraw itself if you changed to another application and came back again.

After implementing my first pass of the Cancel button functionality by calling `PeekMessage()` occasionally, I discovered that my import filter now ran three times slower than it used to. I thought that this would be a perfect application for using a second thread. The dialog could run in its own thread and the primary thread could run the import filter. If the user pressed the Cancel button, I could set a flag in the primary thread that I could easily check every so often. I would not have to call `PeekMessage()` and the thread running the dialog would wait very efficiently.

How wrong I was.

The sample program CANCEL on the CD-ROM demonstrates the various problems that I ran into. CANCEL is an MFC application that puts up a modeless dialog that is supposed to come up and allow processing while the primary thread is busy.

In CANCEL, I launch a new thread, then allow that new thread to create the dialog. Immediately after launching the thread for the dialog, the primary thread goes into a tight loop to simulate the import filter that never goes back to the main message loop.

CANCEL tries to solve the problem in three different ways, as outlined here. You can try each technique by using the View menu once the application starts.

1. Using an MFC user interface thread that brings up a CDialog.
2. Using a raw `CreateThread()` and `CreateDialog()` calls where the mainframe is the dialog's parent.
3. Using a raw `CreateThread()` and `CreateDialog()` calls where the dialog has no parent.

Using the first technique, the dialog does not come up at all until the busy loop finishes in the primary thread. In the CANCEL sample, you can try this by selecting Launch MFC Dialog from the View menu. After looking at SPY, I realized that there were some MFC internal messages that were flying around, so I tried going around MFC and just used direct Win32 calls with `CreateThread()`.

You can try this second technique in the sample by selecting Launch Win32 Dialog from the View menu. This technique does not work either. The window still refuses to come up until the primary thread starts processing messages again.

Again going back to SPY, I watched the messages going between the dialog and the parent. In order to create the new window, the system sends the parent window a series of messages, including deactivate messages. If the parent window is busy and does not service these messages, then the child window, in this case the dialog, blocks and stops running. As soon as the parent window starts processing messages again, the child dialog comes right up, in spite of the fact that it is supposed to be running in a completely separate thread.

I tried to synchronize the startup of the dialog so that the primary thread would continue processing messages for a short time after the new thread was started, but then the problem was just deferred until the user tried to move the dialog or change a control.

Based on this information, I tried specifying a NULL parent when I created the dialog. In CANCEL, you can see this by selecting "Launch Win32 (no parent)" from the View menu. This technique allows the dialog to come up immediately and to run properly, but it has other problems.

Without a parent window, the dialog had its own icon on the taskbar and did not minimize along with the main application. This is standard behavior; it had nothing to do with multithreading. Although it would have been possible to work around this behavior, there was another more serious issue. Because the primary thread was busy, no repaints were being serviced and the window looked awful.

The Verdict

All of these problems could probably have been worked around, but clearly I was trying to force the system to do something that it was not designed to do. The more I hacked it to try to make it work, the more fragile the whole mechanism became. I finally retreated and optimized the `PeekMessage()` loop to control both the main window and the modeless dialog.

The project highlighted to me the dangers of improperly using threads. Unfortunately, the distinction between "proper use" and "improper use" is not always obvious.

Locking GDI Objects

A key part of any application is using GDI to draw the contents of the windows. This means working with GDI objects such as device contexts, pens, and brushes.

GDI objects are per-process owned and per-thread locked. If one thread is using a GDI object, it will be locked and other threads will be prevented from using it. Unlike most other parts of Windows, access to GDI objects is *not* serialized. Threads will not "get in line" to wait for a busy GDI object. Instead, calls will simply fail to work. Even worse, if one thread deletes a device context, it goes away even if another thread was using it. If you select a new pen into a device context while another thread is using that context, then the second thread gets the new pen, too. The results are unpredictable at best.

It is possible to share GDI objects if you use your own synchronization mechanism to protect them. However, this functionality was not implemented in the kernel because it was too inefficient. You would be wise to follow the kernel designers' lead and find another way to solve the problem for your application.

I would strongly discourage trying to share GDI objects between different threads. The Microsoft documentation has very little to say on the matter, and the few sample programs that address the topic only say, "Don't do it."

Summary

In this chapter you saw that a window is always owned by a particular thread and that thread will process all messages for that window. You saw that the primary thread in an application should be the only thread that interacts with the user interface and all time-intensive tasks should be moved to worker threads. Finally, you saw that GDI objects are locked while a thread is using them, and that sharing GDI objects between threads is difficult and overhead-intensive.

Chapter 12

Debugging

This chapter describes various techniques for writing, debugging, and testing a multithreaded program.

Debugging a multithreaded program, if not approached carefully, can be like chasing a butterfly. You can see the problem, get close to it, but when you almost have your hands on the problem it floats away, only to reappear somewhere else. We saw some of this behavior in Chapter 2 in the NUMBERS sample program, where a change as small as redirecting the output to a file instead of the screen had a dramatic effect on the results that were generated.

If you have tried to debug mouse and keyboard message handling in Windows you have encountered problems that are very similar to what you will see with multithreaded applications. For example, a common feature in draw and paint packages is to allow the user to drag a rubber band around a set of shapes. This is usually implemented by handling left button down, left button up, and mouse move. If you try to set a breakpoint for either left button down or for mouse move, then the debugger and the system gets confused when you continue running after the breakpoint because the mouse button is in the wrong state.

This chapter will discuss debugging using both changes in your program and tools available in the debugger. We will use the integrated debugger in Visual C++ v4.x to demonstrate how some of these tools can be applied.

Use Windows NT

First and foremost, if you are going to develop a multithreaded application, use Windows NT. In the course of developing the samples for the book, I spent about 95 percent of my time in Windows NT and 5 percent in Windows 95. In spite of spending little time debugging in Windows 95, the machine crashed several times. The debugger in Visual C++ under Windows 95 seemed particularly vulnerable when several threads were running and the debugger tried to breakpoint the program. On the other hand, Windows NT was rock solid and stayed up regardless of what I threw at it.

When you are developing under Windows NT but targeting Windows 95, you need to pay attention to which calls are supported in Windows 95 and which are not. There are obvious omissions such as I/O completion ports, but there are also calls that are only partially supported.

Planning for Errors

Properly debugging any application starts long before you ever reach the debugger. Programs have bugs in them, especially new ones. This would seem obvious to the most casual developer. Therefore, if you know there are going to be bugs, how about planning to try to make sure you catch them?

If there is one thing that Win32 is good at, it is generating errors. Most of the functions in Win32 return some form of error using `GetLastError()`. Therefore it is imperative that everything you do is checked for validity. Even supposedly "safe" operations like `SelectObject()` in GDI can fail in a multithreaded application. So the rule is: *Error check everything*.

Ever since Chapter 2 I have used the macro MTVERIFY, which checks to see if a Win32 call returns FALSE, and if so, MTVERIFY calls `GetLast-Error()` and displays a message about what happened. This macro saved me many hours of debugging. It caught Invalid Parameter errors when I passed the wrong parameter to `CreateThread()`. It caught Invalid Handle errors when I used the wrong variable. It even caught more subtle errors like calling `WaitForSingleObject()` after the event object had already been destroyed.

MFC and the C run-time library both have ASSERT facilities. The idea behind the ASSERT facility is that you trade off safety for speed. This is very similar to the Debug Build of Windows 3.1 and Windows 95, and the Checked Build of Windows NT. If you are running a Debug build (as defined by Visual C++), the assertion checking will be turned on. Of course the program will run slower, but the point of the build in the first place is for debugging, so that is okay. When you are more confident, you turn on Release Build, the asserts go away, and your program runs faster.

Test your assumptions everywhere. Validate all the conditions on entry to a routine. Do not just check if a pointer is valid. If possible, check to see if the data in the structure the pointer points at is internally consistent.

Bench Testing

If you need to design a new algorithm, a new C++ class, a new module, or anything else that implements a set of functions, build it and test it by itself. Do not place the code in the final application until you are satisfied that the code works properly. The goal is to test the functionality first without worrying about a multithreaded environment. If you have both logic problems and race conditions, it is going to be very difficult to figure out what is really going wrong in a multithreaded environment. If you isolate the functionality and make sure the logic is correct, then any problems that are left are probably threading-related.

This type of development is called bench testing. If an auto mechanic fixes an alternator on a car, he tests it "on the bench" in a test rig before installing it back in the car. That way if the car still does not run properly, the mechanic has eliminated one potential problem and can concentrate on other possibilities.

If possible, I would even recommend bench testing all core multithread algorithms. For example, you saw the Readers/Writers algorithm in Chapter 7. I developed that code on its own using a small test program. The test program could easily be modified to change the test conditions as needed. There were enough subtle problems in the Readers/Writers implementation that, if I had tried to develop it as part of a larger application, I would probably still be working on it.

The Threads Dialog

FAQ 48

How do I debug a specific thread?

The Visual C++ debugger has built-in support for working with threads. For example, when a thread hits a breakpoint the debugger will automatically switch to the context of that thread. This creates some behavior that is surprising the first time you see it. If you set a breakpoint in a routine that many threads are using, the debugger will cycle among the threads as each thread hits the breakpoint.

This happened to me several times. I would set a breakpoint, try to step to the next line, and I would be right back at the breakpoint again. It took me

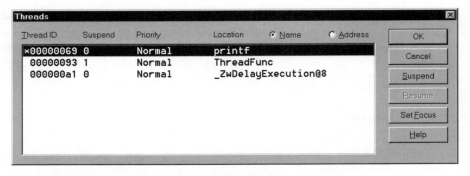

Figure 12-1. The Visual C++ 4.0 Threads dialog.

awhile to realize that the debugger was switching threads. I thought that there was some awful bug in the code that was eluding me.

There are a variety of ways to work around this problem. One way is to suspend all threads except the one that you are interested in. In the debugger, if you open the Debug menu and choose Threads, you will see a dialog similar to the one shown in Figure 12-1.

From this dialog, you can suspend or resume any thread and set the focus of the debugger on a particular thread. To solve the problem above, I would select two of the threads, click Suspend, select the third thread, and click Set Focus.

Logging

Logging is a method by which key points in the program announce their activity. Logging is useful because it allows you to focus on the sequence of operation of particular parts of the program, even if they are widely separated. I will use this technique in Chapter 14, where I have `printf()` statements inserted throughout the code, so that I can see the sequence of events as a DLL initializes. Here is an example of what it looks like:

PROGRAM OUTPUT:

```
DLL:    Process attach (tid = 180)
        Thread launched
DLL:    Thread attach (tid = 54)
        Thread running
DLL:    TheFunction() called
DLL:    Thread detach (tid = 54)
DLL:    Process detach (tid = 180)
```

Not too impressive on the face of it, but consider the difficulty of putting breakpoints at all these locations and then writing down by hand what happened! If you are trying to understand a section of code, logging simplifies matters immensely.

Remember that you can have a console window even in a GUI program. This means that you can use `printf()` and `puts()` in a GUI program. Do not try to use a list box or a multiline edit control because they both suffer from having to rely on message passing and proper repaints, neither of which is guaranteed if your application is misbehaving. A console window will be handled by a system device driver outside of your application that will remain responsive even if your application crashes or is stopped in the debugger.

Logging to *stdout* has the additional benefit that it can be redirected to a file. Logging to a file instead of the screen will decrease the amount of time spent logging and reduce the impact of logging on the application. You can use I/O redirection on the command line to decide where you want the output to go. Once you have a couple of log files, you can use WINDIFF.EXE or something similar to analyze the difference between runs.

The multithread version of the C run-time library uses mutexes to make sure that only one thread at a time tries to print to *stdout*. This is both good and bad from the debugging point of view. It is good because it increases the likelihood that messages will be printed in the order they really happened. It is bad because the threads will have to wait, and therefore the timing can be changed significantly. Note that logging to *stdout* is still not a guarantee that the order in which you see statements printed is really the order of execution. There is a lot of opportunity for a context switch to happen between the time an operation executes and the time the log message is printed.

Be aware that `printf()` has a significant amount of overhead because it has to parse the formatting string. To reduce overhead, use `puts()` to output plain text.

There is also a `TRACE()` macro in MFC that will print text to a debugging window, typically to the Debug tab in the Output pane in Visual C++. This mechanism is somewhat slow and it is easy for the Output pane to get far behind what the program is doing. I avoid using it for debugging thread-related problems because its overhead and performance impact on a running application are not clear.

Memory Trails

Even if you redirect I/O to a file, the impact of the time it takes to do the logging is enough to change the results of execution. When this happens I fall back to a low-level technique I refer to as "memory trails."

To use a memory trail, create a global buffer and a global pointer to that buffer. For example:

```
char gMemTrail[16384];
char *pMemTrail = gMemTrail;
```

At each point you would have printed something to the screen or to the log file, you write a marker to the memory trail. For example:

```
*pMemTrail++ = 'D';
```

Each trace point in your program should write a different letter. Whenever you want, or when your program crashes, you can look at the memory trail with the debugger to analyze what happened. It is obviously not as easy to read as plain text, but it is still a lot better than guessing.

There is a little-used feature of the debugger that can help you look at the buffer. At any point when the program is stopped in the debugger, open the memory window by selecting Memory from the View menu in Visual C++. (This information is current as of Visual C++ 4.x.)

Once the window comes up, double-click on the global variable to highlight it, and drag the selection into the memory window. By default you will see the data presented in byte mode. To switch to a character view, choose Options from the Tools menu, and select the Debug tab. Under Memory Window, set Format to ASCII. Now every time your program stops in the debugger, the memory window will highlight the data that has changed. This is very convenient for seeing what data has been added to the memory trail.

If you need to store more information, you can use an array of DWORDs and put in aggregate values, like this:

```
*pBuf++ = ( 5<<16 | some_useful_value );
```

This would store 5 in the high word and a value to be remembered in the low word. The memory window can be set to Long Hex mode so this data is easy to decipher.

The memory trails significantly reduce the probability of causing interference because they make no system calls and use no synchronization. However, because they are not synchronized, it is possible for memory trails to "lose" information because two threads write at the same time. This could be a significant problem if there are many threads and/or many trace points.

Hardware Debug Registers

IMPORTANT!
> This section is applicable only if you are developing on an Intel-based architecture. The PowerPC and most other CPUs supported by Windows NT do not have hardware debug registers.

Have you ever run into the situation in which a location in memory is becoming corrupted, but you cannot figure out where it is happening? Most often the problem is caused by a stray pointer, but the problem is usually very difficult to track down because what is happening should be "impossible." There is a marvelous little feature built into every Intel CPU since the 386 called the hardware debug registers that can help you track down problems like this.

The debugger can program the debug registers with up to four locations to watch. The debug registers monitor the actions of the CPU. If the CPU changes any of these locations, the program will instantly be stopped in the debugger. At this point you can see what caused the instruction to change. Best of all, the use of the debug registers does not impact the speed of the application.

IMPORTANT!
> The hardware debug registers do not work reliably under Windows 95 even though Visual C++ will try to use them. Setting Data Breakpoints in Windows 95 can cause applications other than the one you are debugging to randomly crash. See Microsoft Knowledge Base article Q137199 on the Microsoft Developer Network CD-ROM.

Using the debug registers is a bit obscure. If you need to monitor a global variable or an element in a global array, choose Breakpoints from the Edit menu, then select the Data tab. In the Expression edit box, enter the variable name. For example:

```
ghThreadHandle
gDataArray[12]
```

The completed dialog is shown in Figure 12-2.

You can monitor many other kinds of expressions with the Data breakpoint tab, but most of them will cause the debugger to use single stepping and evaluate the results in software. Doing so typically makes your program run about 100 times slower. However, if you need to monitor a stack-based variable, there is a workaround for this problem.

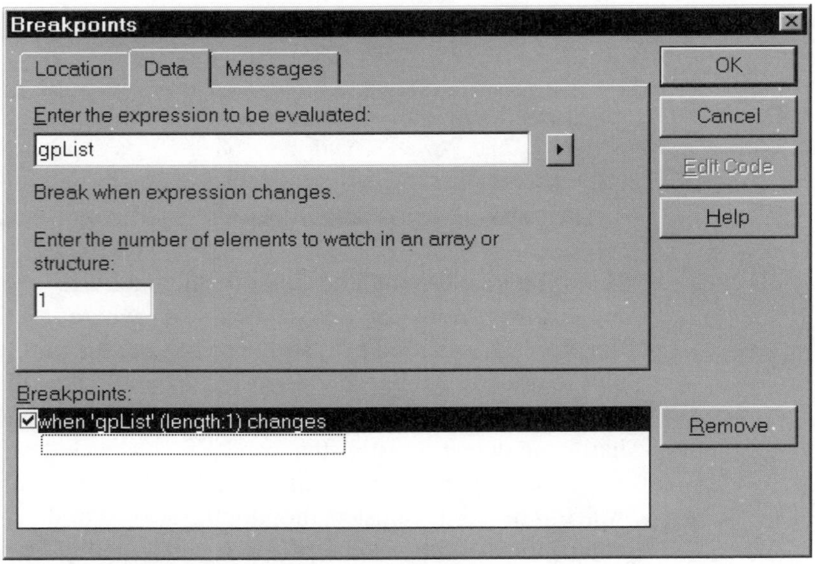

Figure 12-2. Data tab in the Breakpoints dialog.

You need to find out what the address of the variable is. In the debugger, click on the variable, open the Debug menu, and choose Quick Watch. The dialog will show you the contents of the selected variable.

In the Expression edit box in the dialog, put an "&" (without the quotes) before the variable name so the debugger will take the address of the variable. For example:

```
&slot
```

This will make the debugger tell you the address of the variable, even if it is on the stack. Write the address down. In my test, the value was `0x0063fdd4`. The leading "0x" is important; it tells the debugger that the value is in hex.

Now go back to the Data tab in the Breakpoints dialog. Enter the value you wrote down including the "0x". The debugger will interpret this as a command to watch the byte at the given address. To watch four bytes, use a cast like this:

```
DW(0x0063fdd4)
```

The debugger will always use the hardware debug registers for raw memory addresses.

Data breakpoints are documented in more detail in *Visual C++ User's Guide* / Using the Debugger / Using Breakpoints / Using the Breakpoints Dialog Box / The Data Breakpoints Tab.

The Scientific Method

There reaches a point when the preventative measures have all been tried, but your program still crashes for no apparent reason. There are three qualities that you have to have in order to succeed at debugging a multithreaded program:

- Determination
- Patience
- Creativity

As we saw in the beginning of the book, multithreaded programs are not always predictable. Ideally, once a multithreaded program, object, or routine is fully debugged, then it starts to become predictable, but since you are reading this chapter I will assume you are not there yet.

The qualities I described above might also be ascribed to a scientist. Scientists study the world, try to understand what they see, and make predictions about what caused what they see. Debugging a multithreaded program is exactly like this.

With multithreading, timing is everything. Common debugging techniques such as using a breakpoint, adding a `printf()`, or putting up a dialog can have a dramatic impact on your running program that throws off the timing of the problem you are trying to find. The timing can also be thrown off by such things as system activity (what other programs are running and how busy is the processor?) and network activity (how saturated is the Ethernet?) Your goal is to stabilize the environment as much as possible so that results are reproducible. That includes the environment within and outside of your program.

You are probably used to debugging applications that are extremely orderly and logical. Multithreaded programs are neither of these, and so require a different approach. The easiest way to debug a multithreaded program is to act like you are conducting a scientific experiment. The scientific method can be summarized as follows:

1. Observe
2. Predict
3. Test

Typically, the debugger will only give you an approximate idea of what might have happened. The rest is guesswork. If you can get to the point where you see *what* happened, but not *how* it happened, you must start making predictions (otherwise known as guesses) about the cause. Try your predictions one at a time. Change one thing in the program and test what happens. Did the behavior stay the same? Did it change? Did the bug fix itself?

If the behavior stayed then same, then undo the change and try something else. You want to isolate your changes as much as possible so that when the program's behavior changes, you know for sure what caused it.

If the behavior changed, then you are probably getting closer to the problem. Do not overlook the fact that for every bug you see, there are probably others lurking. A problem can be the result of several bugs working together. Keep notes on what you try so that you can backtrack if necessary. There is nothing more frustrating than realizing that something you did 10 minutes ago was important but you forgot how you did it.

If the bug fixed itself, you need to make sure that you understand exactly what the problem was and look over related code to make sure that the problem is completely solved. Bugs in multithreaded applications do not *ever* go away by themselves. They lurk in hiding and show up again at a customer's site at 11 o'clock at night.

What I am trying to say here is that debugging a multithreaded program must be done in a very controlled, methodical fashion. There is nothing more likely to solve the problem than your own intuition and brain power. A little bit of thinking is worth hours of debugging.

Testing

Because multithreaded programs are so sensitive to timing, it is very important to test them on a wide variety of configurations. Faster processors and slower processors will both unleash new opportunities for race conditions. Run your program on the fastest processor you can get your hands on, then run it on something slow, like a 486/25. If the application does a lot of I/O, make sure that you test on a disk or Ethernet with little activity, then test it on a very busy disk or Ethernet.

A good example of the wide variations in performance your program can encounter is the effect of using Remote Access Services (RAS). If you are talking to a server over Ethernet, most requests will be serviced in a few hundred milliseconds. But when you take your program and run it on RAS over a modem, suddenly requests may take several seconds to be serviced and the timing within the program changes dramatically.

Possibly most important of all, test your Release build as well as your Debug build. As we saw in Chapter 7, the optimizer can have a devastating effect on the logic in a multithreaded program.

Ideally, you should have two versions of your Release build, the Asserted version and the Unasserted version. In the default configurations that Visual C++ uses, ASSERT checking drops out when you do a Release build. Because of the additional problems that can be caused by optimization, it is worth having an optimized build that retains the assertion checking. Remember that the ASSERTs themselves will change the timing of your application, so both types of Release builds must be tested.

Summary

I hope this chapter has not made you decide not to use multiple threads, but the difficulties of debugging a multithreaded application should not be underestimated. These difficulties underscore the need to analyze the cost/benefit ratio of adding multiple threads, as well as the importance of properly training developers who will be using them.

In this chapter you saw how to use logging and memory trails to monitor what your application is doing with a minimal impact, you saw some tools in the debugger that can help you track problems, and you saw basic information on how to test a multithreaded application.

Chapter 13

Interprocess Communication

This chapter describes some of the techniques that can be used to communicate between threads in different processes and the issues that can arise when you use these techniques.

So far we have talked almost exclusively about threads that are working together within the same process. There are several new issues that must be addressed when the threads are in different processes and so reside in different address spaces.

Although we have talked about why the use of threads has some benefits over the use of multiple processes, there are also reasons you might want to stay with a multiple-process model. We saw that threads are an advantage because they are very lightweight, have a minimal impact on system resources, and are fast to start up and shut down. Multiple threads also share the same address space and kernel objects, so it is very easy to move data between them.

In contrast, processes are designed to be heavily shielded from each other. If one process dies, other processes in the system will stay running. For some applications, the additional robustness this provides is worth the additional overhead. If multiple threads are running within a single process, then an errant thread could potentially crash the entire process.

Before version 4.0, the graphics subsystem in Windows NT was a separate process. The graphics subsystem could completely crash and the system would keep running. This was a good example of how processes were used as partitioning mechanisms, similar to the way ocean ships are divided with bulkheads and multiple hulls. Using separate processes creates boundaries through which errors will not propagate.

Another reason for using multiple processes exists when an application is being ported from another platform, such as Unix. Traditionally, Unix has not supported threads, but process creation and shutdown were inexpensive. Therefore Unix applications are frequently designed to be implemented with multiple processes and changing them over to a thread model could entail a major rewrite. In this case, porting the application to Win32 and rewriting how the processes communicate might be a cost-effective compromise.

This chapter discusses some of the low-level solutions you need when trying to get processes to talk to each other in Win32. We will start by looking at how to move data using the message queue, then see how to create and use shared memory. At the end of the chapter I talk briefly about some of the high-level solutions, including what they are suited for and why you might need to use them.

Moving Data with the Message Queue

A simple way to move data between two threads within the same process is to use the message queue. We did this in Chapter 4 in EVENTTST when the worker threads told the primary thread to update the list box. It is very easy to define a custom message and put a pointer to any extra data in LPARAM.

If you try to pass a pointer in LPARAM from a thread in Process A to a thread in Process B, then Process B would probably crash if it used the pointer. The problem is that the pointer is to data in the address space for Process A. It is not possible for Process B to see into that address space, and so the pointer would be interpreted in the context of Process B's data.

To solve this problem, Windows defines a message called WM_COPYDATA that is designed to move data between threads, regardless of whether the two threads are in the same process. Like most messages, you need a destination HWND to give as the destination for the message, so the receiving thread will need a window to be able to receive the message.

The message WM_COPYDATA is used like this:

```
SendMessage(hwndReceiver,
            WM_COPYDATA,
            (WPARAM)hwndSender,
            (LPARAM)&cds);
```

The LPARAM argument *cds* must refer to a structure that Windows defines called COPYDATASTRUCT.

```
typedef struct tagCOPYDATASTRUCT {   // cds
    DWORD dwData;
    DWORD cbData;
    PVOID lpData;
} COPYDATASTRUCT, *PCOPYDATASTRUCT;
```

The meaning of the structure members is as follows:

dwData	This parameter is a user-defined value. It is most useful as an "action code" that describes what to do with the contents of *lpData*.
cbData	Size in bytes of the data pointed at by *lpData*.
lpData	Block of data to be passed to the receiving window's thread.

You must use SendMessage() with WM_COPYDATA. You cannot use PostMessage() or any of its variants such as PostThreadMessage(). This is because the system needs to manage the lifetime of the buffer used to move the data. If you use PostMessage(), the buffer will be cleaned up and destroyed before the receiving thread has a chance to process the message.

The lifetime of the various buffers is an important point. To pass a structure of information to a thread with CreateThread() it was necessary to allocate the structure from the heap because the thread would be running after CreateThread() returned. The origin of the block that *lpData* points to is not limited in that way. Because you are using SendMessage(), you can guarantee that the receiving process will be done with the memory when SendMessage() returns. Therefore the block of data can be on the heap or on the stack.

However, the data that the receiving thread gets is owned by the system. This data block is temporary and will disappear as soon as the message has been processed. Because the system owns the memory, it should be regarded as read-only. If the receiving thread needs to make changes to the data or needs to store a more permanent copy of the data, then the receiving thread should make its own local copy.

Creating the Buffer for COPYDATASTRUCT

You need to exercise a little bit of care when creating the buffer that *lpData* in COPYDATASTRUCT will point at. The system does not know anything about the data that is in the buffer; it just sees the data as a block of memory. Therefore you could pass a pointer to a structure that looks like the following because all the data is in one place.

```
struct GoodDataBlock
{
    DWORD dwNumber;
    char  szBuffer[80];
};
```

It would not be legal to pass a pointer to the following structure because the data that *szBuffer* points at would not be copied.

```
struct BadDataBlock
{
    DWORD dwNumber;
    char *szBuffer;
};
```

When you move into the world of C++ it gets even more complex. It is never legal to pass a pointer to an object with virtual functions, because the *vtbl* pointer would point at functions in the wrong process. This restriction eliminates using run-time type checking because run-time types rely on virtual functions. In the following example, the destructor is declared virtual and so a *vtbl* pointer will be created that will not be correctly passed into another process.

```
class BadDataClass
{
public:
    BadDataClass();
    virtual  ~BadDataClass();
};
```

You must also be careful of using embedded classes with virtual functions, or embedded classes that contain pointers of their own. One data type that it is easy to forget about is CString in MFC. A CString contains a pointer to the character data, and so WM_COPYDATA will not make a correct copy of it. The following example has that problem as well as deriving from a class, CObject, that contains virtual functions.

```
class BadMfcDataClass : public CObject
{
public:
    CString strDescription;
};
```

It is almost never safe to use a pointer to *this* as the value for *lpData* in COPYDATASTRUCT. It is too likely that the class contains a virtual function or an embedded class that is unsafe.

The COPYDATA Sample Programs

To demonstrate the use of WM_COPYDATA, I created two MFC applications. The first one, COPYRECV, creates a window containing a multiline edit control and waits for a message to be sent. The second application, COPYSEND, allows you to type in text and send it to the COPYRECV window. COPYRECV will display each thing you send it on a new line. You can then select, copy, or save the text in COPYRECV.

The COPYRECV application creates an SDI window using the MFC class `CEditView`. This provides a convenient way of creating the window with the multiline edit control. The message handler for WM_COPYDATA is in `CMainFrame` because COPYSEND sends its message to the top-level window. The handler for WM_COPYDATA is shown in Listing 13-1.

This handler decides what to do based on the value of *dwData* in the structure. The values ACTION_DISPLAY_TEXT and ACTION_CLEAR_WINDOW are defined by the application. They are not Windows or MFC values.

If you are only somewhat familiar with MFC, notice how easy MFC makes the string handling for what gets displayed in the edit control. MFC allows the use of BASIC-style concatenation operations as well as `Trim( )` functions to remove whitespace.

Listing 13-1. Excerpt from COPYRECV—Handler for WM_COPYDATA

```
LONG CMainFrame::OnCopyData( UINT wParam, LONG lParam)
{
//   HWND hwnd = (HWND)wParam;                    // handle of sending window
     PCOPYDATASTRUCT pcds = (PCOPYDATASTRUCT) lParam;


     // The view is inside the mainframe,
     //and the edit control is in the view
```

Listing 13-1 (continued)

```
CEditView* pView = (CEditView*)GetActiveView();
ASSERT_VALID(pView);

// Find the edit control
CEdit& ctlEdit = pView->GetEditCtrl();

switch (pcds->dwData)
{

case ACTION_DISPLAY_TEXT:
    {
    LPCSTR szNewString = (LPCSTR)(pcds->lpData);
    // Setting a CString equal to a LPCSTR
    // makes a copy of the string.
    CString strTextToDisplay = szNewString;
    // Throw away any \r\n that may already be there
    strTextToDisplay.TrimRight();
    // Now add our own
    strTextToDisplay += "\r\n";

    // Set the cursor back at the end of the text
    int nEditLen = ctlEdit.GetWindowTextLength();
    ctlEdit.SetSel(nEditLen, nEditLen);
    // Append the text
    ctlEdit.ReplaceSel(strTextToDisplay);
    ctlEdit.ShowCaret();
    break;
    }

case ACTION_CLEAR_WINDOW:
    ctlEdit.SetWindowText("");
    break;

default:
    break;
}

return 1;
}
```

The application COPYSEND that sends text to COPYRECV is dialog-based. Dialog-based applications are a standard feature of MFC. COPYSEND finds the COPYRECV window by using `FindWindow()` with the title of

COPYDATA's window. Depending on whether you want to clear the window or transmit text, it builds the COPYDATASTRUCT in different ways. The block of data is sent to COPYRECV using the routine `SendToServer()`. The handlers are all shown in Listing 13-2.

The routine `OnOK()` is the handler for the Send button. Subverting the use of the OK button to be a Send command allowed me to quickly handle the user pressing Enter without writing extra code. The Exit button is handled elsewhere.

As with any structure you use in Windows, it is important to zero the structure before you use it. Even if you plan to fill in all the data members, zeroing the structure can avoid mistakes in the future if someone changes the code.

Listing 13-2. Excerpt from COPYSEND—Build and send a WM_COPYDATA message

```
void CCopySendDlg::OnOk()
{
    CEdit *pEdit = (CEdit*)GetDlgItem(IDC_EDIT_SENDTEXT);
    ASSERT_VALID(pEdit);

    // Get the text from the edit control
    CString strDisplayText;
    pEdit->GetWindowText(strDisplayText);

    COPYDATASTRUCT cds;
    memset(&cds, 0, sizeof(cds));
    cds.dwData = ACTION_DISPLAY_TEXT;
    cds.cbData = strDisplayText.GetLength() + 1; // +1 for the null
    cds.lpData = (LPVOID)(LPCTSTR) strDisplayText;

    SendToServer(cds);
}


void CCopySendDlg::OnClear()
{
    COPYDATASTRUCT cds;
    memset(&cds, 0, sizeof(cds));
    cds.dwData = ACTION_CLEAR_WINDOW;

    SendToServer(cds);
}
```

Listing 13-2 (continued)

```
void CCopySendDlg::SendToServer(const COPYDATASTRUCT& cds)
{
    CWnd *pDisplayWnd = CWnd::FindWindow(NULL, szDisplayAppName);
    if (pDisplayWnd)
    {
        pDisplayWnd->SendMessage(WM_COPYDATA,
            (WPARAM)GetSafeHwnd(), (LPARAM)&cds);
    }
    else
        AfxMessageBox(IDS_ERR_NOSERVER);
}
```

Advantages and Disadvantages of WM_COPYDATA

WM_COPYDATA has one particular feature that makes it unusual. This message will work between 16- and 32-bit applications. Because Win16 does not support most interprocess communication mechanisms, WM_COPYDATA is one of the only ways to move data between 16- and 32-bit applications.

There are also a few disadvantages to using WM_COPYDATA. First, the internal mechanism is not blazingly fast. It is not an effective solution if you need high performance. Any data you pass will need to be copied into the new process. A faster mechanism, shared memory, is discussed in the next section of this chapter. Windows implements WM_COPYDATA using shared memory.

The second disadvantage is that you cannot use `PostThreadMessage()` because WM_COPYDATA can only be used with `SendMessage()`. Therefore the receiving thread must have a message queue and an associated window, even if it is invisible. If the thread does not have a window, you cannot use WM_COPYDATA.

Finally, `SendMessage()` is a synchronous call. The sender cannot continue until the receiver has processed the message. This forces the sender and receiver to be synchronized. If the receiver is busy, it may be some time before WM_COPYDATA is processed and the sender is allowed to continue.

Using Shared Memory

One of the fundamental ideas behind Win32 is that processes are secure from each other. As far as each process is concerned, it has the machine to itself. It is not possible for a process to see any part of another process's address space. This separation is so complete that each process appears to itself to live in the exact same address range. The address in physical memory where a program lives is obscured from the program and the program only sees a logical address. In fact, the physical address where a program lives in memory may change constantly as the virtual memory manager moves parts of the program in and out of virtual storage.

For moving data between processes, the WM_COPYDATA technique is easy and simple, but sometimes you need a very high degree of integration between two processes. You need the processes to actually share data, just like multiple threads do, so that changes within one process are instantly reflected in the other process. To do so, you need to use the lowest level of interprocess communication in Win32, called **shared memory.**

A shared memory area is a region of memory that is explicitly designated to be visible to several processes at the same time. Although you receive a pointer to the memory just like you would with `GlobalAlloc()`, there are significant limitations on how you can use this memory, a topic we will address in the next section of this chapter.

I'll walk you through the following steps in using shared memory, then look at the finer points of using pointers to shared memory.

1. Setting up a shared memory area.
2. Using shared memory.
3. Synchronizing access to shared memory.

You can see a more comprehensive example of using shared memory in Chapter 16, which shows an ISAPI plug-in for the Internet Information Server. The plug-in uses a second process to work around the problem of using a database that is only single-threaded.

Setting Up a Shared Memory Area

Setting up a shared memory region takes two steps:

1. Create a file-mapping kernel object that specifies the size of the shared area.
2. Map the shared area into your process's address space.

The first step uses the call `CreateFileMapping()`. Normally this call allows you to access a file as if it were data in memory, but we will use a special mode that creates a space in the paging file that any process can access by name. `CreateFileMapping()` looks like this:

HANDLE CreateFileMapping(

HANDLE hFile,
LPSECURITY_ATTRIBUTES lpFileMappingAttributes,
DWORD flProtect,
DWORD dwMaximumSizeHigh,
DWORD dwMaximumSizeLow,
LPCTSTR lpName
);

Parameters

hFile	This parameter is normally a handle returned by CreateFile() specifying the file that should be mapped into memory. However, by passing (HANDLE)0xFFFFFFFF we can use a piece of the paging file instead of a regular file.
lpFileMappingAttributes	Security attributes. Ignored in Windows 95.
flProtect	Specifies the protection that should be applied to the file view. Can be one of PAGE_READONLY, PAGE_READWRITE, or PAGE_WRITECOPY. For shared memory between processes you would typically use PAGE_READWRITE.
dwMaximumSizeHigh	High-order 32 bits of the size of the file to map. When using the paging file, this parameter will always be zero because the paging file is not large enough to contain a 4GB shared memory area.
dwMaximumSizeLow	Size of the area to map. For shared memory, this would be the amount of memory to be shared.
lpName	Text name of the memory area. Any thread or process can refer to this file-mapping object by this name. When creating shared memory, this value is not normally NULL.

Return Value

CreateFileMapping() returns a handle if it succeeds, otherwise it returns NULL. GetLastError() returns a valid result in either case. CreateFileMapping() succeeds if a file-mapping by that name already exists, in which case GetLastError() returns ERROR_ALREADY_EXISTS.

`CreateFileMapping()` creates a file-mapping kernel object. Although the need for this kernel object is not apparent in this discussion, it is useful when one process must inherit the handle from another during startup, or for manipulating files that are larger than 2GB. For our purposes, the file-mapping kernel object is the intermediate handle that other processes use to allow access to the shared memory.

Those of you already familiar with `CreateFileMapping()` may wonder why I use the paging file instead of using a dedicated file out on the file system. There are two reasons. The first is that everyone would have to agree on a name and a location for the file within the file system, an unnecessary complication. The second reason is that a file could be "stale." If the machine crashes, the file would be left lying around and it would take special logic to detect this condition and clean up. If you use the paging file for shared memory, neither of these problems will happen.

`CreateFileMapping()` has many uses besides creating shared memory. See the online documentation in Visual C++ for details of what else it can do.

We now have a kernel object, but we still do not have a pointer to memory that can be used. To obtain a pointer from the file-mapping kernel object, use `MapViewOfFile()`.

LPVOID MapViewOfFile(

```
HANDLE hFileMappingObject,
DWORD dwDesiredAccess,
DWORD dwFileOffsetHigh,
DWORD dwFileOffsetLow,
DWORD dwNumberOfBytesToMap
);
```

Parameters

hFileMappingObject	Handle to file-mapping kernel object returned by `CreateFileMapping()` or `OpenFileMapping()`.
dwDesiredAccess	For shared memory, this value will normally be FILE_MAP_ALL_ACCESS. There are numerous other values for other purposes.
dwFileOffsetHigh	High-order 32 bits of the offset within the mapped file. When using the paging file, this parameter will always be zero because the paging file is not large enough to contain a 4GB shared memory area.

dwFileOffsetLow	Low-order 32 bits of file offset. For shared memory, this value would almost always be zero so as to map the entire shared region.
dwNumberOfBytesToMap	The number of bytes to map for this file view. Using the value zero will map the entire space, so that is the easiest for shared memory

Return Value

On success, returns a pointer to the beginning of the mapped view. On failure, returns NULL, in which case you can use `GetLastError()` to find out why.

Here is a short code sample that demonstrates creating a shared memory area that is large enough to hold a DWORD. This would be a useful thing to do to store the ID of a server thread responsible for processing some sort of request. We must store the thread ID instead of a thread handle because handles are only meaningful in the context of their own process. Error checking is left out for the sake of brevity.

```
HANDLE hFileMapping;
LPDWORD pCounter;

hFileMapping = CreateFileMapping(
                (HANDLE)0xFFFFFFFF,  // File handle
                NULL,                // Security attributes
                PAGE_READWRITE,      // Protection
                0,                   // Size - high 32 bits
                sizeof(DWORD),       // Size - low 32 bits
                "Server Thread ID"); // Name

pCounter = (LPDWORD) MapViewOfFile(
                hFileMapping,        // File mapping object
                FILE_MAP_ALL_ACCESS, // Read/Write
                0,                   // Offset - high 32 bits
                0,                   // Offset - low 32 bits
                0);                  // Map the whole thing
*pCounter = GetCurrentThreadId();
```

A subtle but important point is that a memory-mapped file creates a new area in memory where data can be placed, somewhat like `GlobalAlloc()`. It does not ask the system to make an existing area of memory shareable.

Finding Shared Memory

In the previous section I showed you how to create a shared memory kernel object that other processes can find by name and then map a view into their address space. When deciding how to use the shared memory, you must decide whether the shared memory will be used on a peer-to-peer basis or whether it will be created by a server process and opened by several client processes.

If the shared memory will be used peer to peer, then each process must be equally capable of creating and initializing the shared memory. Each process should call `CreateFileMapping()` and then call `GetLastError()`. If the error return is ERROR_ALREADY_EXISTS, then the process can assume that the shared memory area was created and initialized by another process. Otherwise the process should assume that it is the first and proceed to initialize the shared memory.

If the shared memory will be used in a client/server arrangement of processes, then only the server process should create and initialize the shared memory. All of the client processes should use the call `OpenFileMapping()`, which returns a handle to a file-mapping kernel object previously created by `CreateFileMapping()`. The call looks like this:

HANDLE OpenFileMapping(
 DWORD dwDesiredAccess,
 BOOL bInheritHandle,
 LPCTSTR lpName
 );

Parameters

dwDesiredAccess	For shared memory, this value will normally be FILE_MAP_ALL_ACCESS. There are numerous other values for other purposes.
bInheritHandle	If TRUE, this handle can be inherited by child processes. Handle inheritance is not covered in this book.
lpName	Text name of the shared memory area to open. This is the same name that another process would have used with `CreateFileMapping()`.

Return Value

`OpenFileMapping()` returns a handle if it succeeds. It returns NULL if it fails, in which case `GetLastError()` can be used to get more details.

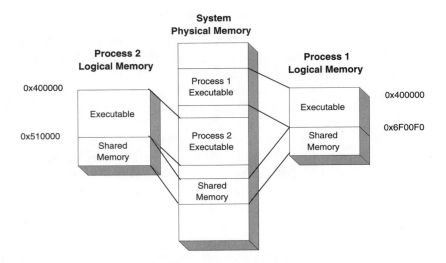

Figure 13-1. Shared memory mapping in multiple processes.

After calling `OpenFileMapping()`, use `MapViewOfFile()` to obtain a pointer to the shared memory area. This would seem simple, but there is a big "gotcha" waiting for you. The pointer returned by `MapViewOfFile()` in the second and subsequent processes is *not* guaranteed to be the same pointer returned in the first process. In fact, the shared memory can be mapped to a different address in each process. A sample of this is shown in Figure 13-1. I will talk more about the ramifications of this later in this chapter.

In practice, the behavior of `MapViewOfFile()` in Windows 95 is to always map the shared memory to the same place. This is because shared memory is placed at an address space that is always available to all processes. It is actually possible for any process in the system to trash your shared memory area, even if that process has never mapped the shared memory area. This is one of the shortcuts that Windows 95 took. The memory security in Windows NT is robust and does not have this shortcoming.

This behavior in Windows 95 should be considered an accident. There is no guarantee that future versions of Windows will have this behavior. If your application uses shared memory between different processes, you should test it under Windows NT to make sure that you are not relying on the addresses being the same.

Cleaning Up

When you are finished using the shared memory area you let go of it by calling `UnmapViewOfFile()` with the pointer returned by `MapViewOfFile()` and calling `CloseHandle()` with the handle to the file-mapping kernel object. `UnmapViewOfFile()` looks like this:

BOOL UnmapViewOfFile(

LPCVOID lpBaseAddress
);

Parameters

lpBaseAddress   Pointer to a shared memory area. This value must match what was returned by `MapViewOfFile()`.

Return Value

`OpenFileMapping()` returns TRUE if it succeeds. It returns FALSE if it fails, in which case `GetLastError()` can be used to get more details.

Synchronizing Access

It may be necessary to create a global flag that indicates when the shared memory area is properly initialized. Even in the earlier example where the shared memory area was a single DWORD, it is possible that a context switch could occur that would allow another process to open the shared memory area and access it before it was properly initialized.

The obvious solution would be to set some "magic" value within the shared memory area, but if a second process were to look at the location and see it was not set, then how would it wait? The second process would have to use a busy loop, something we already know is very bad.

The best solution is to use either a mutex or a Readers/Writers lock. (*Note:* The Readers/Writers lock presented in Chapter 7 was designed to run within a single process. It will need further revision to work properly across processes.) Such a lock could provide protection during startup as well providing synchronization of reads and writes in the shared memory. Other processes should open the mutex by name and wait for it to become signaled (released) before proceeding. When the shared memory area is fully initialized, then the mutex can be released and the waiting applications will eventually be allowed to continue.

Using Pointers to Shared Memory

Using pointers to shared memory is very tricky, especially in C++. All of the restrictions I discussed in *Creating the Buffer for COPYDATASTRUCT* earlier in this chapter apply equally to shared memory areas. However, because the memory is often a large block, there are even more problems.

For example, I saw the following bit of code in a C++ MFC application I was reviewing that used shared memory:

```
HANDLE hFileMapping = CreateFileMapping( ... );
LPVOID pSharedView = (LPDWORD) MapViewOfFile( ... );
CStringArray* pStringArray =  new(pSharedView) CStringArray;
```

Note: The last line of code above uses the "placement new" syntax in C++, which is a special version of new that initializes an existing block of memory instead of allocating a new block. CStringArray is derived from CObject, and the placement new operator is defined by MFC for all CObject-derived classes. Placement new is so named because it creates a new object at a certain place in memory.

What happens here is that the pointer to shared memory is cast to an array of CStrings, and then the array is initialized by calling the constructor. The program then went on to start filling in the CStringArray. The problem is that an instance of the class CStringArray is only about 16 bytes long, and it only contains a pointer to the array data. The array data itself is allocated from the heap, which would cause that array data to be placed in normal memory instead of in shared memory.

Even if the array had worked properly, the individual CStrings would have caused an error because each allocates space for the string from the heap; it does not have a local buffer. Finally, even if the array data was located in shared memory, the pointers to it would be wrong if they were used in another process.

The lesson here is that just about any collection class, be it from MFC or otherwise, is going to be unsafe to use in shared memory.

The __based Attribute

The compiler supports an obscure workaround to some of the problems related to using shared memory. There is a modifier for pointers called __**based** that allows pointers to be defined as 32-bit offsets from a given point instead of absolute addresses in memory.

The following example declares a pointer *lpHead* that is internally stored as an offset from *pSharedView*. In other words, *lpHead* is "based on" *pSharedView*. ListNode is a convenient name for an arbitrary structure.

```
HANDLE hFileMapping = CreateFileMapping( ... );
LPVOID pSharedView = (LPDWORD) MapViewOfFile( ... );

ListNode __based( pSharedView ) *lpHead;
```

Although based pointers are quite useful, you pay a small penalty in processing overhead. Every access with a based pointer requires the processor to add the base pointer to the offset to figure out the actual location.

The __based attribute will be demonstrated in detail in the sample program coming up next.

The SHAREMEM Sample Program

The SHAREMEM sample is an MFC application that demonstrates how shared memory can be used to pass an array of strings. The running application is shown in Figure 13-2. You can run several instances of the program

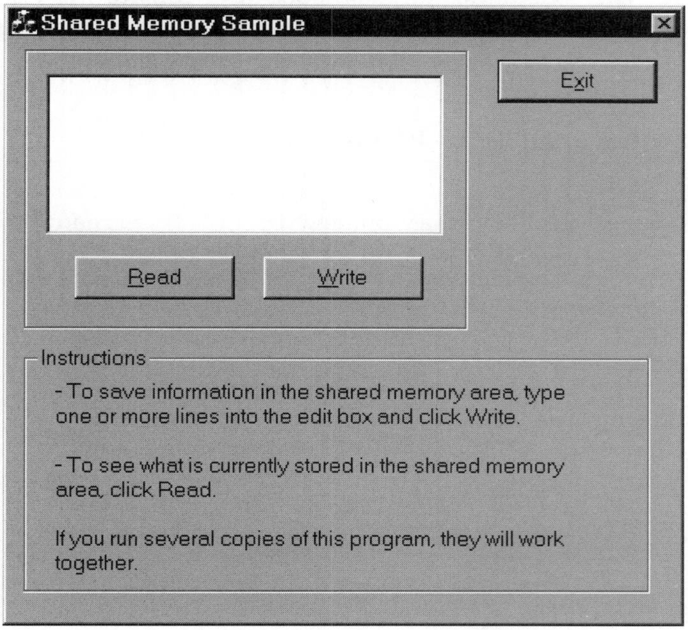

Figure 13-2. SHAREMEM sample program.

and they will all share the same shared memory area. Whatever one writes, all the others can read.

An instance of SHAREMEM will only read from shared memory when you hit the Read button. There is no notification mechanism to signal when shared memory changes.

This sample demonstrates several concepts. It uses a mapped view from a file-mapping kernel object to create the shared memory. It uses a mutex to prevent simultaneous writes or reads while the shared memory is being built. It also demonstrates the usage of the based pointer.

The shared memory is initialized in `InitInstance()`. The code shown in Listing 13-3 works exactly as I have described in the past few sections. There is a mutex that protects the shared memory while it is created. Both `CreateFileMapping()` and `MapViewOfFile()` are called to create the shared data area. `GetLastError()` is checked after calling `CreateFileMapping()` to find out if this process was the first to create the shared memory block, and if so to initialize it.

We do not lock the mutex while we are exiting because other processes can safely access the shared memory while we are unmapping it. Because the file-mapping kernel object is reference counted, it may continue to exist even if the process that created the shared memory exits.

The code is liberally sprinkled with calls to MTVERIFY to make sure everything is working properly. In production code, the calls to MTVERIFY should be replaced with more robust error handling.

Listing 13-3. Excerpt from SHAREMEM—Initialization code

```
// Create a mutex with initial ownership. If it already
// exists, we will block until it is available.
ghDataLock = ::CreateMutex(NULL, TRUE, "ShareMem Data Mutex");
MTVERIFY( ghDataLock != NULL );

HANDLE hFileMapping;

hFileMapping = ::CreateFileMapping(
                (HANDLE)0xFFFFFFFF,    // File handle
                NULL,                  // Security attributes
                PAGE_READWRITE,        // Protection
                0,                     // Size - high 32 bits
                1<<16,                 // Size - low 32 bits
                "ShareMem Sample App Data Block"); // Name
MTVERIFY( hFileMapping != NULL );
DWORD dwMapErr = GetLastError();
```

Listing 13-3 (continued)

```
gpSharedBlock = (SharedBlock*) ::MapViewOfFile(
                    hFileMapping,        // File mapping object
                    FILE_MAP_ALL_ACCESS, // Read/Write
                    0,                   // Offset - high 32 bits
                    0,                   // Offset - low 32 bits
                    0);                  // Map the whole thing
MTVERIFY( gpSharedBlock != NULL );

// Only initialize shared memory if we actually created.
if (dwMapErr != ERROR_ALREADY_EXISTS)
    gpSharedBlock->m_nStringCount = 0;

::ReleaseMutex(ghDataLock);

CShareMemDlg dlg;
m_pMainWnd = &dlg;
int nResponse = dlg.DoModal();

MTVERIFY( ::UnmapViewOfFile(gpSharedBlock) );
MTVERIFY( ::CloseHandle(hFileMapping) );
MTVERIFY( ::CloseHandle(ghDataLock) );
```

The beginning of the shared memory contains the structure SharedBlock. The structure looks like this:

```
// Declare a forward reference to cure a circular dependency.
struct SharedBlock;

extern SharedBlock* gpSharedBlock;

struct SharedBlock
{
    short   m_nStringCount;
    char __based( gpSharedBlock ) *m_pStrings[1];
};
```

The member variable *m_pStrings* is an array of based pointers to char. Although it is defined to be of size 1, this is merely a way to trick the compiler into allowing us to address an array at that point. The technique is identical to how the color palette is managed in a Device Independent Bitmap (DIB).

If there is more than one string, their pointers are written immediately after SharedBlock. After these pointers come the strings themselves, which the pointers point at. All of these pointers are based pointers, so internally they are all indices relative to the beginning of shared memory.

Assuming that three strings were loaded into the shared memory, it would look like this:

Offset from start of shared memory	Contents
0	3 (m_nStringCount)
4	16 (m_pStrings[0] – Based ptr to string 0)
8	25 (m_pStrings[1] – Based ptr to string 1)
12	31 (m_pStrings[2] – Based ptr to string 2)
16	String 0\0
25	Str 1\0
31	String number 2\0

The code that reads and writes the shared memory is shown in Listing 13-4. The pointer juggling in OnWrite() to calculate where everything should be written within the shared area gets quite complicated. Without the benefit of a heap manager to allocate space within the shared memory, it is necessary to resort to such raw storage management.

The OnWrite() routine figures out how many lines there are in the multiline edit control, saves this value to the shared memory, then figures out how much space to reserve for the pointer array. Then it reads lines from the edit control one at a time, saves the string in shared memory, and saves a based pointer to the string in the array. This whole operation is protected by a mutex so that other processes will not interrupt it in the middle.

Listing 13-4. Excerpt from SHAREMEM—OnWrite() and OnRead()

```
void CShareMemDlg::OnRead()
{
    // Make sure the shared memory is available
    ::WaitForSingleObject(ghDataLock, INFINITE);

    CEdit* pEdit = (CEdit*)GetDlgItem(IDC_EDIT);
    ASSERT_VALID(pEdit);
    pEdit->SetWindowText("");
    pEdit->SetSel(-1, -1);
    pEdit->ShowCaret();
```

Listing 13-4 (continued)

```cpp
    for (int i=0; i<gpSharedBlock->m_nStringCount; i++)
    {
        CString str = gpSharedBlock->m_pStrings[i];
        str += "\r\n";
        pEdit->ReplaceSel(str);
    }

    ::ReleaseMutex(ghDataLock);
}

void CShareMemDlg::OnWrite()
{
// Make sure the shared memory is available
    ::WaitForSingleObject(ghDataLock, INFINITE);

    CEdit* pEdit = (CEdit*)GetDlgItem(IDC_EDIT);
    ASSERT_VALID(pEdit);

    int iLineCount = pEdit->GetLineCount();
    gpSharedBlock->m_nStringCount = iLineCount;
    char *pTextBuffer =
        (char *)gpSharedBlock
        + sizeof(SharedBlock)
        + sizeof(char __based(gpSharedBlock) *) * (iLineCount-1);

    char szLineBuffer[256];
    while (iLineCount--)
    {
        // Get the next line from the edit control
        pEdit->GetLine(iLineCount, szLineBuffer, sizeof(szLineBuffer));

        // Terminate it
        szLineBuffer[pEdit->LineLength(
            pEdit->LineIndex(iLineCount))] = '\0';

        // Store the line in shared memory. The compiler
        // silently translates from a based pointer to
        // a regular pointer, so strcpy() works properly.
        strcpy(pTextBuffer, szLineBuffer);

        // Remember where we put it. Convert to a based
        // ptr before storing the ptr.
        gpSharedBlock->m_pStrings[iLineCount] =
            (char _based(gpSharedBlock) *)pTextBuffer;
```

Listing 13-4 (continued)

```
    // Skip to the next open space in the buffer
    pTextBuffer += strlen(szLineBuffer) + 1;
}

::ReleaseMutex(ghDataLock);
}
```

Summary of Using Shared Memory

If you are starting to get the idea that using shared memory is not simple, you are absolutely right. To implement a structure such as a linked list in shared memory, it would be necessary to build a custom memory allocator that can treat the shared memory region as a heap and returned based pointers within that heap. This is not a trivial undertaking. The difficulty highlights the importance of keeping information sharing between threads to a minimum, and to tightly define the interface through which any data is shared.

Here are some guidelines for using shared memory:

- Do not put C++ collection classes in shared memory.
- Never put C++ classes with virtual functions in shared memory.
- Never place MFC objects in shared memory that are based on CObject.
- Do not use pointers that point within the shared memory area.
- Do not use pointers that point outside of the shared memory area.
- It is safe to use "based" pointers but they should be used with care.

Higher Level IPCs

At the beginning of this chapter I said we would be discussing the low-level mechanisms that are available in Win32 for interprocess communication. There are many other ways to communicate between processes, which I will briefly discuss here but will not cover in any detail.

Compared to other platforms, such as Unix, there is somewhat less need in Win32 to use low-level Inter-Process Communication (IPC) because there are standard calls that take care of the most common situations. For example, the system clipboard can be used by any application at any time. It allows arbitrary data to be passed between applications without each application having to figure out how the data is actually moved.

Anonymous Pipes

A pipe is like the plumbing in your house. You put something in one end, and it comes out the other end. An anonymous pipe only "flows" in one direction, and can only be used between processes on the same machine. An anonymous pipe is what allows you to redirect the *stdout* of one program to the *stdin* of another program. Anonymous pipes are only used for point-to-point communication, and are most useful when one process creates another.

Pipes can also be useful because they are an operating-system-provided ring buffer. If you have one thread that needs to feed data to another thread, a pipe is a very simple way to do so. In many samples in this book, we have used messages to give a thread information. The use of messages requires that the receiving thread have a message loop. Using a pipe, you can send information to another thread or process without the receiving end having a message loop.

For more information on anonymous pipes, look up `CreatePipe()` in the *Programmer's Reference* in the online help in Visual C++.

Named Pipes

Named pipes are much more versatile than anonymous pipes. A named pipe can be unidirectional or bi-directional and it will work over the network. Because it is named, an unrelated process can easily attach to it. A named pipe can also be put into message mode, in which you specify that each piece of data put into the pipe will be a certain size, and `ReadFile()` will only read in multiples of that size. This mode can be beneficial when running over the network, because if the pipe were running in byte mode the system would not know that more data is coming and would return partial messages.

Named pipes can be set up for overlapped operations and so can be used with I/O completion ports. Named pipes are point-to-point like anonymous pipes; the server can create new named pipes with the same name as connections occur, so that a single server can communicate with multiple clients.

Because named pipes can be bi-directional, they are useful for establishing a two-way dialogue between threads or processes. The handle to a named pipe is global to a process, so it is possible for several different threads to be reading from the pipe if it is put into message mode. This could be used for a server thread to feed requests to several client threads within the same process.

For more information on named pipes, look up `CreateNamedPipe()` in the *Programmer's Reference*.

Mailslots

Whereas pipes are designed for point-to-point communication, mailslots are a form of broadcast communication. A mailslot is just like your mailbox at home. Anyone can send a letter to you, but only you are allowed to take the letters out of the mailbox. With mailslots, a server process creates the mailslot, any client can write to it, but only the server process can read the mailslot. Mailslots are named and work across the network.

For more information on mailslots, look up `CreateMailslot()` in the *Programmer's Reference*.

OLE Automation

OLE Automation and Uniform Data Transfer are higher-level mechanisms that allow communication across process boundaries and even across machine boundaries. OLE allows objects to communicate in a standard fashion with other objects that might live in a DLL or in another process. OLE can potentially talk to non-Win32 platforms. OLE may use some of the mechanisms described in this chapter, but these mechanisms would be just a few of several transport mechanisms that OLE supports. An OLE example that works across processes is presented in Chapter 17.

DDE

DDE stands for Dynamic Data Exchange, and it dates back to 16-bit Windows. I mention it for the sake of completeness. OLE version 1.0 was based upon DDE. DDE is a system built on message passing that allows applications to pass strings and data structures among themselves. It is still used for purposes such as telling a running application to open a document. However, DDE has some inherent limitations in terms of handling time-outs and creating connections, so I would advise against its use in light of the other mechanisms that are available.

Summary

In this chapter you saw how to move data between two processes by sending the message WM_COPYDATA with a block of memory. You saw how to create and use a shared memory block, the lowest level of interprocess communication. Finally, you saw the problems involved with addressing shared memory, and how based pointers can help work around the problem.

Chapter 14

Building DLLs

This chapter describes how to handle process and thread attach and detach notifications in a DLL, and the problems you can expect using these notifications. It also describes thread local storage and how to use it.

A DLL (Dynamic Link Library) is the standard mechanism in Windows for doing one of three things:

- Providing a consistent set of APIs that any application can call. In this sense, DLLs are sharable modules.
- Providing a library of routines that can be loaded at run-time.
- Reducing memory usage for shared code.

In this chapter we will be discussing those aspects of DLLs that have to do specifically with multithreading. If you need more information about how to create, compile, or use DLLs, I recommend starting with the topic entitled *Overview: Dynamic-Link Libraries (DLLs)* in the Visual C++ online documentation.

UNIX   The way a DLL works is very different from shared library implementations that exist in Unix. Although the net result is similar, the mechanisms are not similar. A DLL is a linked entity that has its own existence. A DLL has its own data that is separate from the process, has its own module identifier, and can be linked either statically or dynamically. For more details see the Win32 documentation.

If you ever wrote a DLL in 16-bit Windows, especially in the early days of Windows 3.0, you may remember an arcane process that included assembly language startup code, numerically identified functions, and the WEP (Windows Exit Procedures) that had a long list of limitations. Today, with Win32 and Visual C++, the burden placed on the developer is much smaller, and building DLLs is much simpler and easier.

Compared to Win16, Win32 has introduced many enhancements to DLLs to make them more suitable for a multitasking environment. Most importantly, a DLL is automatically given a separate copy of its global data for each process that uses it. In Win16 you had to go to extreme measures to make sure that each application that used a DLL would be isolated from the other applications. In Win32 the separation is automatic and transparent. If a DLL has an array that tracks open file handles, there will be a separate copy of the array created every time another application loads the DLL.

Because they are designed to be used as sharable modules or sharable components, DLLs need detailed information about what threads and processes are using them. Win32 provides this information by calling a function in your DLL with status updates.

DLL Notifications

A DLL is a curious creation because it only exists in the context of another application, yet it has its own "personality" while it is loaded. If multiple applications that use the same DLL start up and shut down, then the DLL will have its own existence that does not depend on any particular application. All that matters for the continued existence of the DLL is that something is always running that uses the DLL. In many ways, a DLL is like a receptionist in a business building. Businesses may come and go, and people may come and go, but the receptionist outlasts all of them. On the other hand, if all the businesses move out, then the receptionist will probably go, too.

Just like a receptionist, a DLL needs to keep track of comings and goings, in this case, of when a new process or a new thread starts or stops using the DLL. To receive these notifications you create a function named DllMain()[1] that should be defined as shown here.

Note: If you want to look this up in the online documentation, you should look for the function DllEntryPoint(). This is an abstract name that you would not actually use.

BOOL WINAPI DllMain(

HINSTANCE hinstDLL,
DWORD fdwReason,
LPVOID lpReserved
);

Parameters

hinstDLL	Module handle to this DLL.
fdwReason	*Why this function was called. It can be one of the following values:*
	DLL_PROCESS_ATTACH
	DLL_THREAD_ATTACH
	DLL_THREAD_DETACH
	DLL_PROCESS_DETACH
lpReserved	Gives more details about *fdwReason*. If *fdwReason* is DLL_PROCESS_ATTACH, *lpReserved* is NULL if the library was loaded with LoadLibrary(), and non-NULL if the library was loaded implicitly.
	If *fdwReason* is DLL_PROCESS_DETACH, *lpReserved* is NULL if DllMain() was called using FreeLibrary(), and non-NULL if DllMain() was been called during process termination.

---

[1] The function is named DllMain() if you are using the C run-time library. In the rare cases where you do not use the C run-time library, the name of the function is defined by the linker switch /ENTRY.

Return Value

If *fdwReason* was DLL_PROCESS_ATTACH, then DllMain() should return TRUE if initialization succeeds and FALSE if it fails. If the DLL was implicitly linked and FALSE is returned, then the application will fail to run. If the DLL was being loaded with LoadLibrary() and DllMain() returns FALSE, then LoadLibrary() will return FALSE.

If *fdwReason* was *not* DLL_PROCESS_ATTACH, then the return value will be ignored.

FAQ 49

How do I tell if a new thread starts using my DLL?

The function DllMain() within a DLL will be called whenever a process loads or unloads the DLL, and whenever a thread starts or exits. Whenever a process starts up, the DllMain() in every DLL it uses will be called with the flag DLL_PROCESS_ATTACH. When a thread starts up, the DllMain() in every DLL in use by the process will be called with DLL_THREAD_ATTACH.

Listing 14-1 is the source to a very minimal DLL. It prints status messages whenever DllMain() is called and it provides a single exported function, called TheFunction(), that applications can link against and call. This version of DllMain() does not actually do anything other than to print the messages.

Listing 14-1. ENTRY.CPP, from the SMALLDLL sample

```
/*
 * Entry.cpp
 *
 * Demonstrate a very simple DLL that prints
 * status messages when its functions are called
 * a provides a single entry point called
 * TheFunction() for test purposes.
 */

#include <windows.h>
#include <stdio.h>

BOOL WINAPI DllMain(
    HINSTANCE hinstDLL,    // handle to DLL module
    DWORD fdwReason,       // reason for calling function
    LPVOID lpReserved )    // reserved
{
    DWORD tid = GetCurrentThreadId();
```

Listing 14-1 (continued)

```
    // Why are we being called?
    switch( fdwReason )
    {
        case DLL_PROCESS_ATTACH:
            printf("DLL:\tProcess attach (tid = %d)\n", tid);
            break;

        case DLL_THREAD_ATTACH:
            printf("DLL:\tThread attach (tid = %d)\n", tid);
            break;

        case DLL_THREAD_DETACH:
            printf("DLL:\tThread detach (tid = %d)\n", tid);
            break;

        case DLL_PROCESS_DETACH:
            printf("DLL:\tProcess detach (tid = %d)\n", tid);
            break;
    }
    return TRUE;
}

_declspec( dllexport ) BOOL TheFunction()
{
    printf("DLL:\tTheFunction() called\n");
    return TRUE;
}
```

To get some understanding of what really happens with all of this code, I created the small driver program shown in Listing 14-2. The primary thread automatically attaches to the DLL because the program is linked with the DLL. Once the program has started, another thread is created that calls `TheFunction()` in the DLL and exits.

Listing 14-2. MAIN1.CPP, from the SMALLDLL sample

```
/*
 * Main1.cpp
 *
 * Driver to load the simple DLL, create a
 * thread, call the DLL, and exit.
 */
```

Listing 14-2 (continued)

```c
#include <windows.h>
#include <stdio.h>

_declspec(dllimport) BOOL TheFunction();
DWORD WINAPI ThreadFunc(LPVOID);

VOID main(VOID)
{
    HANDLE  hThrd;
    DWORD   dwThreadId;

    hThrd = CreateThread(NULL,
        0,
        ThreadFunc,
        NULL,
        0,
        &dwThreadId );
    if (hThrd)
        printf("\tThread launched\n");

    WaitForSingleObject(hThrd, INFINITE);
    CloseHandle(hThrd);
}

/*
 * Just call a function in the DLL and exit
 */
DWORD WINAPI ThreadFunc(LPVOID n)
{
    printf("\tThread running\n");

    TheFunction();

    return 0;
}
```

To help identify where information is coming from, I wrote the `printf()` calls so that what the application prints is indented, and what the DLL prints is preceded by "DLL:".

PROGRAM OUTPUT:

```
DLL:    Process attach (tid = 180)
        Thread launched
```

```
DLL:    Thread attach (tid = 54)
        Thread running
DLL:    TheFunction() called
DLL:    Thread detach (tid = 54)
DLL:    Process detach (tid = 180)
```

The first point to notice based on this output is that `DllMain()` is called once with DLL_PROCESS_ATTACH and once with DLL_THREAD_ATTACH. To me this is a little surprising because there are *two* threads. However, Win32 defines the mechanism such that the first thread in each process that calls `DllMain()` will use DLL_PROCESS_ATTACH. All subsequent threads will use DLL_THREAD_ATTACH.

The second point is that `DllMain()` is called in the context of the new thread. This is very important because you need a context to use thread local storage, which we will discuss shortly.

Disabling Notifications

There are some interesting ramifications to `DllMain()` being called in the context of the new thread. Obviously, the sample program MAIN1 never made the function calls to `DllMain()` directly. `DllMain()` was called automatically as a side effect of `CreateProcess()` (which Windows called) or `CreateThread()` (which MAIN1 called). Now look at the case where there were five, ten, or even twenty DLLs attached to the process. Every time you start a new thread, the `DllMain()` in each of those DLLs will be called. Suddenly you are looking at a lot of overhead to perform the bookkeeping.

To help avoid this problem, there is a function in Win32 called `Disable-ThreadLibraryCalls()`. This call is only supported under Windows NT. It does nothing under Windows 95. On a DLL-by-DLL basis, you can instruct Win32 that your DLL does not need notifications. In a program that frequently creates threads, making this little optimization could save a lot of overhead. The call looks like this:

BOOL DisableThreadLibraryCalls(

  HMODULE hLibModule
);

Parameters

hLibModule   Module handle to this DLL.

Return Value

`DisableThreadLibraryCalls()` returns TRUE if it succeeds, otherwise it returns FALSE. On failure, call `GetLastError()` to find out why. This call will always fail if the given DLL uses thread local storage.

If we were to modify ENTRY.CPP in SMALLDLL to disable notifications, the code would look like this:

```
case DLL_PROCESS_ATTACH:
        DisableThreadLibraryCalls(hinstDLL);
        printf("DLL:\tProcess attach (tid = %d)\n", tid);
        break;
```

When I made this change and reran MAIN1, I got the following output. (This is not on the CD-ROM.) Based on this result, you see that you continue to receive DLL_PROCESS_ATTACH and DLL_PROCESS_DETACH, but not the thread notifications.

PROGRAM OUTPUT AFTER ADDING DisableThreadLibraryCalls():

```
DLL:     Process attach (tid = 190)
         Thread launched
         Thread running
DLL:     TheFunction() called
DLL:     Process detach (tid = 190)
```

Problems with Notifications

In case you thought everything was perfectly orderly with DLL notifications, let me lead you back to reality. The first time I wrote MAIN1 I forgot to put in `WaitForSingleObject()`, so `main()` returned right after calling `CreateThread()`. The output I ended up with was as follows:

PROGRAM OUTPUT OF MAIN1 WHEN WaitForSingleObject() WAS LEFT OUT:

```
DLL:     Process attach (tid = 185)
         Thread launched
DLL:     Process detach (tid = 185)
```

This was very interesting. I received no notifications of thread attach, and `TheFunction()` did not print a progress report. It appears that Win32 calls

`TerminateThread()` on all running threads when you call `ExitProcess()`, which is what the C run-time library does when you return from `main()` or call `exit()`.

If you remember, in Chapter 2 I talked about the dangers of using the `TerminateThread()` call. One of the reasons it causes problems is specifically because it prevents DLL notifications from being sent, so a DLL never realizes that a thread or a process has gone away. Because `Terminate-Thread()` is used when a process exits, a program that exits without safely shutting down all running threads could unintentionally leave any attached DLLs in an unstable state.

Effects of Dynamic Loading

FAQ 50

Why do I need to be careful of dynamic linking when writing DLLs?

On the CD-ROM there is a second driver program called MAIN2 that uses dynamic linking to load the library instead of static linking. Other than the information about `LoadLibrary()` and `FreeLibrary()`, the results of running the program are identical to MAIN1. The output looks like this:

PROGRAM OUTPUT OF MAIN2:

```
        Calling LoadLibrary()
DLL:    Process attach (tid = 169)
        Thread launched
DLL:    Thread attach (tid = 166)
        Thread running
DLL:    TheFunction() called
        Calling FreeLibrary()
DLL:    Process detach (tid = 169)
```

Now watch what happens if the applications starts the thread, *then* calls `LoadLibrary()`. We receive a thread detach, but never receive a thread attach! The sample program that does this is in MAIN3. Remember, all of these samples are using the same DLL.

PROGRAM OUTPUT OF MAIN3:

```
        Thread launched
        Calling LoadLibrary()
        Thread running
DLL:    Process attach (tid = 178)
DLL:    TheFunction() called
DLL:    Thread detach (tid = 154)
        Calling FreeLibrary()
DLL:    Process detach (tid = 178)
```

When a DLL is loaded dynamically with `LoadLibrary()` or `Load-LibraryEx()`, `DllMain()` will not receive DLL_THREAD_ATTACH notifications for any of the currently running threads except for the thread that actually called `LoadLibrary()`. `DllMain()` will, however, receive DLL_THREAD_DETACH notifications from those threads. This is the documented behavior, regardless of whether you consider the behavior to be useful.

Failed Initialization

There is one final notification "feature" that you should be aware of. If `DLLMain()` cannot initialize and returns FALSE when it receives DLL_PROCESS_ATTACH, then `DLLMain()` will still be sent DLL_PROCESS_DETACH. Therefore you must be very careful to initialize every variable to a known state before FALSE is returned so that the handling for detach will not crash because of problems like wild pointers or illegal array indices.

Summary of Notification Issues

Because of these issues, you have to take great care in how you structure your `DllMain()` function. Ideally, you should test using driver programs similar to those I have provided to make sure that attach and detach notifications can be correctly handled even if they are missing or out of order.

Here is a quick summary of the issues with notification:

- If a process has more than one thread running when `LoadLibrary()` is called, then DLL_THREAD_ATTACH will not be sent for any of the existing threads.
- `DllMain()` does not receive DLL_THREAD_ATTACH for the first thread; it receives DLL_PROCESS_ATTACH instead.
- `DllMain()` will not receive any notification for threads that are terminated with `TerminateThread()`. This will also happen if an application calls `exit()` or `ExitProcess()`.

DLL Entry Serialization

We are not quite finished with the DLL entry point routine. When Win32 was designed, the following scenario had to be solved:

1. Thread 1 calls `LoadLibrary()`, which sends DLL_PROCESS_ATTACH.

2. While the DLL is processing DLL_PROCESS_ATTACH, Thread 2 calls `LoadLibrary()`, which sends DLL_THREAD_ATTACH.
3. `DllMain()` starts handling DLL_THREAD_ATTACH before the processing for DLL_PROCESS_ATTACH has completed.

FAQ 51

Why should I be careful of starting threads in `DllMain()`?

Without help from the operating system, an unsolvable race condition is created. To solve this problem, Win32 serializes access to the `DllMain()` routine of all DLLs. Within a process, only one `DllMain()` routine in one DLL in one thread at a time can run. In fact, the way the initialization is implemented, each thread in turn calls the `DllMain()` for all attached DLLs.

There is a side effect of this process that you occasionally run into. If you create a thread within `DllMain()`, then that thread will not actually start up until this, and possibly several other, `DllMain()` routines have completed executing. Therefore it is not possible to start a thread in `DllMain()`, wait for it to initialize, and then continue executing.

DLL Notifications in MFC

As of MFC 4.2, implementing the DLL notifications as described above is somewhat tricky in regular DLLs that use MFC (as opposed to extension DLLs that extend MFC). MFC provides its own implementation of `DllMain()` that is required to properly initialize MFC. You cannot replace it with your own without using undocumented internal functions.

A DLL that uses MFC has its own `CWinThread` object that is part of `CWinApp`. When the DLL receives a DLL_PROCESS_ATTACH notification, MFC calls `InitInstance()`. When the DLL receives DLL_PROCESS_DETACH, MFC calls `CWinThread::ExitInstance()`. You can provide your own implementation of these functions because they are virtual. However, there is no virtual function that is called for DLL_THREAD_ATTACH or DLL_THREAD_DETACH. If you must receive these notifications in an MFC application, refer to Microsoft Knowledge Base article Q148791.

MFC 4.x also performs some special handling when a thread built on `CWinThread` starts up. Because of the serialization of calls to `DllMain()`, it is never possible to start a thread from within `CWinThread::InitInstance()` in a DLL. The DLL will hang during initialization if you try to do so.

Feeding Worker Threads

Let's diverge for a moment and talk about using a DLL that creates its own worker threads. One of the key problems to solve is how to tell the worker threads what to do. A very convenient mechanism would be to send messages on the message queue. You would define a bunch of custom messages for the various things that the worker thread could do, point to an allocated data structure using WPARAM and LPARAM, and you'd be in business.

The hitch is that a worker thread does not own any windows and so there is no window handle that other threads can send or post messages to. This is typically not a problem for a GUI thread because a window handle and a message queue are readily available.

You run into the same problem in a DLL because a DLL, multithreaded or not, almost never owns any windows. However, the distinction between a GUI thread and a worker thread is very small. If you call `GetMessage()` in a worker thread, then a message queue will be created, even if you do not have a window. Add to that the `PostThreadMessage()` call we saw in Chapter 11 and we are all set.

In Listing 14-3 is the source code for a worker thread with its own main message loop. In spite of this chapter's title, there is no DLL in this source. The concept would be identical if you placed the code in a DLL.

The primary thread starts up, creates the worker thread, and then waits for the worker thread to signal with an event object that it has initialized. The worker thread starts up, calls a USER function to force the creation of a message queue, sets an event object to signal the primary thread to continue, then queues a timer request for two seconds.

The primary thread queues three messages to the worker in rapid succession using `PostThreadMessage()` and waits for the worker to shut down. `PostThreadMessage()` takes a thread ID instead of a window handle to identify the message queue. The worker thread processes the requests, processes the timer, and shuts down. Messages sent by `PostThreadMessage()` are identified by a NULL window handle.

Listing 14-3. WORKER.CPP, a worker thread with a message loop

```
/*
 * Worker.cpp
 *
 * Demonstrate using worker threads that have
 * their own message queue but no window.
 */
```

Listing 14-3 (continued)

```c
#include <windows.h>
#include <stdio.h>
#include <process.h>
#include <string.h>
#include "MtVerify.h"

unsigned WINAPI ThreadFunc(void* p);

HANDLE ghEvent;

#define WM_JOB_PRINT_AS_IS        WM_APP + 0x0001
#define WM_JOB_PRINT_REVERSE      WM_APP + 0x0002
#define WM_JOB_PRINT_LOWER        WM_APP + 0x0003

int main(VOID)
{
    HANDLE hThread;
    unsigned tid;

    // Give the new thread something to talk
    // to us with.
    ghEvent = CreateEvent(NULL, TRUE, FALSE, NULL);

    hThread = (HANDLE)_beginthreadex(NULL,
                    0,
                    ThreadFunc,
                    0,
                    0,
                    &tid );
    MTVERIFY(hThread);

    // This thread has to wait for the new thread
    // to init its globals and msg queue.
    WaitForSingleObject(ghEvent, INFINITE);

    // The only place in the book we get to use
    // the thread ID!
    char *szText = strdup("Thank for buying this book.\n");
    PostThreadMessage(tid, WM_JOB_PRINT_AS_IS, NULL, (LPARAM)szText);

    szText = strdup("Text is easier to read forward.\n");
    PostThreadMessage(tid, WM_JOB_PRINT_REVERSE, NULL, (LPARAM)szText);

    szText = strdup("\nLOWER CASE IS FOR WHISPERING.\n");
    PostThreadMessage(tid, WM_JOB_PRINT_LOWER, NULL, (LPARAM)szText);
```

Listing 14-3 (continued)

```
    WaitForSingleObject(hThread, INFINITE);

    CloseHandle(hThread);

    return 0;
}

VOID CALLBACK TimerFunc(
    HWND hwnd,   // handle of window for timer messages
    UINT uMsg,   // WM_TIMER message
    UINT idEvent,   // timer identifier
    DWORD dwTime )   // current system time
{
    UNREFERENCED_PARAMETER(hwnd);
    UNREFERENCED_PARAMETER(uMsg);

    PostThreadMessage(GetCurrentThreadId(), WM_QUIT,0,0);
}

/*
 * Call a function to do something that terminates
 * the thread with ExitThread instead of returning.
 */
unsigned WINAPI ThreadFunc(LPVOID n)
{
    UNREFERENCED_PARAMETER(n);

    MSG msg;

    // This creates the message queue.
    PeekMessage(&msg, NULL, 0, 0, PM_NOREMOVE);

    SetEvent(ghEvent);

    // We'll run for two seconds
    SetTimer(NULL, NULL, 2000, (TIMERPROC)TimerFunc);

    while (GetMessage(&msg, NULL, 0, 0))
    {
        char *psz = (char *)msg.lParam;
        switch(msg.message)
        {
        case WM_JOB_PRINT_AS_IS:
            printf("%s", psz);
            free(psz);
            break;
```

Listing 14-3 (continued)

```
    case WM_JOB_PRINT_REVERSE:
        printf("%s", strrev(psz));
        free(psz);
        break;
    case WM_JOB_PRINT_LOWER:
        printf("%s", _strlwr(psz));
        free(psz);
        break;
    default:
        DispatchMessage(&msg);
    }
}

    return 0;
}
```

Thread Local Storage

I want to start this section out by telling you what TLS (thread local storage) is *not*. When I first heard about TLS, I thought it was a memory protection scheme by which memory that was allocated would only be available to a particular thread and would be protected against other threads. This notion was utterly and completely wrong.

TLS is a mechanism whereby a thread can keep a pointer to its own copy of a data structure. Both the C run-time library and MFC make use of TLS. The C run-time keeps values such as *errno* and the strtok() pointer in a thread local structure because their state must be preserved between calls without interference between threads. If each thread has its own copy, no problem.

MFC uses TLS to keep track of handles to GDI and USER objects on a per-thread basis. MFC is very strict that CWnds, CPens and other structures can only be used by the thread that created them. By using TLS, MFC can verify that objects are not being passed between threads.

Thread local storage works by giving each thread an array of 4-byte slots. This array is guaranteed to have at least TLS_MINIMUM_AVAILABLE entries in it. Currently, the guaranteed minimum is 64 entries. A certain slot in the array is assigned to be used for a particular structure. If the structure *WordCount* was at slot 4, then each thread would allocate a *WordCount* structure and set TLS slot 4 to point at it.

TLS is particularly valuable in a DLL because it allows the DLL to work without constantly having the calling functions pass in a pointer to a context. TLS is invaluable in situations where a library is called from hundreds or thousands of places, and adding such a context pointer to all of those places would be almost impossible.

Before you ask about per-process storage in a DLL, remember that all memory allocated, even in a DLL, is allocated in the context of the calling process. Also, your DLL will get a fresh copy of all its global variables for each calling process, compliments of the operating system and virtual memory magic. Unless you work to circumvent these safeguards, your DLL can comfortably ignore the fact that it is being used by several processes at the same time.

Setting Up Thread Local Storage

Using TLS starts with the `TlsAlloc()` function. `TlsAlloc()` allocates a slot in the TLS array and returns an index to that slot. Each thread will have a separate copy of the slot, but all copies will be at the same index.

DWORD TlsAlloc(VOID)

Return Value

On success, this function returns a slot in the TLS array. On failure, this function returns 0xFFFFFFFF. Call `GetLastError()` to find out why.

In a DLL you would typically call this function when you get the notification DLL_PROCESS_ATTACH. You would call `TlsAlloc()` just once to get a slot, then assign that value to a global variable that all threads can use.

It is important that you allocate just a single TLS slot, which will be used by all of your structures. The number of slots available is limited. If you have a large application that must link to many DLLs, running out of TLS slots becomes a real concern. If your DLL allocates four or five TLS slots for itself, then the problem only gets worse.

Once you have a slot, each new thread (including the first one!) needs to allocate a block of memory to store the thread local data. If you have several structures, enclose all of them in a larger structure. Then you must set a value for the TLS slot for the current thread using `TlsSetValue()`:

BOOL TlsSetValue(

```
DWORD dwTlsIndex,
LPVOID lpTlsValue
);
```

Parameters

dwTlsIndex   Index of the TLS slot returned by `TlsAlloc()`.

LpTlsValue   Value to store in that slot.

Return Value

On success, this function returns TRUE. On failure, this function returns FALSE. Call `GetLastError()` to find out why.

Let's look at how this would work in action. The DLL gets a DLL_PROCESS_ATTACH notification. It calls `TlsAlloc()`, which returns 4. The DLL stores this in a global variable. The DLL then allocates a block of memory, say at 0x1f0000. Finally, the DLL calls `TlsSetValue()` so that slot 4 will be associated with address 0x1f0000 for this current thread.

When the next thread attaches to the DLL, the DLL knows that a slot has already been allocated because the global variable with the slot number is set, so it proceeds to allocate a memory block. Let's say the memory block is at 0x203000. To finish initialization for this thread, the DLL calls `TlsSet-Value()` so that slot 4 will be associated with 0x203000 whenever this thread is executing.

Now each thread has its own memory block, and it can retrieve a pointer to it by calling `TlsGetValue()`:

LPVOID TlsGetValue(

    DWORD dwTlsIndex
);

Parameters

dwTlsIndex   Index of the TLS slot returned by `TlsAlloc()`.

Return Value

On success, this function returns the value that was stored by this thread with `TlsSetValue()`. On failure, this function returns zero. Call `GetLast-Error()` to find out why. If the application had actually stored zero in that slot, then `GetLastError()` will return NO_ERROR.

When the first thread calls `TlsGetValue(4)`, it will get 0x1f0000. When the second thread calls `TlsGetValue(4)`, it will get 0x203000. As more threads start up, this process repeats.

When the DLL finally receives the DLL_PROCESS_DETACH notification, it should call `TlsFree()` to release the slot.

BOOL TlsFree(

DWORD dwTlsIndex
);

Parameters

dwTlsIndex   Index of the TLS slot returned by `TlsAlloc()`.

Return Value

On success, this function returns TRUE. On failure, this function returns FALSE. Call `GetLastError()` to find out why.

Privacy Is Absolute

A thread cannot access another thread's TLS slots. It would be nice to have this access at shutdown because you could walk all TLS arrays and make sure that they were properly cleaned up.

The workaround is to maintain your own table of each block of memory that has been allocated. Although the system will clean up the physical memory if you do not, you may be able to prevent data loss or corruption by closing files and other handles that may exist in those data blocks.

A TLS index is only valid within a particular process. As a rule it is not safe to assume that the same TLS index will be used in two different processes.

DLL Startup with TLS

FAQ 52

How do I set up a thread local structure in a DLL?

The example in Listing 14-4 shows the basic implementation for setting up a DLL that supports thread local storage. The listing follows the logic exactly as outlined above.

Listing 14-4. Standard TLS startup in a DLL

```
// This is the shared slot
static DWORD gdwTlsSlot;

BOOL DllMain(
          HINSTANCE hInst,
          DWORD     dwReason,
          LPVOID    lpReserved)
{
    LPVOID lpvData;
    UNREFERENCED_PARAMETER(hInst);
    UNREFERENCED_PARAMETER(lpReserved);
```

Listing 14-4 (continued)

```
    switch (fdwReason)
        {

        case DLL_PROCESS_ATTACH:
            // Find the index that will be global for all threads
            gdwTlsSlot = TlsAlloc();
            if (gdwTlsSlot == 0xFFFFFFFF)
                return FALSE;

            // Fall through to handle thread attach too

        case DLL_THREAD_ATTACH:
            // Initialize the TLS index for this thread.
            lpData = (LPVOID) LocalAlloc(LPTR, sizeof(struct OurData));
            if (lpData != NULL)
                if (TlsSetValue(gdwTlsSlot, lpData) == FALSE)
                    ; // This should be handled
             break;

        case DLL_THREAD_DETACH:

            // Release the allocated memory for this thread.

            lpData = TlsGetValue(gdwTlsSlot);
            if (lpData != NULL)
                LocalFree((HLOCAL) lpData);
            break;

        case DLL_PROCESS_DETACH:

            // Release the allocated memory for this thread.
            lpData = TlsGetValue(gdwTlsSlot);
            if (lpData != NULL)
                LocalFree((HLOCAL) lpData);

            // Give back the TLS slot
            TlsFree(gdwTlsSlot);
            break;

        default:
            break;
    }

    return TRUE;
}
```

There is still a potential problem for any DLL that relies on the code in Listing 14-4 working "properly." If the DLL is loaded dynamically with `LoadLibrary()`, then there may be many threads running for which DLL_THREAD_ATTACH was never sent. Therefore, any class that uses the thread local storage that is allocated above must always check and make sure that the slot is not NULL. If it is NULL, then the memory block needs to be allocated and stored in the TLS slot, as shown in the listing for DLL_THREAD_ATTACH.

_declspec(thread)

There is another, somewhat simpler way to use thread local storage that requires less work on the developer's part. Microsoft Visual C++ allows a variable or structure to be declared so that it will always be thread local. For example, the following declaration, if placed in a DLL, will create a global variable that will be unique within each process.

```
DWORD gProgressCounter;
```

In contrast, this next declaration would be unique on a *thread* basis.

```
_declspec(thread) DWORD tProgressCounter;
```

This mechanism also works well for structures. For example:

```
struct _ScreenObject
{
        RECT        rectBoundingBox;
        COLORREF    crColor;
        POINT       *ptVertices;
}

_declspec(thread) struct _ScreenObject BouncingPolyhedron;
```

All of the work to put the value or structure into thread local storage is handled by the compiler. In many ways, it is much easier to use than the TLS calls. It is not necessary for `DllMain()` to know about all of the structures that need to be in TLS. It is not necessary to create one "super structure" that holds all the other structures. Each structure can be declared where it is needed and the compiler will take care of putting them all together into thread local storage.

Each EXE and DLL that declares objects in this manner will have a special section in the executable file that holds all the thread local variables. When the EXE or DLL is loaded, the operating system recognizes this section and handles it appropriately. The section is automatically set up by the operating system to be local to each thread and no further work on your part is necessary.

When an application (EXE) is loaded, the operating system scans the executable and all statically linked DLLs to find all thread local sections. The size of all the sections is summed together to find the amount of memory that should be allocated for each thread that starts up.

The Tls...() calls and _declspec(thread) do not interact and can safely be mixed. You are not limited to using just one or the other.

Limitations

FAQ 53

What are the limitations of _declspec-(thread)?

If you are using C++, there are some limitations on classes that you create. An object may not be declared _declspec(thread) if it has a constructor or a destructor. Therefore you have to initialize the object yourself when the thread starts up.[1]

There is another limitation that is much harder to work around. A DLL that uses _declspec(thread) will not be properly loaded by LoadLibrary(). The calculation of thread local sections was done when the application started up and cannot be modified as new DLLs are loaded. Although the call to LoadLibrary() will usually succeed under Windows NT, the DLL will generate a protection fault when a function within it runs. See Microsoft Knowledge Base article Q118816 for more information.

Data Consistency

We have talked at length in other places in the book about the need to protect your variables with synchronization mechanisms. Because DLLs are designed to be sharable, and sometimes reusable, components, you never know when a developer will decide to start calling it from four or five threads at the same time.

This problem is particularly important with OLE and Active X, where component reuse is a far more easily realized goal. The sheer simplicity of using controls and automation objects means that developers will probably try to use them in some pretty wild environments.

---

[1] There is a bug in versions 1.0 through 4.2 of the Visual C++ compiler that prevents you from declaring an object to be _declspec(thread) if the object has any private or protected members. See Microsoft Knowledge Base article C2483 for more information.

The guidelines for producing DLLs that will be safe in a multithreaded environment are straightforward:

- Do not use global variables except for TLS slot storage.
- Do not use static variables.
- DO use thread local storage.
- DO use your stack.

If you come from the Win16 world, you are used to making all sorts of compromises to make a DLL work, particularly when dealing with the problem of difference between the data segment and the stack segment. A Win32 application typically has at least a megabyte for its stack, and all pointers are 32 bit, so putting a 16K object on the stack is no problem at all.

Summary

In this chapter you saw how to process notifications that are sent to a DLL to indicate a thread or process is attaching or detaching. You saw that there are some significant limitations on these notifications and that care has to be taken to process them properly. You saw how to use thread local storage and why it is useful. Finally, you saw `_declspec(thread)`, which is a compiler-supported way of doing thread local storage.

Part III

Multithreading in Real-World Applications

Chapter 15

Planning an Application

This chapter provides guidelines on what kind of applications are best suited for multithreading and how best to structure them. The chapter has several "mini-discussions" on issues that influence multithreaded design, including third-party libraries and application architecture.

In the world of software, where new technologies flare up overnight and just as quickly burn out, multithreading is a bit of a curiosity. Threads have been available in one form or another under Unix and other operating systems for several years and have been in the research labs for even longer. However, if you do any research on them, you will discover that threads are discussed in the context of theory and of operating systems at great length, but very little material is written about applying threads in an application.

Reasons to Multithread

? FAQ 54

When should I use threads?

We have already seen some reasons *not* to multithread. For example, the messaging architecture of Windows does a fine job of breaking up MDI management into small tasks. Trying to "improve" an MDI application by using one thread per child window is a recipe for disaster. Not surprisingly, it is also a bad idea to make an application multithreaded just because the tools are available to do so.

So where *are* threads a good idea?

The practical application of threads is in four main areas. Any given application could qualify under several of these areas, and there is arguably overlap between each of them.

1. Offloading time-consuming tasks from the primary GUI thread to make the user interface more responsive
2. Scalability
3. Fair-share resource allocation
4. Simulations

FOR THE EXPERTS

For the purposes of this discussion, massively parallel processing is a completely different problem than the application of a few, or a few dozen, threads on a Windows system.

If you come from the Unix world, it is worth pointing out that threads in Win32 are much cheaper than processes under Unix. Many of the tasks under Unix that you would have solved with multiple processes and with IPCs can be solved under Win32 with the use of threads. More on this later.

Offloading Time-Consuming Tasks

We have already spent some time on this in Chapter 11. The goal of the main message loop is to quickly respond to most messages in Windows and not cause the application to halt by clogging up the message queue. If it takes 15 minutes to successfully calculate a repaint, the user will not even be able to select Exit from the File menu unless some means is found to keep the message queue operational.

In Win16 the popular solution was to call `PeekMessage()` to check for messages in the queue and to respond to them appropriately. This technique was very difficult to implement effectively. The calls to `PeekMessage()` had to be scattered through the code at regular intervals. If `PeekMessage()` was called too often, the application suffered a performance penalty. If it was not called enough, the application was unresponsive and hesitant.

In Win32 the primary thread and the message loop can be left fully functional while a worker thread does the hard work. However, this "simple" scenario needs careful planning to do it properly. Substantial thought has to be given to making the user feel comfortable that the application is doing the right thing. How many times have you used beta software that never put up wait cursors? You sit there clicking away, hoping that the software is paying attention to you, and the software does not give you any feedback at all that something is going on. You wonder, "Has it crashed? Should I reboot?"

Multithreaded programs doing work in the background need to keep the user up-to-date. A wait cursor is not a reasonable solution because the work *is* going on in the background and the cursor should only be showing what is happening in the foreground.

Consider Microsoft Word. Whenever it is background printing, you see a little animation of a printer spitting paper out in the status bar. To prove that the operation is actually proceeding and that more than a cartoon is in progress, Word also displays the page number of the page being printed. Even if printing ends up taking half an hour, the user is assured that everything is working and can get some sort of feel for how long the operation will take.

Let's look at another example. A photo-retouching program frequently has to work with very large bitmaps, easily 2048×2048 true color pixels for a total of 12MB of memory. Obviously, the program is not going to be able to load this bitmap in two or three seconds. In fact, it is entirely possible that opening the file could take several minutes if the machine is slow or the network is congested. Therefore, opening the file seems like an ideal candidate to move to a separate thread.

There are several ways of indicating that an operation is in progress, and all of them require updating the screen in some way. Because we want the thread that opens the file to be a worker thread and not a GUI thread, it will be necessary to set up some means of communication between the worker thread and the primary GUI thread. This could be an event object that is marking some data, but probably it would be a lot easier just to post a message from the worker thread to the primary thread's main window.

The status could be presented to the user by putting a gauge in the destination window, by putting up a percent indicator in a dialog, or in other ways. The important thing to remember is that the user could potentially be opening up several files at the same time. Therefore an indicator on the status bar would probably not be appropriate because there would only be room for one indicator.

In a client/server application, creating a report might be a candidate for a worker thread. The main part of the decision is based on whether the reports are being generated locally or if the reports are being generated on a remote server.

If the report is being generated locally then it may be a prime candidate for being moved to another thread. Reports can take hours to run, and tying up the application for several hours would not be a good thing.

If the report is being generated remotely, then it may be possible to set up a notification mechanism to alert the main message loop when the report finishes. Obviously, it would be a very bad design to continually have to poll the report server as to whether it had finished.

Scalability

Scalability refers to the concept that an application's performance can be improved by adding RAM, disk space, and processors. For the purposes of this discussion, the most important of these is the addition of processors. Somewhere way back in Chapter 1 I mentioned the concept of SMP, or Symmetric Multi-Processor. Unlike a single processor system, which gives the appearance of multitasking by rapidly switching between threads, an SMP system runs several threads at exactly the same time by using a different processor for each thread.

Windows NT can support multiple processors right out of the box. If your application is heavily CPU-bound, then adding processors may be just the ticket to improving performance.

Making effective use of an SMP system requires that your program support multiple threads. If an application has only one thread, it can only make use of one processor.

An application that can perform several independent tasks is typically one of the best candidates to benefit from a scalable architecture. Servers often fall into this category. A database server, a Web server, or a report server all handle requests that are largely unrelated. Each of these tasks would fit neatly into its own thread.

Another type of application that is easily scalable is one that has a single task that can easily be broken apart. An excellent example of this type is a raytracing application. Raytracers have to perform vast amounts of number crunching to calculate each pixel in the destination picture. However, each pixel can be calculated independently and does not rely on any other pixel. By creating one thread for each available processor, a raytracer's performance could be doubled by going from one processor to two.

I want to emphasize that the threads are merely a mechanism for dividing the tasks among multiple processors. Creating multiple threads in a raytracer that only has a single processor available will slow things down because of the system overhead to manage the threads.

Most GUI applications are not scalable because the user can do only one thing at a time. A spreadsheet might be recalculating, redrawing, and printing, all at the same time, but these tasks are tightly tied together because they are all working on the same document. A power user might have three or four documents all active at the same time, but this situation is very different from the server processing several hundred requests per minute. With a few exceptions, such as CAD programs whose recalculations are highly parallel, GUI applications are not a good fit for this category.

Use threads for scalability to easily allow an application to make optimal use of hardware.

Fair-share Resource Allocation

Even in an SMP system, a heavily loaded or **saturated** application server will be using every bit of CPU time to service requests. With scalability you solve the problem of how a heavily loaded server can be improved by spending money on more hardware. However, there is another problem of how to get a heavily loaded server to service requests in a fair manner. The question then becomes how long a client will have to wait before its request gets serviced.

If you properly limit the maximum concurrent number of requests being serviced, then you can assign a thread to each request and the operating system's scheduling algorithms will help enforce that each request is processed with equal priority, and that any particular request does not bog down the server. It is important to limit the number of requests because too many threads will cause the system to thrash excessively. If there are 500 threads and 500 context switches per second, then each thread would only get to run for less than 2 ms out of every second.

By properly applying thread priority, you can also ensure that deserving threads get more than their fair share of processing time. For example, it would be possible to set the system up so that any request that came in from a particular group of workstations would be processed before any others. Using thread priority, you can let Win32 give you the desired result.

Simulations

The fourth and final reason for using multiple threads would be to drive a simulation. In this case, scalability and fairness are not interesting. What is important is to provide independent "players" that can interact with each other in the simulation.

The use of threads for simulations is largely a convenience to the developer. There is nothing that the threads provide that cannot be done sequentially.

Simulating a stretch of highway with 10,000 cars using one thread per car is almost guaranteed to fail. Simulating a parking lot with 100 cars is much more likely to succeed.

Threads or Processes?

The next practical question to answer is whether to use multiple threads or multiple processes. In spite of the emphasis of this book, there are conditions under which using multiple processes instead of multiple threads is an appropriate solution.

Throughout this discussion it is important to keep in mind that processes are expensive. They are expensive to start, expensive to clean up, and expensive for the operating system to keep track of. The difference in overall cost between threads and processes is two to three orders of magnitude. Therefore, it is feasible to envision an environment with 500 threads, but not with 500 processes. Creating and destroying many threads per second is feasible. Creating and destroying many processes per second is not.

One good reason to consider using multiple processes is application integrity. In a multithreaded application, there must be some level of trust that a thread will not crash and bring down the other 50 threads. While this is possible and reasonable to do if the entire application is designed by a single group of people, the danger rises dramatically if you allow plug-ins or extension DLLs, or if there is an embedded programming language.

Consider the case where you have to use a legacy body of code that is not very stable but cannot be rewritten at the moment. By running this section of code in another process, you can perform damage control if the process crashes. The operating system will clean up all of the file handles and other objects that might otherwise be left open. In this scenario, it may be possible to leave the process running instead of incurring the cost of starting and stopping it.

Although we have touched on security very little in this book, the security between processes is inherently much greater than between threads. In a multithreaded program, all data is available to all threads. While this is a great advantage most of the time, for a secure system this openness could potentially be a big security risk. By compartmenting the data in processes, you create a much more secure barrier.

Multithreaded Application Architecture

When designing the architecture of a multithreaded application, there are three key concepts to keep in mind. We have already gone over all these several times in the book, so I will pick selected examples that demonstrate the issues.

1. Keep the surface area between threads to a minimum
2. Minimize race conditions
3. Code defensively

In Chapter 2 we started a background printing job by gathering up all the information a new thread would need, then passing all the data in a block. It was not the epitome of efficiency but it was very easy to understand and it was *safe*. It is the extreme example of numbers 1 and 2 in our list. The surface area between the primary GUI thread and the worker thread was zero. The worker thread had everything it needed to do its work and it did not share this data with the primary thread. Second, the primary thread was responsible for taking care of all operations that were order-sensitive. By the time the worker thread started, there was nothing left whose order mattered.

Number 3 in the list was demonstrated by using code like MTVERIFY, as used in many sample programs in this book. The most unbelievable things can go wrong in a multithreaded application. Test every assumption.

In Chapter 7 we talked about how to effectively protect your data from race conditions. If there is a mechanism in the operating system that might do what you need, use it. For example, instead of writing your own multi-threaded ring buffer, you could use anonymous pipes. Pipes may not be the fastest, the most elegant, or the most efficient solution, but they are already written, debugged, and known to work correctly under multitasking conditions. If it turns out that performance is a problem you can rewrite the code, but otherwise you have saved yourself a sizable headache.

Dividing the Pieces

In operating system design there are two particularly common ways of designing the kernel. Because operating systems are multithreaded by their very nature, they provide a case study in how to assemble multithreaded systems.

The first design is called **monolithic.** In a monolithic kernel, there is one giant piece of code that performs all operating system functions. Everything has access to everything, and there aren't usually tightly defined interfaces to various subsystems within the monolithic kernel. A monolithic kernel is the easiest thing to design by the seat of the pants, because it is easy to work around architectural problems.

The downfall of monolithic kernels is that they eventually collapse under their own weight. All of the "hacks" to fix individual flaws start to interfere with each other. Problems become increasingly difficult to track down because the functionality is so spread out and interdependent.

Monolithic kernels have a high surface area between components. It is almost impossible to completely debug them and guarantee them to be reliable.

Microkernel architecture is the opposite extreme. The kernel of the operating system tends to be very small and to be responsible only for core functions such as memory management and process/thread scheduling. Other functions of the operating system, such as file systems, disk drivers, and communications drivers run in their own processes and can only be accessed with tightly defined interfaces. Microkernel architectures tend to be much more robust and reliable, but may suffer from performance problems if not carefully tuned.

The key to the microkernel architecture is the separation of components. It is very similar to the concept of objects in object-oriented design. Changes are localized and ripple effects of changes tend to be minimized.

When designing your own multithreaded software, strive to follow microkernel architecture. Although it requires substantially more up-front design, it will pay for itself over and over with maintainability and reliability.

Evaluating Suitability of Existing Code

FAQ 55

Can I multithread existing code?

It would be nice to say that an application should always be designed from the ground up with multithreading in mind, but the reality is that existing programs must often be retrofitted for a multithreaded world. In this section I will try to provide some guidelines for what to look for when assessing a body of existing code for conversion to multithreading.

The first thing to look at in a body of existing code is the usage of global variables and static variables. It is a favorite practice in C to keep state information in either a global variable or in a local static variable. This practice will utterly destroy a multithreaded program. Particular examples are global file pointers and global window handles. This is less of a problem in C++ because of the simple usage of member variables.

As we saw in Chapter 8, the C run-time library uses static buffers in a variety of run-time functions, such as `asctime()`. Unless you use the multithreaded version of the run-time library, separate threads calling `asctime()` at the same time will cause bizarre and undefined results.

In the run-time library this problem was fixed by creating a structure in thread local storage that had space for each function that used a static buffer. Each thread therefore has a copy of this structure where it can place static and global data that must be kept on a thread-by-thread basis. For example, when you call `asctime()` in the multithreaded runtime library, a pointer is retrieved to the thread local structure and the result is stored in the structure member variable *_asctimebuf* instead of in a static local variable in the function. In Visual C++ 4.2, the structure is defined in MTDLL.H and is shown in Listing 15-1. (*Note:* Processor-specific fields were removed for this listing.)

In this listing, you can look through the structure and get an idea for the kinds of information that the run-time library has to track separately for each thread.

Listing 15-1. Thread local structure used by the C run-time library

```
/* Structure for each thread's data */

struct _tiddata {
    unsigned long   _tid;          /* thread ID */

    unsigned long   _thandle;      /* thread handle */

    int       _terrno;             /* errno value */
    unsigned long   _tdoserrno;    /* _doserrno value */
    unsigned int    _fpds;         /* Floating Point data segment */
    unsigned long   _holdrand;     /* rand() seed value */
    char *          _token;        /* ptr to strtok() token */
#ifdef _WIN32
    wchar_t *   _wtoken;           /* ptr to wcstok() token */
#endif /* _WIN32 */
    unsigned char * _mtoken;       /* ptr to _mbstok() token */

    /* following pointers get malloc'd at runtime */
    char *          _errmsg;       /* ptr to strerror()/_strerror() buff */
    char *          _namebuf0;     /* ptr to tmpnam() buffer */
#ifdef _WIN32
    wchar_t *   _wnamebuf0;        /* ptr to _wtmpnam() buffer */
#endif /* _WIN32 */
    char *          _namebuf1;     /* ptr to tmpfile() buffer */
#ifdef _WIN32
    wchar_t *   _wnamebuf1;        /* ptr to _wtmpfile() buffer */
#endif /* _WIN32 */
    char *          _asctimebuf;   /* ptr to asctime() buffer */
#ifdef _WIN32
    wchar_t *   _wasctimebuf;      /* ptr to _wasctime() buffer */
#endif /* _WIN32 */
    void *          _gmtimebuf;    /* ptr to gmtime() structure */
    char *          _cvtbuf;       /* ptr to ecvt()/fcvt buffer */

    /* following fields are needed by _beginthread code */
    void *          _initaddr;     /* initial user thread address */
    void *          _initarg;      /* initial user thread argument */
```

Listing 15-1 (continued)

```
/* following three fields are needed to support signal handling
 * and runtime errors */
void *      _pxcptacttab;    /* ptr to exception-action table */
void *      _tpxcptinfoptrs; /* ptr to exception info ptrs */
int         _tfpecode;       /* float point exception code */

/* following field is needed by NLG routines */
unsigned long   _NLG_dwCode;

/*
 * Per-Thread data needed by C++ Exception Handling
 */
void *      _terminate;     /* terminate() routine */
void *      _unexpected;    /* unexpected() routine */
void *      _translator;    /* S.E. translator */
void *      _curexception;  /* current exception */
void *      _curcontext;    /* current exception context */
};
```

The other piece of information that is often global is the error flag, such as *errno* in the run-time library. You can see it included in the Listing 15-1 in the structure member *_terrno*. This solution works for most applications, but the error result should be retrieved with a function instead of a variable. Existing projects can cheat by using #define so that the error variable will automatically turn into a function call.

The next important thing to look for when evaluating existing code is libraries or precompiled objects for which no source is available. These can be tricky to find because they are often buried in the makefile. If you find such a module but cannot get any source, you may be able to get away with wrapping the calls in a mutex but more likely the module will have to be rewritten.

One of the more frustrating problems when using existing code is protecting the various pieces of data in the application. Every shared array, every shared linked list, every shared hash table will have to be protected with a synchronization mechanism. Even worse is enforcing the idea of "logically atomic" operations, similar to SQL transactions, but it takes several changes to a data structure to make its data consistent.

The designers of Windows 95 faced this problem when trying to get 16- and 32-bit applications to coexist while running on top of a 16-bit code base. The solution in Windows 95 was the "global mutex," which gets set whenever any

16-bit application is executing an API call. When the global mutex is set, no other applications, including the 32-bit applications, are allowed to make API calls.

Planning for ODBC

FAQ 56

Can I use threads in my database application?

Multithreading client database code is very tricky. The problem is that a number of components from different vendors must work together and each of these components must be thread-safe. Here are the factors that go into making a decision as to whether you can multithread a database client.

1. **Will more than one thread be talking to the database?**

   If only one thread in your application will be talking to the database, you typically do not need to be concerned. In other words, even if your application is multithreaded, if you only access the ODBC driver from a single thread, then there is no problem for the ODBC driver. The exception to this rule is the DAO, or Data Access Object, as discussed in #4 below. If your client is making full use of threads, then several threads are talking to the database driver at the same time and may in fact be sharing database handles.

2. **Is the JET database engine being used?**

   The JET database is the engine that ODBC and DAO use to talk to Access databases, *x*Base compatible databases, text databases, and Excel databases. As of version 3.00, the JET database was not thread-safe and could not be used by multithreaded clients.

3. **Is the ODBC driver documented to be thread-safe?**

   Unless an ODBC driver is specifically documented to be thread-safe, you should assume it is not. As a rule, a driver will not "just work." The Microsoft SQL Server ODBC driver is documented to be thread-safe.

4. **Is DAO being used?**

   The DAO is an OLE COM object for communicating with databases. The DAO was supported by MFC as of MFC v4.0. The DAO is built on OLE. As of this writing, not only is DAO *not* thread-safe, it can only be used from within the primary thread of an application.

5. **Is MFC being used?**

   Although MFC has had support for ODBC for a long time, it was not until MFC v4.2, released in July, 1996, that the ODBC classes within

MFC, such as `CDatabase` and `CRecordSet`, were fixed to be thread-safe. The "thread-safe" designation applies only to the MFC C++ classes themselves. MFC uses the standard ODBC drivers and the drivers themselves must be thread-safe for MFC to function reliably.

The MFC DAO support is not thread-safe as of MFC v4.2. Chapter 16 shows an example of how to work around this problem when using ISAPI with Internet Information Server.

Third-Party Libraries

With today's emphasis on component software, it becomes increasingly difficult to build an application that does not use at least one third-party component. These components could come in any of the following forms:

- Memory managers (such as SmartHeap by MicroQuill)
- OLE controls (such as the calendar control with Visual C++)
- Database drivers (ODBC, dbTools++)
- Report generators (such as Crystal Reports)
- Image processing libraries (such as LeadTools)
- Communications libraries
- Frameworks (such as MFC)
- Many, many others

Each of these pieces must be separately evaluated for its safety and capabilities in a multithreaded environment. If in doubt, call and ask the company how its application has been tested in a multithreading environment. Be wary of claims that "It will just work."

Summary

In this chapter you saw some of the issues surrounding writing new multi-threaded applications or modifying existing applications to be multithreaded. You saw some discussion of when to use threads versus processes, and you saw how to evaluate third-party libraries and database access code.

Chapter 16

ISAPI

This chapter shows an ISAPI extension DLL for a web server that uses the JET engine under ODBC.

By now you have probably heard of the Internet, the latest Big Thing. The Weather Channel has its own web site, Boston has its own web site, even the White House anted up. With all these big names running their own web servers, server performance has attracted more than a little attention. When Microsoft designed the Internet Information Server (IIS), they came up with a way to add in server extensions so that they will run dramatically faster than the competition's. The technique requires the extension to support multiple threads and to be thread-safe. In this chapter we will take a look at how to build a server extension that talks to the JET engine with ODBC.

Web Servers and How They Work

For those of you who have never dissected a web server, here's a short course. The server receives a request from a client, typically a web browser such as Internet Explorer or Netscape. The request is text-based and arrives on a socket connection, just like we used to demonstrate I/O completion ports in Chapter 6.

The user would have typed in a URL, or Universal Resource Locator, such as `http://www.microsoft.com/visualc/vc42`. This means that the protocol is HTTP, the name of the site is "www.microsoft.com," and the path to the resource on the site is "visualc/vc42."

With a simple request like this, the server would just return the requested file. That file might point to other files, such as bitmaps, that the browser would automatically ask for separately.

Sometimes static text and images are not enough, and some processing must take place to generate the page. Historically this processing has been taken care of by using CGI, or Common Gateway Interface. To use CGI, a client makes a request that points to a program instead of to an HTML page. The server sees that the URL is to a program and launches the program using CGI. For example, this request runs the program "search" in the "cgi-bin" directory:

```
http://www.bigcompany.com/cgi-bin/search?product=toaster
```

(*Note:* Unix does not use file extensions such as EXE to indicate that a file is executable. A file is marked as executable with its permissions in the file system.)

When the server receives a request, it launches the CGI application as a new process. The environment strings for the new process are set with any parameters that were specified in the URL. The sample URL above would cause the server to run a program called "search" and pass "product=toaster" as one of the environment variables. The program then generates its response to *stdout,* which is piped back to the server, which sends the information back to the client.

This arrangement works pretty well, except that a process must be created and destroyed for every single request. The CGI interface was designed under Unix, where processes are relatively cheap, but definitely not free. Even worse for performance, many CGI programs are written in Perl, a versatile language that does the job with a minimum of difficulty, but Perl programs are interpreted and therefore have a high overhead.

ISAPI

Microsoft was very aware of the performance problems with CGI when they designed the Internet Information Server. Microsoft's solution is called ISAPI, which stands for Internet Server API. ISAPI is implemented by the Internet Information Server (IIS) on Windows NT Advanced Server 4.0,

Peer Web Services (PWS) on Windows NT Workstation 4.0, and Personal Web Server on Windows 95B.[1]

ISAPI server extensions can be either filters or applications. A filter is invisible to a web browser. The filter is installed into the web server, and it processes every page the server sends out. In contrast, an ISAPI application must be requested explicitly by a URL. The URL includes the path and name of the ISAPI application, similar to how CGI scripts are requested.

Extensions based on ISAPI are implemented as DLLs instead of as EXEs. To process a request, the server simply makes a call to the DLL instead of having to create a new process. The DLL needs to be loaded once, the first time it is used, and it usually stays resident after that. The startup and shutdown overhead to process a request is reduced to zero and the memory requirements drop dramatically. Imagine having to allocate, initialize, and load 256K (or much more!) of data space and stack in an application for each request that comes in, and you can easily see why many Unix web servers require 128MB of memory.

The ISAPI DLL is in the same address space as the server itself, so no context switches are necessary to switch between the extension and the server. In contrast, it could potentially take many context switches for a CGI script to write all its data to the server using *stdout*, so the savings in overhead on a busy server is substantial.

There are some disadvantages to the ISAPI architecture. Without the barriers of process boundaries, an ISAPI DLL can walk all over the data space of the server. An access violation in the DLL could potentially crash the entire server. With CGI, the process for that request would fail, but the web server itself would keep running because the process boundaries would shield the server from failures in CGI applications. The importance of thoroughly testing ISAPI DLLs cannot be overemphasized.

The next disadvantage is that an ISAPI server extension must be written in C or C++. This constraint restricts the creation of ISAPI DLLs to an exclusive set of system-level developers. Someone familiar only with Perl will not be able to write an ISAPI DLL. However, CGI is still available in IIS and PWS, so Perl developers can still write Perl scripts, but they lose the performance advantages of ISAPI.[2]

---

[1] Release "B" of Windows 95 was an OEM release for shipment on new computers. It was not released to the public as a separate service pack.

[2] This restriction may be changing. As I write this, I have seen discussions of an ISAPI-based Perl interpreter as well as controls that allow writing ISAPI extensions in Visual Basic.

Writing ISAPI DLLs

When writing ISAPI DLLs, it is absolutely critical that you pay close attention to resource usage. In a regular application, if you forget to call `CloseHandle()` a few times, the system will just clean up when the user exits. However, an Internet Server could run for months without stopping. Consider the case of an ISAPI function that forgets to free a single resource for each request that is processed. The ISAPI function could be missing a call to `CloseHandle()`, or maybe even `DeleteCriticalSection()`. On a busy server, you could easily lose a few hundred or even a few thousand handles per hour. Eventually, the system will run out of space and crash.

The sheer volume of requests that an ISAPI extension can process can be hard to grasp. Writing software that is mission-critical that might run for weeks or months without stopping takes a certain dedication to details. Again, thorough testing is of paramount importance.

The fact that your ISAPI extension is a DLL and not a process in its own right also causes a few problems. You never know what thread will be used to call the DLL, nor is there a primary thread that is responsible for maintenance or other special functions. Therefore mechanisms such as thread local storage are not particularly useful because no thread has any assigned responsibilities. Even if you try to assign responsibilities, you do not have control over what the individual threads are doing.

FOR THE EXPERTS

It is possible for an ISAPI DLL to create its own thread, but some care must be taken when doing so. The logical place to start the thread would be in `DllMain()` when the DLL is loaded. However, you run into problems because of DLL startup synchronization (see Chapter 14). You should also be careful to gracefully shut the thread down if it is maintaining any state information that must be preserved.

Threads in IIS

I will go out on a limb here and guess that the Internet Information Server was implemented using I/O completion ports. As you saw in Chapter 6, completion ports imply the use of multiple threads. The Internet Information Server is fully multithreaded and is capable of processing multiple requests at the same time. Because of this, ISAPI DLLs must be thread-safe and must be able to support any number of concurrent threads.

Depending on the design of the DLL, making it thread-safe could be very simple or very difficult. A simple ISAPI server extension might just generate a bitmap of a counter. In this case there would be no need to do any synchronization because each thread could operate completely independently.

A more complex example would be an inventory management system that has to read and write to a database. This could be a very complicated proposition. Different threads may have to share data so the real-world view stays consistent. For example, you would not want different threads to try to give out three futzilators when only two are available.

A common solution to this problem is to use a database, but the database driver would have to be completely thread-safe to work properly in the multithreaded ISAPI environment. We looked at some of the issues surrounding using database drivers in Chapter 15. From Microsoft, only the driver for SQL Server is stated to be thread-safe.

The IS2ODBC Sample Program

The sample program for this chapter demonstrates one possible way to use a non-thread-safe database driver with an ISAPI DLL. The sample program IS2ODBC (read it as "IS-to-ODBC") uses a process outside of IIS to run the database engine. Requests to the database server process are serialized and processed one at a time. This is obviously not a high performance solution, but it fills the gap between no database at all and purchasing, installing, and maintaining SQL Server.

To make the whole thing work, there are four pieces. These are:

- The Web server
- The IS2ODBC ISAPI DLL
- The database process
- The Web browser

I will go through each of these pieces, how it works, and how it talks to the other pieces. First, you may be interested in seeing the extension running.

Running the Sample

I am afraid that IS2ODBC will win no prizes for ease of installation. The procedure changes depending on which server you are running and requires ODBC to be correctly installed for Microsoft Access databases. Here is a basic summary for most Microsoft servers. Depending on how your system is configured, there may be additional issues with rights and security.

In Windows NT 4.0 Workstation and Windows 95B, the Web server is not installed by default. You can install it by going into Network in the Control Panel.

These instructions assume you will be running the server and the browser on the same computer. More details are available in README.TXT in the IS2ODBC directory on the CD-ROM.

1. Configure the database in ODBC as described in the READ ME.
2. Copy IS2ODBC.DLL to your "scripts" directory.
3. Copy DBSERVER.EXE to your "scripts" directory.
4. Copy QUERY.HTM to your "wwwroot" directory.
5. Make sure your Web server is running.
6. Load the file QUERY.HTM into the browser with the command `http://localhost/Query.htm`.
7. Choose one of the queries.

Overview of Operation

Here is the sequence of events when the Web server receives a URL that uses IS2ODBC. For the sake of discussion, let's say that the URL is:

```
http://localhost/scripts/Is2Odbc.dll?Sort=Title
```

The host name is "localhost", which is a standard alias for the machine you are running the program on. The path to the ISAPI extension is "scripts/Is2Odbc.dll". The server will see that this is a DLL and assume that it is an ISAPI DLL. Finally, the URL specifies the parameter "Sort=Title". I'll talk more about this shortly.

The Web server first makes sure that IS2ODBC.DLL is loaded, then passes the query on to the DLL. IS2ODBC needs the database process DBSERVER to service the request, and so starts the database process if it is not running.

IS2ODBC then waits until the database process is not busy, passes the request from the URL to DBSERVER, and waits for a response. DBSERVER runs the query, creates a text result and signals IS2ODBC to continue. IS2ODBC takes the result text and sends it back to the web browser.

Both IS2ODBC and DBSERVER were written using MFC. MFC provides helper classes that simplify writing both ISAPI extensions and database applications.

Browser Page

Everything starts with the Web browser. A picture of the Web page for this sample is shown in Figure 16-1. This page gives a brief description of the sample, then allows the user to click one of three URLs to start a query.

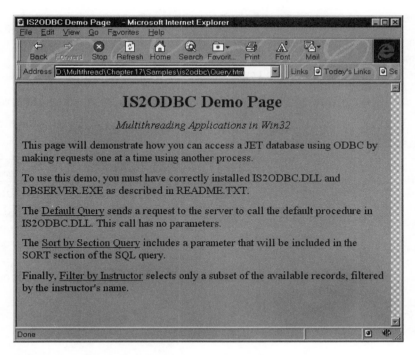

Figure 16-1. The Web page for IS2ODBC.

This Web page allows three different requests: a default query with no parameters, a sorted query, and a filtered query. This page could be extended by using forms so that the user would have finer control over the filter or the sorting.

The ISAPI Application

The ISAPI example application OS2ODBC was created with the ISAPI Extension Wizard in Visual C++ 4.2. MFC provides a class called `CHttpServer` that is used for implementing ISAPI extensions. The class handles many of the miscellaneous details necessary to make sure that everything works.

When the Web server receives the URL from the Web browser, it sees that the URL refers to a DLL and so passes the request to the DLL. At this point MFC helps out by interpreting the contents of the URL and turning the text string into parameters that can be handed to a member function.

You will find the parse map that controls this translation near the beginning of IS2ODBC.CPP. It is shown in Listing 16-1. The macro `ON_PARSE_COMMAND()` declares the default procedure to have two parameters, both of

Listing 16-1. MFC parse map for IS2ODBC

```
BEGIN_PARSE_MAP(CIs2OdbcExtension, CHttpServer)
      // Added Optional Filter and Sort arguments
      //
      ON_PARSE_COMMAND(Default, CIs2OdbcExtension, ITS_PSTR ITS_PSTR)
      ON_PARSE_COMMAND_PARAMS("Filter=~ Sort=~")
      DEFAULT_PARSE_COMMAND(Default, CIs2OdbcExtension)
END_PARSE_MAP(CIs2OdbcExtension)
```

which are strings ITS_PSTR. The `ON_PARSE_COMMAND_PARAMS()` declares the names of the parameters as they will appear in the URL. The `DEFAULT_PARSE_COMMAND()` declares which function will be called if the URL does not specify a procedure name. We are not using procedure names, so `Default()` will always be called.

The parse map allows MFC to call the `Default()` member function, which will handle the request.

Data Interchange

The source for the `Default()` member function is shown in Listing 16-2. You can see the parameters *pszFilter* and *pszSort,* which correspond to the parameters in the URL. One of the first things you will notice is that this function returns `void`. This seems strange because it is easy for the function to fail. However, the result of this function is a generated Web page. If the function fails, it is its responsibility to generate a Web page that describes the error. Since the Web server knows nothing about what the extension is doing, it is impossible for the server to generate a meaningful error message.

The functions `StartContent()` and `WriteTitle()` are provided by MFC to generate the appropriate HTML tags for a text-based Web page.

Listing 16-2. URL handler for IS2ODBC

```
void CIs2OdbcExtension::Default(
      CHttpServerContext* pCtxt, LPTSTR pszFilter, LPTSTR pszSort)
{
    StartContent(pCtxt);
    WriteTitle(pCtxt);
```

Listing 16-2 (continued)

```
CMutex myMutex(FALSE, MUTEX_DB_REQUEST);
CSingleLock myLock(&myMutex, FALSE);

// Wait to get access to the DBSERVER server
// If another request is outstanding then we will not get in.
if (myLock.Lock(TIMEOUT_MUTEX))
{
    // Create events for signaling DBSERVER
    CEvent startEvent(FALSE, TRUE, EVENT_START_PROCESSING);
    CEvent doneEvent(FALSE, TRUE, EVENT_DONE_PROCESSING);

    //
    // Allocate memory for our data structure in shared memory.
    //
    HANDLE hFileMapping = NULL;
    DbRequest* pDbRequest = NULL;

    MTVERIFY( hFileMapping = CreateFileMapping((LPVOID) -1, NULL,
        PAGE_READWRITE, 0, sizeof(DbRequest),
        FILE_DB_REQUEST));

    MTVERIFY( pDbRequest = (DbRequest*) MapViewOfFile(
                hFileMapping, FILE_MAP_ALL_ACCESS, 0, 0, 0));

    //
    // Fill in our DB request.
    // Make sure we detect the default argument "~" and replace it.
    //
    strcpy(pDbRequest->sqlFilter, "");
    if (strcmp(pszFilter, "~") != 0)
        strcpy(pDbRequest->sqlFilter, pszFilter);

    strcpy(pDbRequest->sqlSort, "");
    if (strcmp(pszSort, "~") != 0)
        strcpy(pDbRequest->sqlSort, pszSort);

    // Tell DBSERVER to do the DB Query
    startEvent.SetEvent();

    // Wait for result from DBSERVER
    // If Server has died, we can tell user
    CSingleLock waitForDoneEvent(&doneEvent, FALSE);
    if (waitForDoneEvent.Lock(TIMEOUT_EVENT))
```

Listing 16-2 (continued)

```
      {   // got result from server
          *pCtxt << _T("The Results from the DB are:<p>");
          *pCtxt << pDbRequest->sqlResult << "<p>";
      }   // end if
      else
      {   // Got no response from server
          *pCtxt << _T("Sorry, but the Database Server "
                       "never responded with the results.<p>");
          *pCtxt << _T("Please check that it is running.<p>");
      }   // end else
      doneEvent.ResetEvent();

      // Close request data structure
      UnmapViewOfFile(pDbRequest);
      CloseHandle(hFileMapping);

  } // end if
  else
  {   // Other threads are busy accessing the server
  *pCtxt << _T("Sorry, the server is too busy to "
  "handle your request right now.<p>");
  }   // end else


  EndContent(pCtxt);
}
```

To exchange data with DBSERVER.EXE, Default() first locks a mutex to indicate that the server is busy. Only one ISAPI thread can lock the mutex at a time so mutual exclusion of the database engine is assured.

Next, Default() creates a named shared memory area, such as we discussed in Chapter 13. The shared memory is created in the paging file so that IS2ODBC and DBSERVER do not have to agree on a location in the file system. The parameters from the URL are copied into the shared memory area so that DBSERVER knows what kind of query to do.

Default() then sets the event *startEvent* to tell DBSERVER to perform the query. DBSERVER copies its results back into shared memory and sets the event *doneEvent*. If DBSERVER does not respond within an appropriate amount of time, Default() assumes that something is wrong and prints an error.

You will also notice that `Default()` uses a time-out when waiting for the mutex. If it cannot acquire the mutex within the time period given by TIMEOUT_MUTEX, currently 10 seconds, then the user is told that the server is too busy to service the request. This could happen if the server is very busy and many threads are waiting in line on the mutex to use DBSERVER.

Summary

This chapter showed the sample ISAPI extension IS2ODBC, which uses a separate process outside the Web server to make database requests to a database that is not thread-safe. This sample uses many of the concepts in this book, including thread synchronization, interprocess communication, and MFC synchronization classes.

Chapter 17

OLE, ActiveX, and COM

This chapter describes the multithreading models that are built into COM and presents an application that demonstrates free-threading. The difference between the apartment model and free-threading is discussed, as well as how each works in a DLL versus an EXE.

Although this is a book about multithreading and not about OLE or ActiveX per se, I think that this chapter will make a lot more sense if I start off by talking about what OLE, ActiveX, and COM really are. If you are already familiar with OLE, skip this section and go straight to the *COM Threading Models* section.

OLE stands for object linking and embedding. Back in version 1.0 in the early 1990s, that was a very good description of what the technology was designed to do. For example, it allowed you, the developer, to write applications that can embed or link a spreadsheet from Microsoft Excel into whatever new business application you were designing.

Today, OLE can still do that, but it can do many other things, too. The suite of technologies called OLE includes drag and drop, structured storage, in-place activation, uniform data transfer, and a multitude of other interfaces. OLE is really a collection of standard interfaces for accomplishing a variety of tasks, all of which are based on COM, the Component Object Model, which I'll talk about in a bit. These interfaces allow Word and Excel to talk to each other, Visual Basic to talk to graphing and calendar controls, and Wordpad and the desktop to allow drag and drop between each other. Because of all this new functionality, much of which has nothing to do with linking and embedding, Microsoft created the name ActiveX to describe the technologies that are not directly related to linking and embedding.

Most of the discussion surrounding ActiveX has been around the Internet, but ActiveX is actually the new name for all technologies built on top of COM that are not part of object linking and embedding. In other words, Microsoft is trying to use the term OLE to describe just those technologies that are actually responsible for object linking and embedding. Because the term ActiveX was brought into the game later, much of the documentation still refers to all of the various technologies as OLE. Therefore the terminology in the documentation you read may not be consistent. If you are still confused, just remember that OLE and ActiveX are the names for a set of technologies built on top of COM.

COM stands for **Component Object Model.** The simplest way to describe COM is to say that it provides interfaces to objects in the form of a C++ class, then allows you to call member functions of that C++ class across application boundaries, across 16- and 32-bit boundaries, and even across network and CPU-type boundaries. You can ask a COM object if it supports a particular interface and the object will return a pointer to that interface if it exists. There are also functions that allow a COM object to describe its interfaces so that they can be called from Visual Basic or from Java.

COM is both a specification and a set of services within Windows that implements that specification. COM is implemented as part of several DLLs, just like GDI or USER. A COM object is an object written to use the COM specification. COM provides the functions for finding a COM object and communicating with it.

As a sample of one way all of this could be used, you might say to COM, "Create me an Excel document object." COM would start Excel, create a document, and return a pointer to a C++ class. This C++ class implements the interface called IUnknown, which is the most fundamental COM interface. In C++ terms, IUnknown is the base class upon which all other interfaces are based. Given IUnknown, you can ask for any other interface the object supports.

The idea of COM can be a little bit hard to grasp because C++ cannot directly express the fundamental idea behind COM. In COM, you deal only with interfaces, never with objects. An analogy in the real world would be if you asked where the airport was, and someone told you where to find the entrances to the airport. You still would not know where the airport itself was, but that would not matter because you would have all the information you needed to get there. The airport entrances go to the airport, but all you need to know is where the entrances themselves are.

In COM, the objects themselves are the equivalent of the airport and the interfaces are the equivalent of the entrances. When you ask for an object from COM, it will only give you an interface; it will never give you a pointer to the object itself. In C++, this concept is expressed as a C++ class that has public member functions but no public member data. However, the pointer to this interface is not a pointer to the object itself. The concept of interfaces does exist in other languages, most notably in Java. COM and Java work very well together.

Once you have an interface to an object, you can call any function that is part of that interface. An interface could be one of the technologies that is part of OLE, or it could be something you create. One of the key problems that COM solves is figuring out how to cross process boundaries so that an object in one process can use an interface for an object that might live in a DLL, in another process, or even on another machine that uses a different kind of CPU. COM can transparently move arguments and parameters between address spaces as needed.

COM Threading Models

OLE version 1.0 started with Win16, long before most people had ever heard of threads or Win32. When the Component Object Model was introduced in version 2 of OLE, a few people were trying out a new operating system called Windows NT 3.1, but the vast majority were still running 16-bit Windows. Therefore, there was no such thing as a "threading model."

Today there are three separate threading models. I will start by giving a quick summary of each of them, then go into the last two in more detail. The first model is a degenerate case of the second model.

The original model from Win16 is still the default. This is the single-threaded model. An OLE server that runs only a single thread has no need for anything else. However, the obvious limitation is that there is no support for multiple threads.

The second model is available in Windows 95 and Windows NT 3.51 and later. It is called the **apartment model.** In the apartment model, each thread is an "apartment" where COM objects can live. A COM object must do all of its work in that apartment. Therefore, any particular COM object can be run in only one particular thread. In Windows NT and Windows 95, a process using the single-threaded model is really a process with a single apartment.

The apartment model can support multiple threads, but because a particular object must run in a particular thread, it is not scalable. For a technology such as OLE Databases, if the database were forced to run in a single thread it would have to process each incoming request sequentially.

The final threading model was first available in Windows NT 4.0. It is *not* available in Windows 95. This newest threading model is called the **free-threaded** model. In this model, any object can run in any thread.

Before I start into more detailed descriptions of these models, I should mention the concept of client/server from the OLE point of view. Anything that implements an OLE object is a server, and anything that calls that object is a client. In an environment such as in-place activation, where one application starts up inside another application's window, both applications implement OLE objects that are working together. In this case, you cannot call one application "the server" and the other application "the client" because the roles switch back and forth depending on who is calling whom. The designation of "client" or "server" applies on a per-object basis, so one application can be a client and a server at the same time.

The Apartment Model

In the apartment model, an object is associated with a particular thread, and calls to that object will be made only in the context of that thread. You will find the apartment model to be available in COM in Windows NT 3.51 and 4.0, as well as in Windows 95. Windows NT 3.5 supports only the single-threaded model.

An apartment in COM is the place where an object is created, does its work, and is destroyed. In a server, COM will serialize calls to an apartment-model object so that only one call is ever being made to an object at a time. This model works the same as message queues for windows, where a particular thread owns a window and that thread services all requests for that window.

The meaning of the threading model on the server is very clear, because COM has to know which thread an object can run in. What is less obvious is that a client also has a threading model. When a client requests a pointer to an interface, it asks for that pointer from a particular thread (the "apartment"). The client may only use that interface pointer from within that apartment.

It is possible to create an interface pointer that can be used by another apartment. To do so, you need to use the COM functions `CoMarshalInterThreadInterfaceInStream()` and `CoGetInterfaceAndReleaseStream()`. These functions will not be discussed in this book.

The apartment model operates internally by using the message queue. COM creates an invisible window for each thread that is registered to be apartment model. As we have seen, messages for a window will be processed only by the thread that created the window, so that using the message queue automatically forces the proper thread to process calls to COM objects. A side effect of this technique is that threads that use the apartment model must have a message loop or calls to COM objects will not be dispatched.

If several calls are made to the same COM object, these calls are each put into the message queue. One call will be dispatched each time the server enters its message loop. This technique forces synchronization and mutual exclusion because only one call can be processed at a time.

COM enters its own message loop internally when a client makes a call to a COM object, thereby allowing window messages to be processed as well as allowing calls back into other COM objects in the apartment. Therefore an apartment can act as both a client and a server at the same time.

The Free-threaded Model

The free-threaded model was introduced in Windows NT 4.0. In the free-threaded model, calls to objects within an out-of-proc (implemented as an EXE and not as a DLL) COM server are made with threads that belong to COM. In other words, even if your application has only started a single thread, COM has its own pool of threads that it uses to call your COM object.

If the server is in-proc (implemented as a DLL), then the calls are usually made directly from the client to the server without COM intervening, although there is an exception to this that I will discuss shortly. This use of direct calls is one of the reasons that apartment-model clients cannot pass pointers between threads. Because the client has direct function pointers that bypass COM, there is no chance for COM to serialize access to the DLL if multiple threads try to make calls at the same time.

There is a fundamental difference between in-proc and out-of-proc servers in who creates the threads. With in-proc servers, the threading is controlled completely by the number of threads that are running within the client application. In-proc servers, once they are running, typically act like a normal multithreaded DLL in how they interact with the application. With out-of-proc servers, the threads are created by COM.

The free-threaded model does not rely on or use Windows messages, so there is no need to have a message loop. Bypassing the message loop allows calls to free-threaded objects to be processed significantly faster than calls to apartment model objects. The penalty is that the application is completely responsible for protecting the objects. Synchronization may be as simple as placing a mutex lock on the entire object, but it is very important to make sure that the object is protected. In comparison, with the apartment model, requests are always processed one at a time, so synchronization is not necessary.

A client can also be declared as free-threaded. A free-threaded client can safely pass a pointer to an interface between threads, and can make calls into that interface from any thread at any time. This means that the client can issue simultaneous requests with the same object, and so a free-threaded client may be using the same interface pointer in five different threads at the same time.

Declaring a Threading Model

A COM client or server must declare the threading model that it supports. For executable (EXE) files, each thread that will be using COM must call `CoInitialize()` or `CoInitializeEx()` before using any COM functions. The threading model is chosen at this time. `CoInitializeEx()` looks like this:

HRESULT CoInitializeEx(

```
void * pvReserved,
DWORD dwCoInit
);
```

Parameters

pvReserved	Reserved for future use, must be NULL.
dwCoInit	One of the values from the COINIT enum. In Windows NT 4.0, the following values are allowed:

> COINIT_MULTITHREADED
>
> COINIT_APARTMENTTHREADED

Return Value

`CoInitializeEx()` returns S_OK if it succeeds, E_INVALIDARG for an invalid argument, or RPC_E_CHANGED_MODE if this thread had previously called `CoInitializeEx()` with a different value for *dwCoInit*.

`CoInitialize()` internally calls `CoInitializeEx()` with a threading model of COINIT_APARTMENTTHREADED. If you are using compound documents, you must initialize OLE using `OleInitialize()`, which internally calls `CoInitialize()`. If you are using compound documents, you cannot use free-threaded objects in any threads that have called `OleInitialize()`.

A server implemented as a DLL works a little differently. Instead of registering its threading models at startup, the threading models that a DLL supports are stored as part of its registry entry. Under its CLSID entry, the DLL places a key under InprocServer32 called "ThreadingModel." The value can be any of the following:

Value	Meaning
(not present)	Single-threading model
Apartment	Supports the apartment model
Free	Supports free-threading
Both	Supports apartment or free-threading models

As an example, the registry entry for one of the OLE DLLs, OLE-AUT32.DLL, has a key as follows:

```
HKEY_CLASSES_ROOT
    CLSID
        {00020420-0000-0000-C000-000000000046}
            InprocServer32
                ThreadingModel="Both"
```

Mixed Model

It is possible for an application to use the apartment model in some threads and the free-threaded model in other threads. To confuse the terminology, all of the threads that are registered as free-threaded are said to live in their own apartment. Therefore there would be one free-threaded apartment with multiple threads, and one or more "standard" apartments, each of which has a single thread.

Each of the apartments behaves as you would expect. The standard apartments would use the message queue for delivery and so would be synchronized, and the free-threaded apartment would operate without the message queue and would not be synchronized.

Interoperability

It is possible that a client and a server have declared different threading models. If both the client and the server are out-of-proc, then COM can take care of making the two communicate safely. If a free-threaded client calls into an apartment model server, then COM will serialize the requests so that the server can handle them one at a time. If an apartment model client calls into a free-threaded server, then the server is allowed to handle requests normally.

If the server is in-proc, then COM can still take care of making the two interoperate but it may require additional overhead to do so. Servers are typically designed to be in-proc to allow calls to be made directly from the client to the server without COM having to help. This arrangement provides a significant speed increase. If a free-threaded client tries to use an apartment model, in-proc server, then COM must intervene by transferring the requests to the main apartment (the first thread that called `CoInitializeEx()`) and serializing each request to the in-proc server.

The AUTOINCR Sample Program

On the CD-ROM you will find a sample called COMDEMO. This sample contains the Visual C++ project to build a COM object called AUTOINCR. There are also two subdirectories with sample programs that use this object. One sample program, MFCCLI, is written in MFC and is itself multithreaded. The other sample program, VBCLI, is written in Visual Basic. The CLI stands for Client.

The COM object implements two auto-increment variables, each of which increments every time it is read. One increments slowly, taking about 15 seconds, and the other increments quickly, taking about 2 seconds. The server is implemented as a DLL and is therefore an in-proc server.

Although the basics of how the object works are straightforward, there are some expert-level features to allow interoperability with Visual Basic.

This object was built using the ActiveX Template Library (ATL), version 1.1.[1] You will need to have the ATL installed to compile this sample program.

---

[1] As of October, 1996, the ActiveX Template Library could be downloaded from `http://www.microsoft.com/visualc/v42/atl`. Version 1.1 of the ATL requires Visual C++ 4.2, so it can be used only if you have the subscription edition of Visual C++.

The ATL provides a big helping hand for creating lightweight COM objects. To reduce distribution size, particularly over the Internet, ATL can create objects that do not use MFC or the C run-time library. Using a Wizard in Visual C++, the ATL can help you create either an in-proc or out-of-proc server that implements one or more objects. Another of ATL's tricks is that it can create objects with dual interfaces. Such objects can be called with IDispatch (otherwise known as OLE Automation) or with custom C++ interfaces.

ATL takes care of generating the code necessary to register and unregister the server. In the file AUTOINCR.H, there is a declaration that looks like this (slightly reformatted):

```
DECLARE_REGISTRY(CAutoIncr,
        _T("ComDemo.AutoIncr.1"),
        _T("ComDemo.AutoIncr"),
        IDS_AUTOINCR_DESC,
        THREADFLAGS_BOTH)
```

This declaration says that the server name is "ComDemo", the object name is "AutoIncr" and the version number is 1. The description of the object will be taken from the string resource IDS_AUTOINCR_DESC. Finally, the flag THREADFLAGS_BOTH instructs the ATL server registration routine to put "Both" into the registry under "ThreadingModel".

In AUTOINCR.CPP is the implementation of the object itself, called CAuto-Incr. The object contains two counter member variables, *m_iValue1* and *m_iValue2*, which are initialized to zero in the constructor. The member functions get_SlowCounter() and get_FasterCounter() simulate work by sleeping for a while, then they return the current value of the counter and increment the count. The code is straightforward and is shown in Listing 17-1.

Listing 17-1. Implementation of CAutoIncr

```
CAutoIncr::CAutoIncr()
{
    // Initialize Counters
    m_iValue1 = 0;
    m_iValue2 = 0;
}

STDMETHODIMP CAutoIncr::get_SlowCounter(WORD* pValue)
{
    Sleep(15000); // simulate work being done.
    if (pValue)
```

Listing 17-1 (continued)

```
    {   // Return value and increase for next time
        *pValue = m_iValue1++;
        return S_OK;
    }
    return E_POINTER;
}

STDMETHODIMP CAutoIncr::get_FastCounter(WORD* pValue)
{
    Sleep(2000); // simulate work being done.
    if (pValue)
    {   // Return value and increase for next time
        *pValue = m_iValue2++;
        return S_OK;
    }
    return E_POINTER;
}
```

The `AutoIncr` object does not use any synchronization mechanisms to coordinate access to the object because there is nothing that can go wrong if a context switch happens at a bad moment. However, if the object's actions were any more complex it would have been necessary to place the routines in a critical section.

Registering the Object

Before you can run either of the client programs, you must register the server in the registry. You can do this either by building AUTOINCR, which registers the DLL as part of the build process, or by running REGSVR32.EXE, which is part of Visual C++. For example:

```
regsvr32 comdemo.dll
```

After installing the object, it will show up in the object browsers available from Visual C++ or from Visual Basic. The Visual Basic Object Browser window is shown in Figure 17-1. The information shown says that COM-DEMO includes a single object, called `CAutoIncr`, and this object has a single interface, called IAutoIncr.

Once the server is registered, you can run either of the two sample programs. One sample program is in MFC and the other uses Visual Basic. The

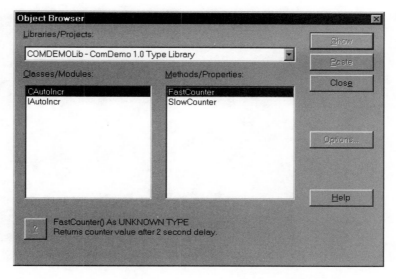

Figure 17-1. Visual Basic browse window showing COMDEMO.

MFC sample is free-threaded (under Windows NT 4.0) and the Visual Basic sample uses the apartment model.

Running MFCCLI

The first sample program is called MFCCLI. It is a client program written in MFC that uses the COMDEMO server. Figure 17-2 shows this program running. This client registers itself as a free-threaded client. It can call the AutoIncr object using either the primary thread or background threads.

Although the demonstration is very simple, there are several concepts being illustrated. Any time you retrieve a value using the primary thread, the entire application hangs until the value is returned. Calls to COM objects are synchronous and so do not return until completion. Because the object's methods take several seconds to execute, the entire application locks up until the call finishes because messages are not being processed.

If you click on one of the background buttons, a new thread will be created that asks for one of the object's values. If the server used the apartment model, then the requests would be processed sequentially. Clicking the Slow Counter "Get (Background Thread)" button three times would take 45 seconds to complete. Because the server uses free-threading, all of the requests will be processed simultaneously.

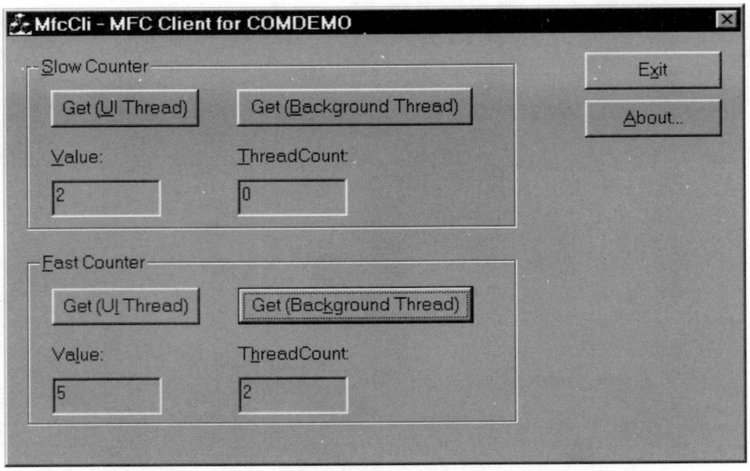

Figure 17-2. The Main window for MFCCLI.

Because the client is free-threaded, the interface pointer can be handed between threads without problem. If the client had been apartment model instead of free-threaded, passing the pointer between threads would have been prohibited and it would have been necessary to use the calls described earlier to pass an interface pointer between threads.

Running VBCLI

The second client program is called VBCLI. Its main window is shown in Figure 17-3. This application is written in Visual Basic 4.0. In contrast to MFCCLI, Visual Basic is an apartment model client. COMDEMO registers itself as supporting both the apartment model and the free-threading model, so VBCLI can successfully load the COMDEMO server. If COMDEMO had been registered as only free-threaded, then COM would have had to step between the two to make the free-threaded server talk correctly to an apartment model client.

Everything in VBCLI will be done sequentially because Visual Basic cannot start multiple threads to create multiple outstanding requests. When you click on Slow Counter or Fast Counter, the appropriate variable in AutoIncr will be read. The slow counter will take 15 seconds and the fast counter will take 2 seconds. As with the buttons that used the primary thread in MFCCLI, the application hangs while the request is being processed.

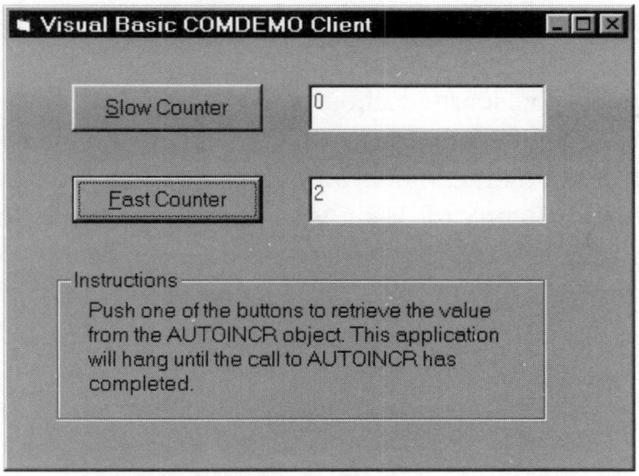

Figure 17-3. The Main window for VBCLI.

If you start up both VBCLI and MFCCLI together, you will see an example of a server that is running mixed model. The COMDEMO server is using the apartment model to talk to the Visual Basic application and the free-threading model to talk to the MFC application. Each application will create its own instance of an AutoIncr object, so the counters for VBCLI will be separate from the counters for MFCCLI.

Automation objects are typically very easy to use with Visual Basic. If you are interested in the implementation details, VBCLI loads AUTOINCR when the form loads at application startup using the following code:

```
Set AutoIncr = CreateObject("ComDemo.AutoIncr.1")
```

The object name looks just like the declaration in COMDEMO for what will be placed in the registry. The variable *AutoIncr* is declared in the global declarations like this:

```
Dim AutoIncr As Object
```

FastCounter and *SlowCounter* are properties of the AutoIncr COM object. The Fast Counter button reads the *FastCounter* property with this code:

```
FastCounterValue.Text = AutoIncr.FastCounter
```

Summary

In this chapter you learned about COM threading models. The apartment model is based on the Windows message queue and guarantees synchronization. The free-threading model does not use the Windows message queue and incurs the difficulty of doing your own synchronization. You saw how to use these in an in-proc and an out-of-proc server. Finally, you saw the COM-DEMO sample object that illustrated many of the concepts in this chapter.

Appendix

The MTVERIFY Macro

The MTVERIFY macro is used in most of the samples in this book to catch errors and help determine their cause. An example of the macro being used looks like this:

```
MTVERIFY( CloseHandle(hThread) );
```

The function `CloseHandle()`, like many Win32 functions, returns TRUE if it succeeds and FALSE if it fails. If it fails, you can call `GetLast-Error()` to determine the reason. `MTVERIFY()` uses this functionality to produce error messages like the following if `CloseHandle()` fails.

```
The following call failed at line 50 in Demo.c:
    CloseHandle(hThread)

Reason: The handle is invalid.
```

I will explain the macro by breaking the listing into parts and explaining each part. `MTVERIFY()` uses several obscure calls in Win32 and in the C run-time library. I will explain these calls as we go. Here is the header to the file. There is no executable code, so there is nothing to explain yet.

```
/*
 * MtVerify.h
 *
 * Error handling for applications in
 * "Multitheading Applications in Win32"
 *
 * For simplicity, this code includes the complete function PrintError
 * as a static function. For the examples in this book, this works fine.
 * To use PrintError() in an application, it should be taken out,
 * placed in its own source file, and the "static" declaration removed
 * so the function will be globally available.
 */
```

The following `pragma` will embed a command to the linker to link against the USER32 library, even if the library is not specified in the link command:

```
#pragma comment( lib, "USER32" )
```

The header file `crtdbg.h` defines a set of debugging functions that was introduced in Visual C++ 4.0. Although it is somewhat obscure, it provides access to such functionality as breaking into the debugger and putting up "Abort, Retry, Ignore" boxes like MFC uses. We need it for the `_ASSERTE()` macro.

```
#include <crtdbg.h>
```

The header file `MtVerify.h` defines two macros. `MTVERIFY()` makes sure that a call succeeds, and prints out an error message based on `GetLastError()` if it fails. `MTASSERT()` is somewhat less functional. It does not use `GetLastError()` and so does not print a reason for the error.

`MTVERIFY()` uses the preprocessor symbols `__FILE__` and `__LINE__` to provide detailed information in the error description. It also uses the "stringizing" operator, which in the macro below is the #a. The stringizing operator takes a macro argument and treats it as if it were a quoted string.

```
#define MTASSERT(a) _ASSERTE(a)

#define MTVERIFY(a) if (!(a)) \
        PrintError(#a,__FILE__,__LINE__,GetLastError())
```

What follows is the function prototype for `PrintError()`. This function gets calls when `MTVERIFY()` fails.

```
// Function prototype, in case the routine is moved out of this file.
void PrintError(
    LPSTR linedesc, LPSTR filename, int lineno, DWORD errnum);
```

Next comes the implementation for `PrintError()`. It gets passed all the information that was collected from the preprocessor by the `MTVERIFY()` macro. If your application is running in a window, this function puts up a message box, similar to what MFC uses when it asserts. If your application is a console app, `PrintError()` describes the problem to *stderr*.

```
static void PrintError(
    LPSTR linedesc, LPSTR filename, int lineno, DWORD errnum)
{
        LPSTR lpBuffer;
        char errbuf[256];
#ifdef _WINDOWS
        char modulename[MAX_PATH];
#else // _WINDOWS
        DWORD numread;
#endif // _WINDOWS
```

The next part, the Win32 call `FormatMessage()`, has to be one of the best-kept secrets in Win32. Among other things, this function can produce readable error messages for the values that `GetLastError()` returns. These error messages will be in the local language, so it can save a lot of work in localization. In this case, `FormatMessage()` will allocate the buffer needed to hold the text. This way we do not have to worry about over-flowing the buffer.

```
FormatMessage( FORMAT_MESSAGE_ALLOCATE_BUFFER
            | FORMAT_MESSAGE_FROM_SYSTEM,
        NULL,
        errnum,
        LANG_NEUTRAL,
        (LPTSTR)&lpBuffer,
        0,
        NULL );
```

Now we create a string with the error message. This function uses the Windows function `wsprintf()` instead of using `sprintf()` from the C run-time library.

```
wsprintf(errbuf,
 "\nThe following call failed at line %d in %s:\n\n"
 "    %s\n\nReason: %s\n", lineno, filename, linedesc, lpBuffer);
```

If this is a console application, get a handle to *stderr* and use `Write-File()` to display the error message. Wait three seconds to make sure the user sees it. If this is a GUI application, display a message box with the error. Force the window to the front so it does not get lost.

```
#ifndef _WINDOWS
        WriteFile(GetStdHandle(STD_ERROR_HANDLE),
            errbuf, strlen(errbuf), &numread, FALSE );
        Sleep(3000);
#else
        GetModuleFileName(NULL, modulename, MAX_PATH);
        MessageBox(NULL, errbuf, modulename,
            MB_ICONWARNING|MB_OK|MB_TASKMODAL|MB_SETFOREGROUND);
#endif
```

Finally, exit using a value appropriate for the operating system. The value EXIT_FAILURE is defined in `stdlib.h`.

```
        exit(EXIT_FAILURE);
}
```

I found the MTVERIFY macro to be tremendously useful. It saved me many hours of debugging and kept me from guessing at the reason for a failure because I did not feel like looking up a reason code. Between tricks of the preprocessor and the obscure `FormatMessage()` call, `MTVERIFY()`'s error information is quite complete and quickly pinpoints problems even when you are not in the debugger.

Index

Addison-Wesley Developers Press

Addison-Wesley Developers Press publishes high-quality, practical books and software for programmers, developers, and system administrators.

Here are some additional titles from A-W Developers Press that might interest you. If you'd like to order any of these books, please visit your local bookstore or:

 FAX us at 800-367-7198 (24 hours a day)

 CALL us at 800-822-6339 (8:30 AM to 6:00 PM eastern time, Monday-Friday)

WRITE to us at Addison-Wesley Developers Press
One Jacob Way
Reading, MA 01867

REACH us online at http://www.aw.com/devpress/

International orders, contact one of the following Addison-Wesley subsidiaries:

Australia/New Zealand
Addison-Wesley Publishing Co.
6 Byfield Street
North Ryde, N.S.W. 2113
Australia
Tel: 61 2 878 5411
Fax: 61 2 878 5830

Latin America
Addison-Wesley Iberoamericana S.A.
Blvd. de las Cataratas #3
Col. Jardines del Pedregal
01900 Mexico D.F., Mexico
Tel: (52 5) 568-36-18
Fax: (52 5) 568-53-32
e-mail: ordenes@ibero.aw.com
     or: informacion@ibero.aw.com

United Kingdom and Africa
Addison Wesley Longman Group
Limited
P.O. Box 77
Harlow, Essex CM 19 5BQ
United Kingdom
Tel: 44 1279 623 923
Fax: 44 1279 453 450

Southeast Asia
Addison-Wesley
(Singapore) Pte. Ltd.
11 Cantonment Road
Singapore 089736
Tel: 65 223 8155
Fax: 65 223 7155

Europe and the Middle East
Addison-Wesley Publishers B.V.
Concertgebouwplein 25
1071 LM Amsterdam
The Netherlands
Tel: 31 20 671 7296
Fax: 31 20 675 2141

All other countries:
Addison-Wesley Publishing Co.
Attn: International Order Dept.
One Jacob Way
Reading, MA 01867 U.S.A.
Tel: (617) 944-3700 x5190
Fax: (617) 942-2829

Win32 Programming

Brent E. Rector and Joseph M. Newcomer
ISBN 0-201-63492-9, $54.82 w/CD-ROM

Comprehensive and detailed—with over 140,000 lines of code included on the accompanying CD-ROM—*Win32 Programming* is your ultimate resource. Concentrating exclusively on 32-bit programming, it offers an in-depth look at the user interface and graphics aspects of the Windows API and demonstrates how to use the API effectively. In addition, many low-level operating system functions and facilities are covered.

Win32® Network Programming

Windows 95® and Windows NT™ Network Programming Using MFC

Ralph Davis
ISBN 0-201-48930-9, $44.95 w/disk

Windows® 95 and Windows NT™ coexist in many networked environments, and the two operating systems share a common networking API. However, there are some important differences in their capabilities and implementation. *Win32® Network Programming* shows programmers how to build networked applications that leverage 32-bit features and functionality, covering both Windows 95 and Windows NT 4.0.

Win32® Client/Server Developer's Guide

Douglas J. Reilly
ISBN 0-201-40762-0, $39.95 w/disk

Win32 Client/Server Developer's Guide is an essential guide to client/server technologies, tools, and strategies for developing distributed Windows applications. Beginning with a grounding in what client/server is and the best uses for it, this book proceeds to discuss how the client should pass requests on to the server, how the properly designed server handles processing requests, and how to improve performance through the use of a file retrieval system like Btrieve.

MFC Internals
Inside the Microsoft® Foundation Class Architecture

George Shepherd and Scot Wingo
ISBN 0-201-40721-3, $39.95 w/disk

MFC Internals is a guide to what goes on inside the
Microsoft Foundation Classes, giving you unique and in-depth
information on undocumented MFC classes, utility functions
and data members, useful coding techniques, and critical
analysis of the way various MFC classes work and how
they all fit together.

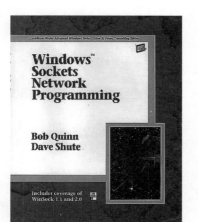

Windows Sockets Network Programming

Bob Quinn and Dave Shute
ISBN 0-201-63372-8, $49.44 w/disk

This book describes how to develop 16- and 32-bit WinSock
applications, and focuses on designs that will run on any
WinSock implementation. It highlights the differences that exist
between WinSock DLLs, and other traps and pitfalls in network
application development, and shows you how to avoid them.
It covers every function in version 1.1 of the WinSock
specification, and provides a detailed tour of the newest
features in WinSock version 2.

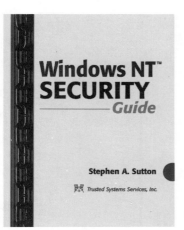

Windows NT™ Security Guide

Stephen A. Sutton
ISBN 0-201-41969-6, $29.95

Your computers are at risk, whether they are connected to a
corporate intranet or the Internet, have access to a sensitive
database, or simply sit on your desk when you're not there. In
the *Windows NT Security Guide,* Steve Sutton, a security expert
and corporate trainer, shows you how to maximize Windows
NT's various security protections and avoid many of its pitfalls.
This book explains NT's security features from a step-by-step,
how-to perspective with numerous realistic examples.